REMEMBER ME, AND I WILL REMEMBER YOU

REMEMBER ME, AND I WILL REMEMBER YOU

DHIKR: THE SOUL OF ISLAM

Tallal Alie Turfe

Visiting Professor
Department of Religious Studies
University of Detroit Mercy

REMEMBER ME, AND I WILL REMEMBER YOU
DHIKR: THE SOUL OF ISLAM

Copyright © 2016 Tallal Alie Turfe.

All rights reserved. No part of this book may be used or reproduced by any means, graphic, electronic, or mechanical, including photocopying, recording, taping or by any information storage retrieval system without the written permission of the author except in the case of brief quotations embodied in critical articles and reviews.

iUniverse books may be ordered through booksellers or by contacting:

iUniverse
1663 Liberty Drive
Bloomington, IN 47403
www.iuniverse.com
1-800-Authors (1-800-288-4677)

Because of the dynamic nature of the Internet, any web addresses or links contained in this book may have changed since publication and may no longer be valid. The views expressed in this work are solely those of the author and do not necessarily reflect the views of the publisher, and the publisher hereby disclaims any responsibility for them.

Any people depicted in stock imagery provided by Thinkstock are models, and such images are being used for illustrative purposes only.
Certain stock imagery © Thinkstock.

ISBN: 978-1-5320-0904-4 (sc)
ISBN: 978-1-5320-0906-8 (hc)
ISBN: 978-1-5320-0905-1 (e)

Library of Congress Control Number: 2016917865

Print information available on the last page.

iUniverse rev. date: 11/09/2016

A gift to my daughter, Summer, for her patience and perseverance in self-actualizing as a daughter and as a mother. Summer, you represent the hope and dream that every parent desires. You have blessed my life greatly. You have fought through some tough times with incredible determination and courage and have been successful at everything you have done. You have a special place in my heart. You can't imagine all the happiness that you brought to my life. Forever, I will remember you as you have remembered me.

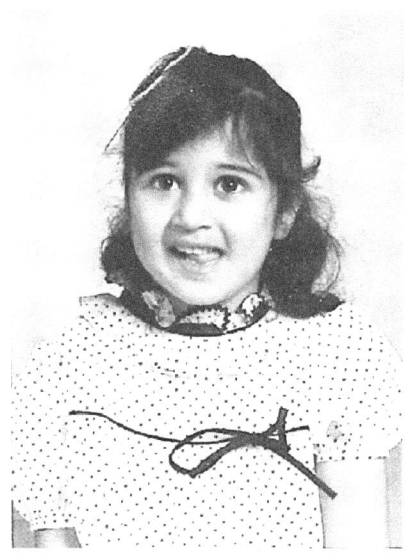

Contents

Preface ix
Acknowledgments xi
Remember: A Poem xiii
Prologue xv
Introduction xvii

Chapter 1	Blessings of Dhikr 1
Chapter 2	Energy of Dhikr 5
Chapter 3	Straight Path of Dhikr 12
Chapter 4	Theology of Dhikr 27
Chapter 5	Types and Praises of Dhikr 38
Chapter 6	Virtues, Effects, and Benefits of Dhikr 51
Chapter 7	Dhikr: Memory, Brain, and Heart 63
Chapter 8	Philosophy of Dhikr 70
Chapter 9	Dhikr: Books of God, Prophets, and Imams 79
Chapter 10	Dhikr: Prophet Muhammad Inspired by the Story of Joseph 91
Chapter 11	Dhikr of Tragedy at Karbala 96
Chapter 12	Dhikr: Creatures and Inanimate Objects 105
Chapter 13	Psychology of Dhikr 112
Chapter 14	Power of God's Dhikr 126
Chapter 15	Dhikr: Islamic Battles 134
Chapter 16	Dhikr: Unity in Islam 145
Chapter 17	Transformation of Dhikr 160
Chapter 18	Monotheistic Aspects of Dhikr 165
Chapter 19	Eschatology of Dhikr 172
Chapter 20	Dhikr: Remembering Others 180

Epilogue 187

Appendix A   Selected Occurrences of Dhikr in the Qur'an 191
Appendix B   Selected Qur'anic Verses on Dhikr...............................193
Appendix C   Dhikr of the Ninety-Nine Beautiful
             Names of God 202
Appendix D   Selected Sayings of Dhikr (Remembrance) 204
Appendix E   Selected Shi'a Hadiths on Dhikr 207
Appendix F   Selected Sunni Hadiths on Dhikr 215
Appendix G   Selected Examples of Recommended
             Supplications (Sunni and Shi'a Hadiths) 221

References..227
Index of Subjects and Names...241

Preface

I am American born, and I had no formal training in Islamic studies. I taught myself the Arabic alphabet so I could read the Qur'an in its original language. English translations of the Qur'an aided my understanding of the Arabic verses. For more than a half century, I taught young people about the Islamic faith, which further strengthened my knowledge and understanding of the religion. I also spoke to adult groups and at interfaith institutions.

As the growing Muslim community needed more Islamic centers and teachers, I became more involved in studying, writing, and lecturing about Islamic topics. Religious scholars recognized my knowledge of Islam, and they frequently invited me to give presentations on the topic. Some of these topics centered on the common ground between Sunnis and Shi'as, such as the Qur'an, hadiths (traditions), and the core fundamentals of Islam as well as the respect for unity in diversity. In addition, I made presentations to the broader interfaith community.

I have authored five other books on religion, some of which are in several languages: (1) *Patience in Islam: Sabr*; (2) *Unity in Islam: Reflections and Insights*; (3) *Energy in Islam: A Scientific Approach to Preserving Our Health and the Environment*; (4) *Children of Abraham: United We Prevail, Divided We Fail*; and (5) *Know and Follow the Straight Path: Finding Common Ground Between Sunnis and Shi'as*.

I have served on a number of boards and was chairman of the Greater Detroit Interfaith Round Table of the National Conference for

Community and Justice, currently the Michigan Roundtable for Diversity and Inclusion. I was a member of former president Bill Clinton's Call to Action: One America race relations group. Dubai Television identified me as a prominent and influential Arab American.

In October 1995, I was the first Muslim to be presented with the Knight of Charity award by the Vatican-based Pontifical Institute for Foreign Missions. I was inducted into the International Heritage Foundation Hall of Fame for my global humanitarian efforts.

In August 2000, I was one of two hundred political and religious leaders from around the world who participated in the Millennium World Peace Summit at the United Nations in New York. I have given other presentations on Islam at the United Nations—for example, education and parenting for peace, global ethics, and public diplomacy.

My wife, Neemat, and I have been married for more than fifty years, and we have five children and twelve grandchildren.

Tallal Alie Turfe

Acknowledgments

This book is dedicated to the Twelfth Infallible Imam, Mohammad al-Mahdi, and may he pardon me for any errors I may have made.

This book is also dedicated to my parents, Hajj Alie Turfe and Hajjah Hassaney Turfe, who were constant and steadfast in their Islamic faith and good deeds. They inspired me to learn about Islam and its message to mankind.

It is hoped that this book will inspire those who wish to obtain a greater understanding of Islam as well as introspective reflection of what is important in becoming a more unified and knowledgeable Muslim community.

The eminent and renowned scholar Ayatollah Imam Abdul Latif Berry, founder of the Islamic Institute of Knowledge, spurred me to enhance my knowledge of Islam and write books on the subject. I am very grateful to him for opening my mind to the many facets of the religion and for nurturing me to explore the depths of its philosophy. He always urged me to undertake a study of the contemporary facets of Islam, thereby enlightening Muslims and non-Muslims in America and abroad.

Remember: A Poem
Tallal Alie Turfe

Call upon your heart to free you from the dark—
Free your restless spirit in need of a spark
From the agony and sadness still inside.
Remember your Lord above who will provide,
And speak His praises to awaken your soul,
Finding peace and comfort in reaching your goal.

Prologue

Wake-Up Call

Picture yourself in a grave, a tiny square of sod the size of which only holds the casket. There is no exit, no door, and no way to get up and leave the grave. You are immovable in a small hole in the ground with no way to turn, no one to talk to, no shoulder to lean on. You are literally in a zone of total darkness, as fear of the unknown shrouds your helpless body.

Shocked by the sudden aura of powerlessness and uncertainty of what lies ahead, you are frightened and all alone. There is no escape! Suddenly a thought overwhelms you as to the meaning of life and death. Its mystery is answered as you become aware that death is the door to eternity, while life is its key. What lies beyond that door is eternal bliss or damnation.

Reflecting on life's journey and the good and bad that you have done along the way, you begin to evaluate and judge yourself. You begin to ask the most important questions: "Why didn't I pray to God? What prevented me from doing so? Why didn't I remember God by at least uttering simple praises, such as 'There is no God but God,' 'God is the greatest,' 'All praise is for God,' or 'Glory to God'?"

After a short pause of silence, you unravel the enigma of this dilemma as you swiftly come to the realization that you were wrapped up in the life of the world that is nothing but sport and play. You took life for granted, and your spiritual well-being was weakened and distressed. Terrified, you shout out, "O my God, please return me back so I can repent and atone for my sins and negligence in life!" But it's too late; there is no return. Time has run out, as you now await your fate.

La ilaha illallah
(There is no God but God)

Introduction

When we think about something we are in need of, we cannot overcome that thought until the need is satisfied. Whether in need of food or water, our minds constantly think about that need until we have something to eat or quench our thirst. Similarly, one who understands how much he or she is in need of God will constantly think about God. When we have faith and the desire to receive God's grace and mercy, we will turn to the remembrance of Him.

We must always stay tuned to the remembrance of God. Otherwise, we lose our sense of direction and purpose in life. What is most important is that we live mainly to connect with God and give thanks to Him. Often, we find ourselves complaining about the challenges of the present and worries of the future. But as we take the time to remember, as we take the time to gain perspective, we realize how truly blessed we are. Remember God, and He will strengthen and lead us to move ahead into the future. To move ahead, we must also be steadfast in meditation and prayer.

Relative to prayer, we often hear people say (a) they don't have time, (b) it's too difficult to memorize the prayer, (c) they don't believe prayer makes any difference, or (d) they don't think prayer is important. Even for those who do pray, they may just go through the motions without concentration, they may not pray on time, or they may miss prayers.

- **Don't have time:** According to an Informate Mobile Intelligence survey conducted in December 2014, people in the United States check their Facebook, Twitter, and other social media accounts a staggering seventeen times a day. The time spent on smartphones alone was an astounding 4.7 hours per day. Considering that the average American is awake for just more than fifteen hours a day, this means that they spend approximately a third of that time on smartphones (Chang 2015). By comparison, a Mason and Nielson survey in 2014 revealed that the average time spent each day on smartphones increased from 1.6 hours in 2011 to 3.3 hours in 2013 (Scott 2014). Undoubtedly, smartphone usage is growing rapidly. Moreover, the time spent on other media further erodes into the number of hours left to do other things. Other reasons cited for not having time to pray are (1) being too lazy to pray; (2) not knowing where to begin; (3) not knowing what to do in prayer; (4) spending time on other essential tasks, such as showering, dressing, eating, working, and homework; (5) dealing with pressures of time itself; (6) facing indecision due to confusion and disorientation of deciding what to do next; (7) oversleeping; and (8) treating prayer as a low priority each day.

- **Difficult to memorize:** Some people do not know the Arabic language and have difficulty in pronouncing the prayer words. Even though Arabic can be read phonetically in English, still they are uncomfortable in reciting the prayer. Not being able to pronounce Arabic words correctly discourages them from praying; they think their prayer will not be accepted. Moreover, for those who can recite the prayer in Arabic, they may not be able to understand its meaning.

- **Doesn't make any difference:** People may think that even if they pray, God will not hear them. They feel that God has somehow shut them off and won't listen to them. They may not have a very strong belief in God in the first place. Or it may be because they don't think it will change anything because of their lack of belief. Still, others feel God is going to do whatever He wants irrespective of what they ask for. They stopped prayer because they weren't getting anything out of it.

- **Don't think it is important:** There are people who just can't bring themselves to ask for anything. Too many people lead satisfied, complacent lives. They may be too proud to ask God for something they want. They feel that what they are praying about is not important enough. They feel their world revolves around their careers, daily routines, television, and visits to restaurants and the mall, thereby resulting in not much to pray about. They just don't want to bother God with their trivial little problems. They don't understand prayer or how important it is in faith and in life. They are not persuaded that prayer matters.

According to a report by Common Sense Media, the total time teens and tweens in America spend watching television and movies, playing video games, reading, listening to music, and checking social media is about 9.0 hours daily. Importantly, this does not include time spent using media at school or for their homework (Wallace 2015). According to GlobalWebIndex, the time spent online alone accounts for over 6.0 hours daily, while time spent on social networks is 1.77 hours in 2015, up from 1.72 hours in 2014, 1.67 hours in 2013, and 1.61 hours in 2012. Microblogs have risen too, now capturing 0.81 hours per day in 2015 (Mander 2015).

An online survey conducted in November 2014 by Cowen and Company of Internet users eighteen and older found that Facebook still leads the US market by a wide margin:

Average daily time spent with selected social networks among US Internet users by age, November 2014 (Minutes)

	18–29	30–44	45–60	60+	**Average**
Facebook	51.0	49.2	37.4	30.6	**42.1**
Tumblr	50.6	18.1	18.4	13.9	**34.2**
Instagram	29.9	18.7	10.2	9.0	**21.2**
Pinterest	25.6	26.2	15.4	0.0	**20.8**
Twitter	23.5	16.0	17.2	13.2	**17.1**
Snapchat	19.8	8.9	13.6	6.0	**17.0**
Tinder	14.2	13.9	32.5	10.0	**14.9**
Ello	9.7	17.5	60.0	3.0	**13.2**
LinkedIn	9.3	9.2	11.3	9.0	**9.8**

Source: Cowen and Company, "Twitter/Social User Survey," November 10, 2014.

Facebook is the top social network when it comes to daily time spent, with individuals averaging forty-two minutes a day on the site. Nevertheless, users utilize several of these social networks daily, which accounts for 1.77 hours a day cited earlier. Interestingly, Facebook is the leader in each age category, with the exception of the forty-five to sixty age group. Here, Ello almost doubles the time spent on Facebook.

There are a number of surveys that have been done regarding time spent by users on electronic media. One of the most reliable surveys is that done by the Nielsen Company, which provides measurement and analysis of online audiences, advertising, video, consumer-generated media, word of mouth, commerce, and consumer behavior. One such survey done by Nielsen revealed that the average time American adults eighteen years and older spent with electronic media was eleven hours and seven minutes per day in 2014, up from ten hours and fifty-three minutes per day in 2013:

Average daily time American adults (18+) spent with electronic media fourth quarter (2014 vs. 2013)
(Hours: minutes)

Media	Q4 2013	Q4 2014
Live TV	5:04	4:51
Radio	2:46	2:43
Smartphone	1:07	1:25
Internet on a PC	1:01	1:06
Timeshifted TV	0:32	0:33
Game Console	0:12	0:13
DVD/Blu-Ray	0:09	0:09
Multimedia Device	0:02	0:07
Total	**10:53**	**11:07**

Source: Nielsen Company Surveys (March 5, 2014; March 13, 2015).

Considering that most people are awake from sixteen hours to eighteen hours a day, eleven hours of electronic media usage seems like a lot. About eight of those hours are probably work related. As Nielsen found, the more screens we have available, the more apt we are to look at them (i.e., "technology begets technology"). However, much of the time spent with electronic media probably happens while performing other things, at the same time (i.e., multitasking) (Richter 2015; Petronzio 2014). For example, a person may be watching television while using his or her smartphone or some other electronic media at the same time.

Moreover, smartphones have a number of features that more than likely are not included in the 1:25 number in the table. Some of these features are smartphone (app + web), smartphone video, smartphone streaming audio, and smartphone social network. If these features were included, then the number would be much higher, more in line with the numbers cited earlier. Nonetheless, the Nielsen survey underscores that the trend in time spent with electronic media is on the rise.

What do we do when we first wake up? According to an online survey of 7,446 respondents conducted in March 2013 by IDC, our interaction with each other through our phones begins within the first fifteen minutes of waking up. It is estimated that four out of five smartphone owners are checking their phones, and among these people, nearly 80 percent reach for their phones before doing anything else:

Percent accessing smartphones after waking up

After Waking	All Respondents	18–24-Year-Olds
Within fifteen minutes	79%	89%
Immediately	62%	74%
Immediately and use as alarm clock	44%	54%

Source: IDC Research Report, sponsored by Facebook, March 2013.

This study was designed to understand how smartphone owners use their phones over the course of a day, with an emphasis on social and communication applications and services. Note that the eighteen- to twenty-four-year-olds have a higher incidence of accessing their smartphones than the average of all respondents. What we need is a wake-up call for *dhikr* (remembrance) of God.

Time management is a concern for how we conduct our daily activities. It is the process of planning and exercising conscious control over the amount of time spent on specific activities, including prayer. However, the combined total time of the five daily prayers only takes about one half hour to perform, which includes the ablution. We will discuss the concept of dhikr (remembrance), which will answer each of the concerns as to why people don't pray in the hope to enlighten them to begin to pray. Moreover, it is not just the failure to pray but for those who pray their failure in how to pray accurately. But before beginning to build upon their prayers, they need to take the time to build upon their foundations, just as the early Muslims did. Start with early steps, like performing dhikr or learning God's Beautiful Names.

The purpose of this book is to examine the meaning and significance of the following Qur'anic verse:

> Then you remember Me; I will remember you. Be grateful to Me, and do not reject faith. (Qur'an 2:152)

The Arabic word for "remembrance" in this verse is known as *dhikr*. Toward this examination, we will discuss dhikr as it applies to various facets of the human persona and its interaction with the remembrance of God. While remembrance is a mental and verbal exercise in extolling the greatness of God, it is also a recognition that either leads to or results from an appropriate action.

This verse expresses our constant remembrance of God by calling upon Him for His favors. Whether in times of comfort and happiness or in times of distress and suffering, we invoke the remembrance of God for His grace and mercy. The second part of this verse reminds us of our gratitude to God. Our recitation of praises in the remembrance of God also expresses our gratitude to Him. Moreover, our gratitude leads back to further recitations, a virtuous cycle of worship. Recitation is the spirit of remembrance, and its foundation is the Qur'an, the ultimate reminder. Whether remembrance (dhikr) emanates from the heart or the conscience, our reliance is on constantly seeking guidance from God.

Dhikr is almost always translated as "remembrance," "remember," or "reminder" in the Qur'an. In addition, *dhikr* can be depicted as "to glorify," "to exalt," "to praise," "to think," "to mention," "to recite," or "to record." In Islam, dhikr has a set of meanings, some of which are the following:

- **Friday Prayer**: "O you who believe! When the call is made for payer on Friday, then hasten you all unto the remembrance of God and leave off (all) trading, that is better for you, if you do know!" (Qur'an 62:9).
- **Prayer**: "And if you be in fear (and cannot pray as prescribed) (pray you) then (as you may) on foot or riding, but when you are safe, remember God as He has taught you (through His Apostle) what you knew not." (Qur'an 2:239).
- **Qur'an**: "This We recite unto thee of the signs and the Wise Reminder." (Qur'an 3:58).

Dhikr has many definitions, some of which are the Qur'an, prayer, supplication, learning, and teaching. These variations in translation give an indication that dhikr is actionable in recollection and reflection. In the Qur'an, dhikr is often used in expressions about God, reminding us of His covenant with mankind.

The word *dhikr* appears prominently in prayers that call upon God to protect and guide the believers to the straight path. However, dhikr of God includes more than prayers. It also includes all that one does in accordance with God's will and is revealed not only in the Qur'an but also through the hadiths (traditions) of Prophet Muhammad. Furthermore, verses in the Qur'an instruct people not to forget but to remember God and His commandments. As such, while dhikr brings us close to God and to mankind, it also brings us closer to our souls. Dhikr is to the soul what life is to the body. This connection to our souls in this world lays the foundation for tremendous benefits and success in the hereafter.

The counterpart to remembering is forgetting. Some information never makes it to long-term memory. Other times, the information gets there but is lost before it can attach itself to long-term memory. Other reasons include decay, displacement, and interference. Decay occurs when we do not rehearse information or don't contemplate it. Information not used for an extended period of time decays or fades away over time. Failing to remember something doesn't mean the information is gone forever. Sometimes, the information is there, but for various reasons we can't access it. This could be caused by distractions going on around us. Displacement is another reason why we can forget information in the short-term memory (i.e., old memories replace new ones). Another reason for forgetting is interference, which can either be proactive when old memories interfere with new ones or retroactive when new information distorts old memories. A study by Altmann and Schunn based on existing memory theory concluded that both decay and interference might occur together (Altmann 2012).

According to Vogel, there are at least two reasons psychologists think we forget information:

+ We store information in our memory but are unable to remember it when we need to but perhaps can at a later date. In this case, information is inaccessible.
+ The human memory simply forgets information permanently, and the physical traces of the memory disappear, in which case information is unavailable (Vogel 2008).

We talk about prayer, we teach about prayer, and then we forget to pray. Prayer is a form of dhikr (remembrance) of God. At times, we forget the power of prayer and remembrance of God. Unquestionably, it is a discipline that we can get better at. There are reasons why we forget to pray. Our inability to retrieve the memory of prayer time is a major reason. We know that there is the memory of prayer, but we just can't seem to retrieve it. Somehow, that memory has decayed over time, faded, or just disappeared. As memories compete with other memories, prayer time experiences interference from other priorities, such as attending a football game, watching a favorite television program, or using our smartphones to access social media. As we remember God, He remembers us. We remember God through prayer, because God made prayer the essential duty of man.

Often, we think of memory as an energetic mechanism connected with retention and retrieval of information about past experiences. However, when we examine the Islamic concept of remembrance, we note that it usually leads to or results from purposeful action. We also note that remembrance is an integral part of worship in the lives of believers.

Remembrance in the Islamic faith centers on God and the Qur'an. Retaining something in our memory means that we have been attentive and conscious to it. Hence, being attentive and conscious means that we will be able to retain it in the future. Remembrance is the compass that directs and guides the tapestry of our lives that is woven into an album of memories. From time to time, we access the web of that album to remember something that we have previously experienced. For example, each year during the month of Ashura, we recall from our memory the events leading to the tragedy at Karbala in which Imam Hussein and the followers of Ahl al-Bayt (Household of Prophet Muhammad) were martyred.

The title of this book is itself a reminder: *Remember Me, and I Will Remember You*. God has commanded us to always remember Him. As Muslims or even as believers from other Abrahamic faiths, we must be in constant remembrance of God. This book will allow us to understand the importance of remembrance and how we can better use it to improve our health and lifestyle. We often take life for granted not realizing that remembrance is part and parcel of our lives. It is the intent of the author to shed light on the concept of remembrance and its importance, as a reminder of our gratitude to the Creator for His grace and mercy.

We will examine the interaction of remembrance of God with the pillars of Islam. In addition, a list of the Beautiful Names of God as well as the types and praises of remembrance will be discussed. The theology, philosophy, and psychology of remembrance will be explored as well as its virtues, effects, and benefits. Furthermore, we will discuss that by remembering God and praising Him we experience His blessings that help us self-actualize as Muslims, in this world and in the hereafter.

As we remember God, He will direct us to the straight path. In turn, God expects us to understand the Qur'an, the purpose of the universe, earth, nature, environment, our emotions, and interactions with mankind. We will also come to the realization that remembrance of God is a key factor in unifying the Muslim community. May God help us realize the importance of remembrance (dhikr), appreciate it, and empower the mind, heart, and soul to embrace it!

AHL AL-BAYT

Chapter 1

Blessings of Dhikr

Dhikr is also known as *zikr, zekr,* or *thikr*. There are many English translations for the word *dhikr*, including "to remember," "to commemorate," "to bear in mind," "to praise," "to extol," "to mention," and "to recollect." It is the name of devotional acts whereby short phrases or prayers are repeatedly recited silently within the mind or aloud. Dhikr is also used to refer to the Qur'an in the sense of a reminder and warning. The Qur'an is the ultimate source of dhikr to be reminded of God and His straight path; it is the ultimate source of commemorating God. Every command in the Qur'an is a reminder that came from God. Dhikr is sometimes accompanied by the repetition of one of God's Beautiful Names or some other expression of praise of one's faith.

One can practice dhikr at any time during the day by reflecting on God's mercy or one of God's other attributes. While there is no specified time for dhikr, the morning and evening are the best times to mention God (Qur'an 33:42; 18:28). Another example of dhikr is the five daily prayers that are offered at prescribed times. In addition, dhikr can be counted on a string of beads or a set of prayer beads (*misbaha*). Moreover,

Muslims believe that constantly reciting the dhikr praises (e.g., glorifying the oneness of God) is one of the best ways to enter heaven.

We often talk about our struggles, traumas, and deaths of loved ones. Yet no matter what happens in our lives, we all have something to be thankful for. Rather than complaining about disappointments and adversities that seem big setbacks at the time, we should count our blessings daily and be thankful for the Creator who brought us into existence. We should always remember God for His grace and mercy. By remembering God, He will remember us.

Count our blessings! Stop and consider what our blessings are. Be grateful for the problems we don't have. If we concentrate on God's blessings, we will feel much better because the remembrance of His blessings is the remedy that relieves us of a myriad of character disorders.

Dhikr (remembrance): Remedy for selected character disorders

Abrasive	Doubtful	Manipulative
Addictive	Egotistical	Pessimistic
Antisocial	Envious	Prejudicial
Apathetic	Faithless	Resentful
Arrogant	Fearful	Self-Destructive
Authoritative	Greedy	Selfless
Complacent	Hateful	Skeptical
Cruel	Helpless	Stressful
Depressive	Impatient	Stubborn
Diffident	Impulsive	Unruly
Discouraged	Insecure	Unstable
Disrespectful	Irresponsible	Withdrawn

By remembering God constantly, we receive many of His blessings to help us overcome our character disorders, such as arrogance, cruelty, depression, impatience, insecurity, and stress. God rewards the believers who perform dhikr (remembrance):

> And the men who remember God much and the women who remember God (much), for them has been prepared forgiveness and a great recompense. (Qur'an 33:35)

A sign of a believer is that he or she is always performing dhikr:

> Those who remember God standing, and sitting, and reclining on their sides and think (seriously) in the creation of the Heaven and the Earth; saying "O Our Lord! Thou has not created (all) this in vain! Glory be to Thee! Save us then from the torment of the (Hell) fire." (Qur'an 3:191)

> O you who believe! Remember your God by remembering (Him) frequently, and glorify Him morning and evening. (Qur'an 33:41–42)

Dhikr (remembrance) cures the heart that is disturbed by the feeling of unrest and discontent. Finding rest and contentment depend on the remembrance of God:

> O mankind! Indeed has come unto you an exhortation from your Lord, and a cure for (the diseases) what is in your hearts and a guidance and mercy for the believers. (Qur'an 10:57)

> And those who believe and their hearts are set at rest by God's remembrance; Certainly! By God's remembrance (only) are the hearts set at rest. (Qur'an 13:28)

Faith is connected with the remembrance of God. Whether in silence or by use of the tongue, remembering God is a sign of genuine faith. Dhikr by the use of the tongue achieves full realization when heavy in the heart. A sign of the reality of life is that we need to extol the Giver of life and not to take Him for granted. To truly believe in God necessitates glorifying and praising Him continually, not just from time to time.

One's spirituality is manifested in remembrance of our gratitude for God's blessings. Remembrance opens up a channel of communication between the believer and God. By way of remembrance, God's blessing removes the rust from one's heart (Qur'an 83:14). Otherwise, those whose hearts are neglectful in the remembrance of God are on a collision course with their own faith. We should never be diverted away from the remembrance of God:

> O you who believe! Let not your wealth nor your children divert you from the remembrance of God; and whosoever does that, these are then the losers. (Qur'an 63:9)

Another blessing of remembrance is that it protects us from the Day of Judgment. Those who are overwhelmed with emotion in remembering God in their privacy, without fanfare in drawing attention from others or boasting about their act of remembrance, are the ones who receive God's blessing. Their reward for remembrance of God will beautify their place in paradise. Remembrance of God is the easiest act of worship, because aside from prayer one does not have to perform ablution, prostration, or even the direction that prayer requires. Rather, one can remember God at any time or at any place, at any hour, sleeping or awake, eating, driving a car, or in any other capacity.

Dhikr is refuge from the many problems we face in life, such as social, psychological, financial, family, and health. By constantly remembering God, the Infinite, we minimize our problems as finite. Yet to obtain the full impact of dhikr, it must not be done hurriedly or unconsciously, rather slowly in order for the heart to intertwine the mind with the soul. Toward this end, the problems we face, in fact, become minimized and inconsequential. With God on our side, our worries diminish because it is His blessings that sustain us.

No limitations are placed on remembrance with respect to time and condition. There is nothing that is more equivalent than the remembrance of God. Moreover, the perfection of remembrance is manifest when the realization of that remembrance is from God's blessings. Toward this end, we must make our intention to remember God.

Chapter 2

Energy of Dhikr

In Islam, what is important is the purity of our intention (*niyyah*). What people think and feel underscores the essence of intention.

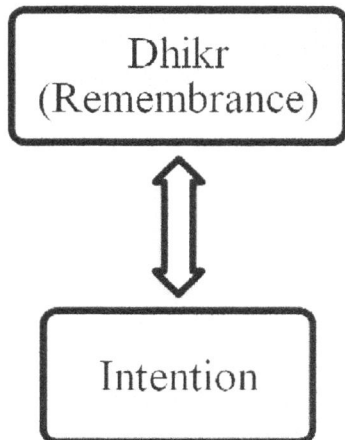

Intention relative to our motives should always be in the direction of satisfaction and approval of God. As a consequence, God evaluates our deeds according to the intentions behind them. All the good deeds will become useless if the intention is corrupt. Our dhikr (remembrance) has no value if the intention is impure. The intention is located in the heart. If the heart is at the point of unrest, then the intention will be impure. Before we begin our dhikr of God, we make our intention to do so. The strength of our emotion brings about a strong intention. Intention requires energy to bring it into concentration. Let us examine positive energy and negative energy as it relates to the dhikr of God.

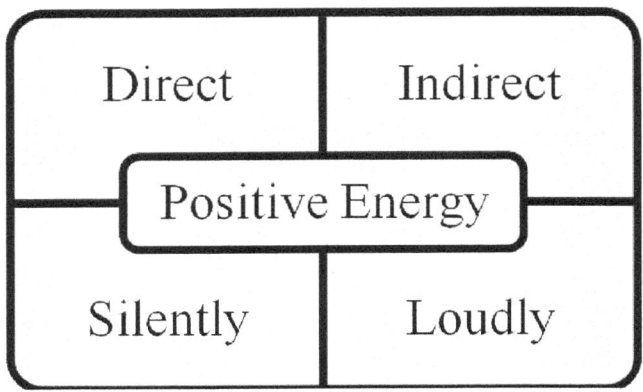

Positive Energy: Along with prayer, dhikr of God is the ideal way to raise the level of positive energy. With positive energy, we can clear our negative thoughts. Remembrance boosts one's positive energy in manifold ways, such as erasing a bad memory or coping with an unfortunate incident. However, for positive energy to work, one's remembrance must be sincere, honest, and passionate. Dhikr is a form of meditation, which is the way we build the bridge between our consciuos physical mind and our subconscious spiritual mind. We begin each day by making our intention to remember God. This intention puts us in the proper frame of mind.

Positive energy of remembrance overcomes negative energy of Satan. Dhikr can be direct or indirect. Direct remembrance involves reciting and repeating the praises of God by providing a direct link between the believer and God. By repetition, the heart and mind come into balance and the exercise of remembrance becomes automatic. The remembrance of God is placed in direct correspondence with God's own remembrance of us (e.g., "Remember Me, and I shall remember you," per Qur'an 2:152).

Indirect remembrance necessitates that the conscience becomes the guardian in ensuring that each word or thought is continously seeking the pleasure of God (Cornell 2007). When remembering God, it is best to perform it silently rather than loudly (Qur'an 7:205). Silent utterance of remembrance is done humbly and quietly, especially if in the presence of people who are asleep. Loud utterance of remembrance should not be excessively loud; rather, it should be in the medium range of loudness. However, at times, it may be necessary to arouse others by uttering remembrance loudly, not excessively, in order to enliven their hearts relative to remembrance (Badawi 2011).

Prophet Muhammad underscored the importance of group prayer:

> The Holy Prophet has said, "God says: 'My servant if you remember Me in privacy, I will also remember you in privacy; and if you remember Me in an assembly, I will also remember you in an assembly that is better and greater (than your assembly).'" (Ala al-Din Ali al-Hindi, *Kanzul-'Ummal*)

During Hajj (pilgrimage) and Eid prayers, Muslims regularly assemble as a group chanting the following loud dhikr of God:

> Group dhikr at Hajj (pilgrimage): "Labbaik Allah humma labbaik, labbaik la sharika laka labbaik, innal hamda wan-ni'mata laka wal mulk la sharika lak" (Here I am, O God! Here I am, at Your service! You have no partner. Here I am. All praise, grace, and dominion belong to You. You have no partner).
>
> Group dhikr at Eid prayers: "Allahu Akbar, Allahu Akbar, la ilaaha ill-Allah; Allahu Akbar, Allahu Akbar, wa Lillah il-hamd" (God is the greatest, God is the

greatest, there is no God but God; God is the greatest, God is the greatest, and to God belongs all praise).

Group dhikr at end of prayer: When a prescribed prayer is completed, Muslims chant the praise of Prophet Muhammad and his progeny along with "La ilaha illallah" (There is no God but God).

During dhikr, we need to exercise our lungs by taking deep breaths, which will help us relax, thereby improving our level of concentration. With each exhalation, envision all the stress, anxiety, and negativity leaving your body. With each inhalation, picture the light, which collects the mass of nerve cells in the upper abdomen behind the stomach, kidneys, and other internal organs, beginning to enlarge. Imagine the warmth of the spiritual energy as it passes through your muscles and organs. Imagine your entire body filled by this spiritual light from the inside out.

Negative emotions are extremely powerful. They can incapacitate lives quickly by causing disparity in the energy system. This sets off a chain of emotional imbalance, such as frustration, agony, mental instability, uncontrolled anger, inferiority complexes, fear, and anxiety. Emotional imbalances, such as fear and anxiety, create negative energies that eventually culminate in illness (Turfe 2010).

Negative Energy: If we start our day with a negative feeling, then we set up a pattern to react to situations in a negative way. Negative thoughts create negative energies, which establish negative activities or situations, thereby creating negative thoughts again. Interacting with people with personal problems can drain our own energies; however, it is a charitable Islamic obligation to practice empathy and help those in need to overcome their troubles. Some of the people experiencing the stresses are of the best believers. Dealing with them actually improves our dhikr because it reminds us of our own blessings, and our faith strengthens along with the person we are helping. However, in some cases, the people we interact with are bad, and in dhikr, it is preferred and highly recommended to be focused and not allow negative aspects from bad people to be an impediment to our concentration on remembrance:

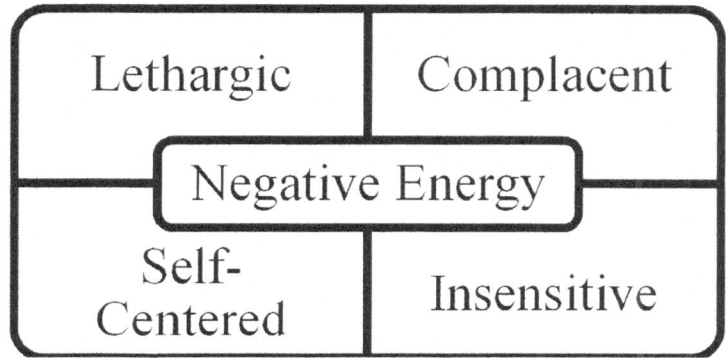

As negative energy accumulates, its gravitational pull causes us to engage in negative thoughts and feelings, such as being lethargic or complacent. Lethargy, or laziness, is a lack of energy that is accompanied by depression, decreased motivation, stress, or apathy. Lethargy stops us from remembering God.

Complacency is a feeling of contentment or self-satisfaction whereby one does not want to be bothered about life in general, be it remembrance of God or otherwise. This gravitational pull also attracts more negative energy from our surroundings, which intensifies the force. We need to understand how negative energy affects us, so we can seek a solution to remedy the problem. If we don't seek a solution, then negative energy will continue to affect our subconscious mind to the point that it overtakes our thoughts and feelings (Turfe 2010).

It will be difficult to remove obsessive thoughts from our conscious mind. We begin to experience erratic behavior, such as being self-centered or insensitive, that can have a devastating effect on our behavioral patterns both with our surrounding environment and ourselves. People who have a sterile, insensitive imagination are oblivious to remembrance because they are wrapped up in themselves and don't care about anyone else.

Negative thoughts and feelings might overpower our conscious mind and prevent us from enjoying life. We may become despondent, depressed, or withdrawn. As the intensity of negative energy builds, we begin to look for an escape mechanism. Escape is not the solution; it only gets worse. Dhikr is severely impacted, because we lose concentration and our thoughts begin to drift (Turfe 2010).

What we need is to learn how to protect and free ourselves in order to build an effective defense mechanism. The following is a plan of action:

> Increase the intensity of remembrance and meditation so as to prevent us from engaging in negative thoughts and feelings.
>
> Remembrance and meditation help us focus our attention inside ourselves rather than on the outside world.
>
> Become habitual in reciting the praises of God and asking for God's blessing and guidance in order to remove the negative energy that is already stored in our personal energy field.
>
> By creating a protective shield around our energy field, we can distance ourselves from engaging in problem areas that might have a negative impact on our thoughts and feelings.

We can use mind power to transcend problems. The most effective process for doing this is prayer, meditation, and remembrance of God. Toward this end, we need to raise our own energy level, so it transforms any external negative energy into positive energy. Negative energy can only cling to negative energy. Positive energy repels it.

We are capable of both positive energy and negative energy (i.e., of sharing light and darkness). Our behavior, be it positive or negative, can deeply transform the behavior of others (Turfe 2010). In dhikr, the electric current brings about mindfulness and concentration:

> Your remedy is within you, but you do not sense it.
> Your sickness is from you, but you do not perceive it.

> You presume you are a small entity, but within you is enfolded the entire universe. You are indeed the Evident Book, by whose alphabet the Hidden becomes Manifest. Therefore, you have no need to look beyond yourself. What you seek is within you, if only you reflect. (Imam Al ibn Abi Talib)

We begin our remembrance by being mindful of our gratitude to God as we seek His mercy and forgiveness. The power of remembrance (*dhikr*) is from within, and that power is patience (*sabr*) and faith (*iman*) that lead us to the straight path.

AHL AL-BAYT

Chapter 3

Straight Path of Dhikr

God has showered His blessings on Ahl al-Bayt (Household of Prophet Muhammad) and empowered them as guides to the straight path. Every Muslim is obligated to recite blessings (*salawat*), especially during prayer. If it is not recited during the prayer, then one's prayer becomes invalid. The Qur'an reminds us that blessings were given to Prophet Muhammad:

> Verily God and His Angels send blessings on the Prophet! O you who believe! Send your blessings on him and you greet him with a salutation worthy of the respect (due to him) (ya ayyuha alladhena amanu sallu 'alayhi wa sallamu tasliman). (Qur'an 33:56)

> O God! Please bless Muhammad and the Household of Muhammad (allahumma salli 'ala muhammadin wa ali muhammadin). (al-Haythami 1965; al-Suyuti 2000)

The first blessing is a directive from the Qur'an, while Prophet Muhammad declared the second blessing. The second blessing resulted from the companions of Prophet Muhammad asking about the necessity of the second blessing, to which the Prophet responded:

> Narrated 'Abdur-Rahman bin Abi Laila: "O God! Send Your Salat (Graces, Honours and Mercy) on Muhammad and on the family of Muhammad as You sent Your Salat (Graces, Honours and Mercy) on Ibrahim and on the family of Ibrahim, for You are the Most Praiseworthy, the Most Glorious. O God! Send Your Blessings on Muhammad and the family of Muhammad, as You sent Your Blessings on Ibrahim and the family of Ibrahim, for You are the Most Praiseworthy, the Most Glorious)." (*Sahih Bukhari*, Vol. 4, Book 60, Hadith 3370)

The question arises as to why the necessity for the two blessings:

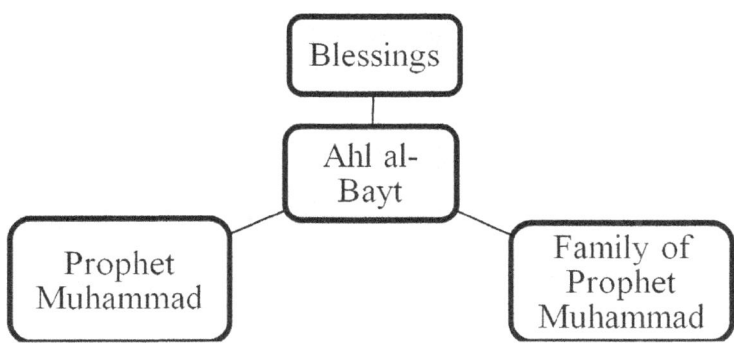

We are reminded by two verses in the Qur'an. The first verse is mentioned above (Qur'an 33:56), while the following verse is the basis for the first verse:

> And stay you in your abodes and display not your finery like the display of the ignorance of yore, and establish your prayer and give away the poor-rate, and obey God and His Apostle (Muhammad); verily, God intends but to keep off from you (every kind of) uncleanness

> O you the People of the House, and purify you (with) a thorough purification. (Qur'an 33:33)

Sunni and Shi'a scholars concur that this verse is attributed in remembrance to those whom God has purified: Prophet Muhammad, Imam Ali, Fatima, Imam Hassan, and Imam Hussein of Ahl al-Bayt. Therefore, it stands to reason that God had a purpose for those whom He purified.

God does not make mistakes, so the purification of Ahl al-Bayt is sound and, therefore, a declaration for all Muslims to obey and follow. Furthermore, the word "intends" in the verse means the continuous will and intention of God. Moreover, Prophet Muhammad remembering to mention his progeny in the blessing is testimony to the importance of inclusion of his Ahl al-Bayt.

Islam is a way of life, and it establishes rules and responsibilities in an orderly fashion, not in a chaotic fashion. Therefore, it is logical to assume that as Prophet Muhammad received the orderly pronouncement of blessing and peace in the Qur'anic verse, then the House of the Family of Prophet Muhammad (Ahl al-Bayt) should likewise receive the same blessing and peace that corresponds with the Prophet's declaration. We find the following Sunni hadiths that confirm the above:

- *Sahih Bukhari*, Vol. 4, Book 60, Hadith 3370
- *Sahih Muslim*, Vol. 1, Book 4, Hadith 907
- *Ibn Majah*, Vol. 2, Book 5, Hadith 904
- *Abu Dawud*, Vol. 1, Book 2, Hadith 976
- *Al-Tirmidhi*, Vol. 1, Book 3, Hadith 483
- *Al-Nasa'i*, Vol. 2, Book 13, Hadith 1286
- *Ahmad ibn Hanbal*, Vol. 4, p. 241, 243–244

A poem by Al-Shafi'i, the imam of one of the four Sunni schools of thought, also confirms the remembrance of blessings upon Ahl al-Bayt:

> O members of the Household (Ahl al-Bayt) of the Messenger of God! (Our) love for you is an obligation,

which God has revealed in the Qur'an. Your lofty station such that if one does not invoke blessings on you (while offering prayers) one's prayers will be of no avail. (al-Haythami 1965)

Likewise, some of the many Shi'a hadiths that record the dhikr (remembrance) of blessings upon Ahl al-Bayt are the following:

Ali bin Ibrahim reported from his fathers who reported from ibn Abu Umayr who reported from Abdulla bin Sinan who reported from Imam as-Sadiq that the Prophet said: "Invoking salawat (blessings) upon me and my Ahl al-Bayt carries away hypocrisy." (*Al-Kafi*, Vol. 4, p. 251)

Imam Ja'far as-Sadiq said: "Every invocation (du'a) sought from God, Almighty and Glorious, is barred (prevented) by the sky unless it is coupled with salawat (blessings), benediction upon Prophet Muhammad and Aale Muhammad (Ahl al-Bayt)." (*Al-Kafi*, Vol. 2, p. 493)

As noted, the above sources further confirm that blessings and peace should be given to both Prophet Muhammad and his progeny of Ahl al-Bayt. With the blessings that God bestowed upon Prophet Muhammad, the Prophet became the mercy for the universe (*rahmatun-lelalamin*). Let us give our blessings to Prophet Muhammad and the Imamat as we pursue the straight path. The opening chapter of the Qur'an, *al-Fatiha*, is the most frequent recital in our lives, whether in daily prayers, upon the birth of a newborn baby, at funerals, at weddings, as an invocation or benediction at an event, or for other occasions. It is a prayer for guidance.

The five daily prayers constitute a total of seventeen parts (*rakats*). *Al-Fatiha* is the only chapter (*sura*) in the Qur'an that is compulsorily recited in the obligatory prayer. It is recited, at least, in each of the first two parts of the prayers, or ten times daily. Including the five daily prayers and the recital of *al-Fatiha* for other occasions, Muslims recite *al-Fatiha* over five thousand times yearly.

In our prayers, we ask God to guide us (*ihdina*) to the straight path (*sirat al mustaqim*), which is the path of faith, righteous deeds, truth, and patience. It is the clear path that guides us to the light (*nur*). Whoever wants to find the straight path will find it, if they are sincere and righteous. The straight path is a blessing (*ni'mah*) from God, and the ultimate ni'mah is the ni'mah of Islam (Turfe 2015)! In seeking the ni'mah, we must obey God and Prophet Muhammad to receive guidance:

> And whoever obeys God and the Apostle (Muhammad) these shall be with those God has bestowed favors upon them; of the Prophets, and the Truthful, and the Witnesses, and the Righteous ones; and excellent are these as companions! (Qur'an 4:69)

The words *hadiyya* (gift) and *hidaya* (guidance) are connected in that the straight path is a gift of guidance:

Straight Path
(Sirat al Mustaqim)

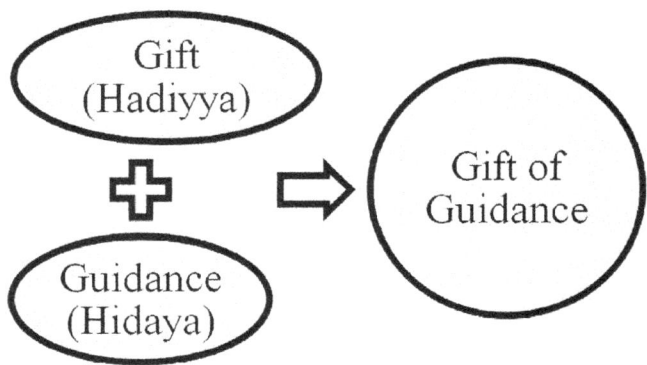

Any deviation from the straight path is regarded as misguidance. Daily, we remember to seek God's grace to guide us (ihdina) to the straight path:

> Verily, this is My Path, leading straight, so follow it, and do not follow (other) paths for they will scatter you away from His Path; thus He enjoins you, so that you may be righteous (and guard yourselves against evil). (Qur'an 6:153)

As God has done us a favor by guiding us to the straight path, we must express our gratitude and be thankful for His guidance and blessing. There is no limit to the amount of hidaya (guidance) one can receive from God. Of course, Prophet Muhammad and Ahl al-Bayt received the most hidaya. As a guide, God revealed to us the Qur'an, which is also a hidaya. As *al-Fatiha* reminds us of the basics of our faith, we must constantly invoke the dhikr (remembrance) to praise and worship God for His benevolence and mercy. We ask God to guide us to seek righteousness and refrain from the company of evil people.

Even Prophets, Messengers, and Infallible Imams were chosen and guided by God to perfect them as they walked the straight path. Not only did they walk the straight path, but they also became the straight path. For example, Prophet Muhammad was the straight path during his life, and his successor *(wasi)*, Imam Ali ibn Abi Talib, and every succeeding Infallible Imam thereafter was also the straight path. We must follow their example of dhikr by remembering to walk the straight path in order to perfect ourselves in every circumstance and aspect of our lives (Turfe 2015).

To be *mustaqim* (straight) is vital to our proper behavior and attitude in life. Once it is followed, the dhikr (remembrance) of the straight path transforms the whole of life by bringing about a positive change in character and action that purifies the self. We seek God's guidance to remove any obstacle or bad intention so that we can remain steadfast along the straight path:

> Whoever holds firmly to God is already guided to the Straight Path. (Qur'an 3:101)

Psychology, as it is practiced in Western societies, neglects or pays little attention to the concept of the soul. As such, people forget their gratitude to God for His hidaya and ni'mah, thereby forgetting to follow the straight path:

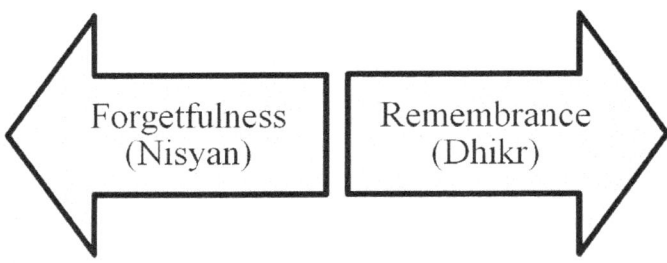

Remembrance (dhikr) leads to divine guidance, while forgetfulness (*nisyan*) is deviation from the straight path. Nisyan is a state of one forgetting his true nature, thereby diverging from the path of righteousness (Chittick 2005). However, guidance (hidaya) results in the remembrance (dhikr) of the straight path (sirat al mustaqim) in order to triumph over that which had been forgotten (nisyan):

Remembrance (dhikr) of the true nature of that which had been forgotten results in restoring one's dignity. The Qur'an warns us of the following:

> And be not like unto those who forsook God! So He made them forsake their own selves; these are the transgressors. (Qur'an 59:19)

When people abandon dhikr of God, they are deserting their own souls. Dhikr is for our benefit. Some people drink alcohol to forget, while the righteous performs dhikr to remember. For Muslims, spiritual happiness and psychological health are connected and often reflect each other. Islamic beliefs are important for our psychological health because they instill proper direction in life, guiding us to the straight path, which leads to self-actualization of the Islamic personality. Even our du'as (supplications) are gifts of guidance, as we not only make du'as for ourselves but for others as well.

It is energy that sparks our patience (sabr) in the remembrance (dhikr) of God in order to guide our hearts to be humble and open for knowledge, thereby leading us to the straight path:

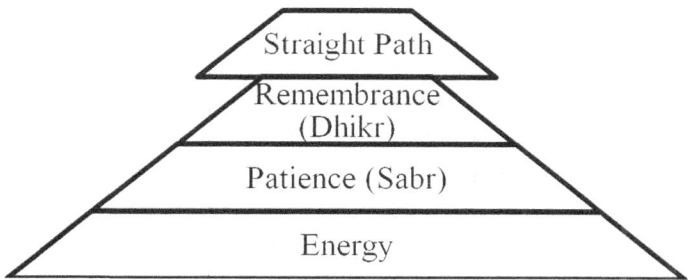

Patience (sabr) enables us to endure the trials and tribulations of life with all its hardships and adversities. It is patience that self-actualizes the unity within our self in order to bring about an Islamic personality that nurtures us to become better Muslims. Patience will help us be what we want to be because attainment is within reach if we persevere. Patience frees us from forgetfulness (nisyan) and prepares the self toward the straight path.

The straight path (sirat al mustaqim) is the connection between remembrance (dhikr) and the Qur'an:

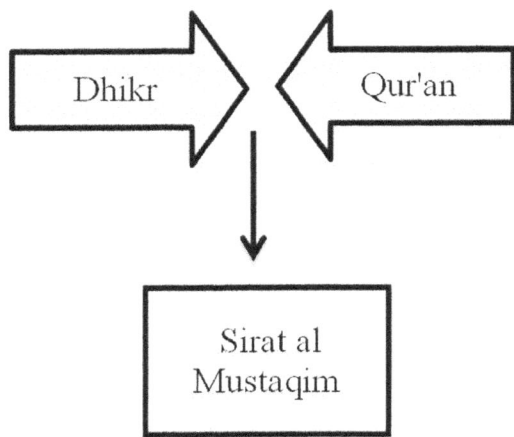

Whoever keeps to the dhikr (remembrance) of God and the Qur'an will be on the sirat al mustaqim (straight path). It is a path of those on whom God bestowed His gift. It is a path of those connected to God. The challenge is to find one's way to the straight path, which requires constant dhikr and reciting the Qur'an. Appendix B cites selected Qur'anic verses on dhikr. Remembrance of the straight path is the connection that links the Qur'an and Ahl al-Bayt as we cling tenaciously to the Rope of God (Qur'an 3:103):

Those who follow Ahl al-Bayt are called Shi'a. Interestingly, according to the Qur'an, the Shi'a were also followers of Prophet Noah (Qur'an 37:79–83). Therefore, Prophet Abraham was a follower (Shi'a) of

Prophet Noah. The followers of Prophet Moses were also Shi'a because Prophet Moses himself was a Shi'a (Qur'an 28:15). Even Prophet Jesus was a Shi'a in that he came to fulfill and follow the law of Prophet Moses in the Old Testament (Matthew 5:17–18). Moreover, we can conclude that Prophet Muhammad was a follower (Shi'a) as was Prophet Abraham, Prophet Moses, and Prophet Jesus.

As Shi'as, the Prophets and Infallible Imams followed the straight path. Likewise, our self-realization becomes manifest when we obtain a deeper understanding of the straight path and the inseparability of the Qur'an and Ahl al-Bayt. The linkage of the Qur'an and Ahl al-Bayt is referred to as al-thaqalayn (two weighty things), which means that obedience to both the Qur'an and the Imamat of Ahl al-Bayt are compulsory and cannot be separated from one another:

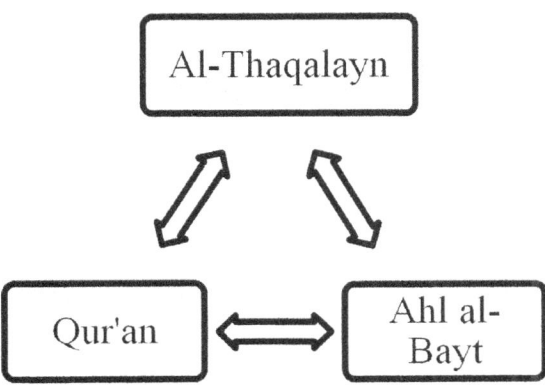

Sunni hadiths confirm that al-thaqalayn refers to the Qur'an and Ahl al-Bayt:

- *Sahih Bukhari, al Ta'rikh al Kabir*, Vol. 3, p. 96
- *Sahih Muslim*, Vol. 6, Book 44, Hadith 6225
- *Abu Dawud, Tadhkirat Khawass al-Ummah*, p. 322
- *Al-Tirmidhi*, Vol. 6, Book 46, Hadiths 3786, 3788
- *Al-Nasa'i, Al-Khasais*, p. 96, Hadith 79
- *Ahmad ibn Hanbal*, Vol. 5, p. 182, 189, 350, 366, 419

In addition, Ahl al-Bayt is also referred to as Ahl al-Dhikr:

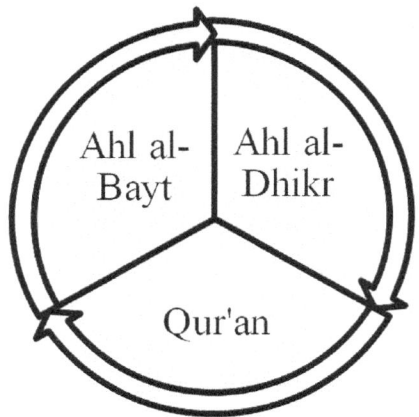

It says in the Qur'an:

> And We sent not before thee but men (as Our apostles), We revealed unto them; so ask you the people of Dhikr (the Qur'an) if you know not, with clear proofs (miracles) and scriptures; and We sent down unto thee the Dhikr (The Reminder, i.e., Qur'an) that thou may make clear unto mankind what has been sent down unto them, that they may reflect. (Qur'an 16:43–44)

> And We sent not before thee, but men unto whom We did reveal, so ask you the people of the Reminder if you know not. (Qur'an 21:7)

From the above verses, it can be understood to mean that Ahl al-Dhikr (People of the Reminder) is also Ahl al-Bayt (People of the House). The Dhikr, or Reminder, is known as the Qur'an. Since the Qur'an was revealed to Prophet Muhammad, it stands to reason that Ahl al-Dhikr is referring to the members of his family (Ahl al-Bayt). Unlike the previous scriptures (Torah and Injil), the Qur'an has not been distorted. Hence, it logically follows that Ahl al-Dhikr is referring to those at the time of Prophet Muhammad. The Imams of Ahl al-Bayt have the guidance and knowledge and are deeply embedded in understanding the Qur'an (Dhikr). So ask those of Ahl al-Dhikr in order to understand the complete meaning of the Qur'an. In addition to the concept of Ahl al-Dhikr, the Infallible Imams can also be referred to as Ahl Ilm (People of Knowledge) or Ahl Aql (People of Intellect).

Moreover, any issues that need to be addressed or disputes reconciled, we must turn to the Qur'an to solve them. We need to know who are the Ahl al-Dhikr referred to in these verses. These verses instruct us to refer to those who know and can differentiate the path to the truth. Those who know are Prophet Muhammad and his progeny (Ahl al-Bayt) who were given the knowledge and wisdom by God to discern, interpret, and understand the Qur'an.

As for religious scholars who believe that the above verses refer to the people of the Torah and Injil (Bible), there are verses in the Qur'an (2:79; 3:72; 3:78; 5:13–14) that reject this premise stating that portions of the Word of God were altered and distorted by the Jews and Christians who claim that it was from God. Hence, the Qur'an is instructing the Muslims to not refer to either the Jews or Christians on issues about which the Muslims themselves are confused. In support of this, we find hadiths from Sahih Bukhari that also reject the notion that the Qur'anic verses are in reference to the Torah and Injil (Bible):

> Narrated Abu Hurairah: The people of the scripture (Jews) used to recite the Torah in Hebrew, and they used to explain it in Arabic to the Muslims. On that, God's Messenger said, "Do not believe the people of the scripture or disbelieve them, but say: 'We believe in God and that which has been sent down to us (Qur'an 2:136).'" (*Sahih Bukhari*, Vol. 6, Book 65, Hadith 4485)

> Narrated Ubaidullah bin Abdullah bin Utba: Ibn Abbas said, "O assembly of Muslims! How do you ask the people of the scriptures, though your book (i.e., the Qur'an) that was revealed to his Prophet is the most recent

information from God and you recite it (the Qur'an) that has not been distorted? God had informed you that the people of the scriptures distorted and changed what was revealed to them, with their own hands and they said (as regards their changed scriptures): 'This is from God,' in order to get some worldly benefit thereby." Ibn Abbas added, "Isn't the knowledge revealed to you sufficient to prevent you from asking them? By God, I have never seen any one of them asking you (Muslims) about what has been revealed to you." (*Sahih Bukhari*, Vol. 3, Book 52, Hadith 2685)

Consequently, we should not refer questions to the people of other scriptures; rather, we should completely rely on the Qur'an. Then, the question becomes, who are the best interpreters of the Qur'an when we have questions? Certainly, we turn to the Sunnah of the Prophet and his progeny. Imam Ja'far as-Sadiq said,

> We are the People of Remembrance (Ahl al-Dhikr) and we are the ones who will be questioned ... I swear by God, it is we who are the Ahl al-Dhikr, to whom all questions must be referred by the command of God.

The following is a Shi'a hadith confirming that al-thaqalayn refers to the Qur'an and Ahl al-Bayt:

> In the presence of many of his Companions, the Prophet declared: "I am soon about to be received ... I am telling you before I am taken up that I shall leave you, as representatives after me, the Book (Qur'an) of my Lord, and my progeny, the people of my Household, the Ahl al-Bayt that the All-Gracious, All-Knowing, told me that they shall not be separated until they meet me on the Day of Resurrection ... Do not precede them, for you would go astray, and do not fall behind them, for you

would perish. Do not teach them, for they are of greater knowledge than you." (*Bihar al-Anwar*, Vol. 23, p. 108)

As to who is Ahl al-Bayt, the following hadith from *Sahih Muslim* refers to al-thaqalayn as the reminders (dhikr) of the Qur'an and Ahl al-Bayt:

> Yazid bin Hayyan said that Zaid bin Arqam said … One day the Messenger of God stood and addressed us at a watering place called Khumm … He praised and glorified God, and he exhorted and reminded us, then he said, "O people … I am leaving among you two weighty things (al-thaqalayn), the first of which is the Book of God in which is guidance and light. Follow the Book of God and hold fast to it … and the people of my Household (Ahl al-Bayt), I remind you of God with regard to the people of my Household (Ahl al-Bayt), I remind you of God with regard to the people of my Household (Ahl al-Bayt), I remind you of God with regard to the people of my Household … the family of Ali, the family of Aqil, the family of Ja'far, and the family of Abbas." (*Sahih Muslim*, Vol. 6, Book 44, Hadith 6225)

As can be noted, the Prophet reminded (dhikr) them that he has left behind his Ahl al-Bayt three times, and he linked his Ahl al-Bayt with the Qur'an (i.e., the two weighty things, *al-thaqalayn*) and that they are from the family of Ali, Aqil, Ja'far, and Abbas. Undeniably, there is no question that both Shi'a and Sunni hadiths confirm that Ahl al-Bayt is that of Prophet Muhammad and his progeny and no one else.

Al-thaqalayn of the Qur'an and Ahl al-Bayt remain connected, complementing each other in leading and guiding the people to the remembrance of God's blessing on these two weighty things. In understanding the significance and meaning of the straight path, we are guided by the Qur'an and Ahl al-Bayt.

Al-thaqalayn implies the religious leadership (Imamat) of Ahl al-Bayt as authorities and guides of the Ummah (community). In addition, al-thaqalayn also infers that the Twelve Infallible Imams of Ahl al-Bayt, like the Qur'an, is free from falsehood and error. To be linked with the Qur'an concludes that these Twelve Infallible Imams must also be infallible and free of sin. Al-thaqalayn manifests itself in the theology of Islam, which constitutes the Articles of Faith and Branches of Faith.

Chapter 4

Theology of Dhikr

We are often not impacted by theological sermons because we hardly ever revisit what we have learned from them. Think and reflect about the Friday prayer sermons at the mosque. How often have we forgotten what the sermon was about? Think about how much impact a sermon would have if we often remember to revisit the things we heard. Undoubtedly, we need a theology of remembrance (dhikr).

We need to remember not just a sermon or a verse from the Qur'an but also previous truths—for example, the Articles of Faith and Branches of Faith of Islam. We need to remember what we already know about these pillars of Islam. We need to revisit important things—for example, the Qur'an. We need to remember the Creator who gave us the faculty to think, to dwell, to analyze, and more importantly to remember God, the Beneficent, the Merciful.

As a student of Imam Ali ibn Abi Talib, guided by his maxims and sermons, the following is a definition of Islam:

> Islam is the attitude, the zenith of which is endurance; endurance is remembrance; remembrance is submission;

submission is certainty; certainty is believing; believing is acceptance; acceptance is adherence; adherence is action; action is behavior, the essence of which is patience.

This definition of Islam heightens and underscores the interaction of dhikr with the Articles of Faith and Branches of Faith:

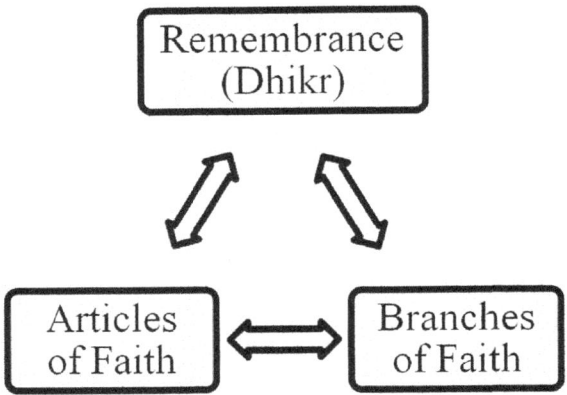

Articles of Faith (*Usul al-Din*): The three major categories of the Articles of Faith are (1) belief in God, (2) belief in the Prophets, and (3) belief in the hereafter. The belief in the unity of God, the justice of God, the angels, the Imamat (succession of Prophet Muhammad), and the Books of God derive from these three categories. For example, the Books of God are revealed to the Prophets who in turn deliver God's divine revelation to mankind. These pillars are reflected in the following diagram:

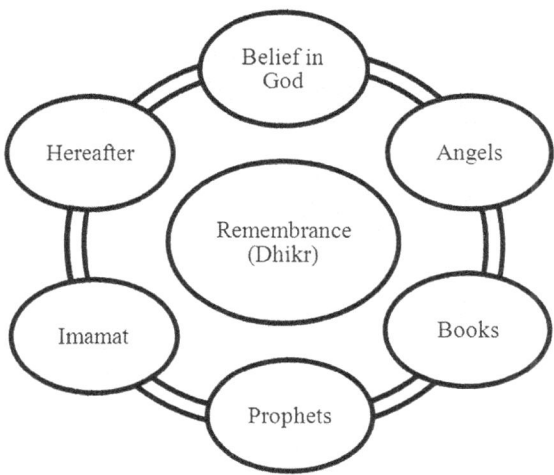

Worship is a human response toward recognition of who God is and our capacity to remember the many benefits and blessings He has bestowed upon us. Indeed, it is in the remembrance of God that a basis for worship exists. God and His works must be brought to mind regularly for the purposes of contemplation and celebration and as a barrier to keep us from sinning.

God commanded Prophet Abraham to sacrifice his son as a test of faith and obedience. God promised Prophet Abraham that his descendants would inherit his legacy and become the fathers of great nations (Qur'an 2:124). Essentially, God made a covenant—not just with the Prophets but also with all mankind—to practice fundamental ethical laws and truth (Qur'an 33:7–8). Our dhikr reaffirms the truth that we are wholly reliant on God for all our needs.

Through individual self-refinement (*tazkiya*) of our souls, we secure our faith through devotion (*ikhlas*) to God. Our reliance (*tawakkul*) on God guides us to the straight path and manifests itself in seeking God's contentment (*qana'a*), gratitude (*shukr*), generosity (*infaq*), and patience (sabr). We seek reliance and remembrance (dhikr) by complete obedience to Him. This obedience takes the shape of piety (*taqwah*), love, and loyalty to God.

How we come to learn about God is by way of revelation through the Prophets. All the Prophets had a role to perform. The summation of their spiritual works became fully realized with the final revelation—the Qur'an. Each of the five Major Prophets (Noah, Abraham, Moses, Jesus, and Muhammad) delivered the message of God. These Prophets delivered to mankind the spiritual works by which we can perform good deeds in our remembrance of God. There are twenty-five Prophets listed by name in the Qur'an of which the five mentioned above are Major Prophets. However, there were many other Prophets whose names were not cited in the Qur'an (Qur'an 40:78).

The Prophets taught us about death and the hereafter:

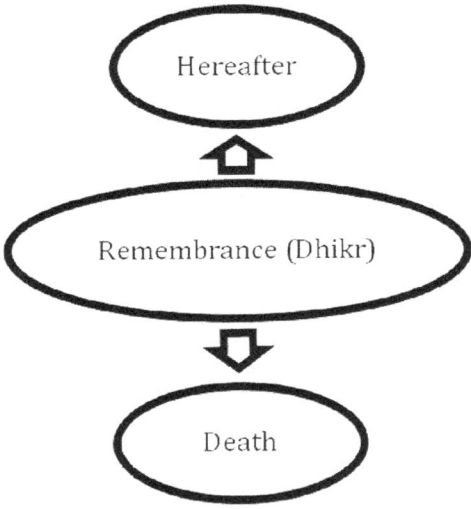

Death and resurrection (*ma'ad*) is inevitable, and the Day of Judgment (Yawm al-Qiyamah) is ever so near:

> The Day when they will hear a (mighty) Blast in (very) truth: that will be the Day of Resurrection. (Qur'an 50:42)

A new life will begin in the hereafter. Our patience and perseverance in the previous life (this life) will then be rewarded. How well we remembered God will weigh heavily in this reward. The reality of death is that it is so very near. The nearness becomes more profound when we realize that we cannot go back to the previous life to correct our wrongs. We had the golden opportunity to express our dhikr of God and embrace the pillars of Islam in the previous life. For those who missed this opportunity, they will fall short of God's grace and mercy.

Branches of Faith (*Furu' al-Din*): The Branches of Faith are many. Some of them are (1) prayer and supplication, (2) fasting, (3) alms, (4) pilgrimage, and (5) struggle (jihad):

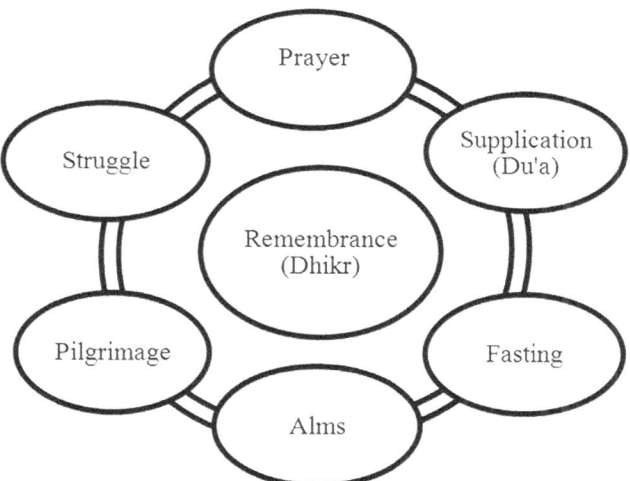

Prayer (*salat*) and supplication (*du'a*) are acts of worship within the nucleus of remembrance (dhikr). While prayer is compulsory in Islam, supplication is voluntary but highly recommended. Dhikr draws us inward, creating an inner sense of harmony and peace. Prayer is emphasized in the following verse:

> Verily, I (alone) am God: There is no god but I: worship thou (only) Me, and establish prayer for My remembrance! (Qur'an 20:14)

Prayer may be classified into two categories: (a) mandatory or compulsory prayers (*wajib*) and (b) supererogatory or recommended prayers (*nawafil*). There are six types of mandatory or compulsory prayers: (a) daily prayer (*salat wajib*); (b) sign prayer (*salat ayat*), to be recited at the solar or lunar eclipse; (c) death prayer (*mayyit*); (d) circumambulation prayer during hajj pilgrim (*towwaf*); (e) prayer that becomes mandatory upon one's taking an oath or making a solemn promise to God (*nazr*); and (f) makeup prayer (*qadha*) (Amini 1997).

As to the mandatory or compulsory prayers, five times daily we prostrate in prayer in remembrance of God. We leave our worldly affairs and business aside as we focus on our Creator and purpose in life. Since the five prayers are spread throughout the day, they keep us alert and focused so as not to become attached to the nonspiritual, material aspects of life. To merely pray, for example, without steadfastness and self-restraint in our prayer weakens our resolve. With remembrance in our prayer, our focus is heightened as we experience the true nature of patience (sabr). Prayer is also a protection from deviating off the straight path:

> Recite that which has been revealed to you of the Book and keep up prayer; surely prayer keeps (one) away from indecency and evil, and certainly the remembrance of Allah is the greatest, and Allah knows what you do. (Qur'an 29:45)

The mental attitude we practice in prayer manifests itself in our daily actions and activities. Remembrance and patience guard the dignity of the prayer and ensures that our behavior will reflect the true essence and meaning of prayer. We must be active in our search for truth through prayer. Remembrance and patience in prayer guide us to a higher level of understanding, thereby setting us on the straight path of truth as we confront the tumultuous world that is full of discord and disenchantment.

In addition, dhikr of God is also referred to as du'a (supplication). Think of supplication as sort of a prayer, a request for help from God.

It carries a sense of worship and adoration with it, a respectful appeal to God. We may ask God for His forgiveness or to thank Him for His blessings. While prayer is mandatory in Islam, supplication is highly recommended to strengthen one's inner self. Du'a means to call, and it is frequently used to call for something needed. The Qur'an underscores the importance and value of du'a:

> And says your Lord: "Call you unto Me, I will answer you." (Qur'an 40:60)

> And when My servants ask thee about Me, then (say unto them) verily I am nigh; I answer the prayer of the supplicant when he beseeches unto Me, so let them hearken unto Me and believe in Me so that they may be led aright. (Qur'an 2:186)

In du'a (supplication), we feel that God listens to our calls as we open up to Him with our needs, such as the problems and painful experiences we encounter in our lives. The constant practice of supplication renders relief and comfort and even helps purify our intentions in this world and the hereafter, thereby leading us to the straight path of peace and serenity. Consequently, by reinforcing our faith in God, we, in effect, unite our bodies with our souls.

In addition to asking God to address our needs, the most important practice of supplication is to feel the higher level of spirituality that comes about from the remembrance of God. The supplications of Imam Ali Ibnul-Husayn Zaynul-Aa'bideen in his *Al-Sahifah Al-Sajjadiyyah Al-Kamilah (The Psalms of Islam)* relate to the myriad of worries and problems that we face in life. As we recite these supplications, our feeling of unity and spirituality is heightened, resulting in the purification of our hearts.

While the mandatory or compulsory five daily prayers consist of seventeen units (rakats), the daily supererogatory prayers consist of thirty-four units (rakats) (Amini 1997). Imam Ali ibn Abi Talib has said,

> Supererogatory prayer (nafilah) results in a believer's becoming near to God. (*Bihar al-Anwar*, Vol. 87, p. 36)

Imam Ja'far as-Sadiq said,

> Truly sometimes one half; or one third, or one fourth, or one fifth of prayer ascends upward (i.e. is accepted by God); only those portions of prayer ascend upwards that are accompanied by heart's presence; and because of this reason. We are assigned to recite supererogatory prayers so that through their means the shortcomings of daily prayers could be compensated. (*Bihar al-Anwar*, Vol. 87, p. 28)

Fasting (*sawm*) means to abstain primarily from eating, drinking, smoking, and sex from dawn to sunset. It is incumbent upon Muslims to fast during the month of Ramadan, the ninth month of the Islamic lunar calendar. Muslims who are sick, traveling, or frail due to old age are exempt from fasting. However, missed fasts must be done at another time when the Muslims restore their health or complete their travel (Qur'an 2:185). There are other recommended fasts outside the month of Ramadan, such as the fast during the first and third days of the month of Muharram, the months of Rajab and Sha'ban, and the first and last Thursday of every lunar month, just to mention a few.

It is highly recommended to recite the entire Qur'an during the month of Ramadan. As such, we heighten our remembrance of God by practicing self-restraint, which is an expression of taqwah (piety). During the month of Ramadan, we reflect upon the words of God by reciting verses from the Qur'an, the Book sent to mankind during this holy month. We guard against our temptations and frailties of character by offering ourselves in deep remembrance and meditation as we reinforce our metaphysical relationship with God.

One of the pillars of Islam is alms. We are reminded (dhikr) by the verses in the Qur'an that stress the importance of remembering to give to charity:

> Men whom neither merchandise nor any sale divert from the Remembrance of God and constancy in prayer and paying the poor-rate; they fear the day the hearts and eyes will be transformed (in a world wholly new), that God may give them the best recompense for what they have done and increase for them, out of His Grace; and God provides sustenance for whomsoever He wills without measure. (Qur'an 24:37–38)

It was Imam Ali ibn Abi-Talib who used to spend his days and nights giving alms to the poor, even while in prayer. It was Imam Ali who did not deny a beggar seeking charity as he gave away his ring that caused the revelation of the following verse:

> Verily, your guardian is (none else but) God and His Apostle (Muhammad) and those who believe, those who establish prayer and pay the poor-rate, while they be (even) bowing down (in prayer). (Qur'an 5:55)

With alms, there are two forms of obligatory charitable payments: zakat and khums. Zakat is a compulsory act. Every Muslim has to pay zakat (i.e., 2.5 percent of his or her total accumulated wealth beyond one's personal needs). It is paid annually. It serves as the welfare contribution to poor and deprived Muslims. It is payable in three kinds of assets: wealth, production, and animals. Sunnis and Shi'as both adhere to the zakat principle of alms.

Khums requires an obligatory charitable payment of 20 percent of the net profit of one's annual earnings or surplus of the past year's income. Generally, khums is given to the poor and needy, orphans, and pilgrims. Shi'as adhere to the principle of khums and zakat. Although the composition of payment differs, khums and zakat generally serve the same purpose. They both assist the poor and needy. Zakat is obligatory for every Muslim. Part of the khums is also given to descendants of Prophet Muhammad who are in need (Turfe 2013).

All Muslims are also encouraged to participate in voluntary charity (*sadaqah*). Charitable deeds are of value when they are done without any self-serving motives. Voluntary charity does not have to be monetary. It can be a kind gesture, word, smile, or warm embrace. To judge a dispute between two people fairly is a form of voluntary charity. Helping an elderly person who has trouble walking is yet another example.

Pilgrimage (Haj) is a place and time when we express our gratitude to God for His blessings through remembrance and submission to Him.

> Haj is in the months well-known, whoever then undertakes the pilgrimage therein ... then when you march from Arafat remember God near the Holy Monument, and remember Him as He has guided you, although you were surely before this, of those who had gone astray. Then march you on from whence the other people march on and seek pardon of God; verily God is Forgiving, Merciful. And when you have performed your rites, remember God as you remember your fathers, rather with a more intense remembrance. (Qur'an 2:197–200)

Muslims from all over the world gather together in unity and in humility to purify their faith through prayer. They seek to cleanse themselves of their worldly weaknesses that inhibit their steadfastness and self-sacrifice to God. At the pilgrimage, they have the opportunity to express their solemn sacrifice to God and to ask for His forgiveness and guidance in order to perfect themselves as Muslims. Muslims utter a sense of obedience by saying, "I bow (my will) to the Lord and Cherisher of the Universe" (Qur'an 2:131).

In making the pilgrimage to the Sacred Mosque (Ka'bah) in Mecca, the holy shrine founded by Prophet Abraham, Muslims utter the words "Labaik! Allahuma labaik!" (I am ready to obey Your Orders, O God!). What the pilgrimage teaches us is to strive and fight in defense of truth, a struggle that first comes from within ourselves. This test of self-sacrifice continues after the pilgrimage where the person is expected to practice Islam in all its beauty and manifestations.

In Islam, there are two forms of struggle (jihad): major and minor. The major jihad is the struggle against egoism. The minor jihad (struggle) is a two-fold concept in Islam that means to (a) defend Islam against all aggressors and (b) to enjoin good by prohibiting evil. In dhikr of God, we endeavor toward struggle (jihad) and self-sacrifice for the sake of God. Self-sacrifice may require fighting in God's cause. One has to be careful in his or her definition here. Like in other faiths, some claim to be fighting for God, when in reality, they are the oppressors.

Defense is an aspect of jihad for the cause of righteousness and justice. Defending Islam by way of physical activity against the oppressor is one aspect of jihad, while scholarly work, charity, and contributions of some sort are other aspects. Jihad is not always physical—quite the contrary. It is primarily nonphysical, and the self-sacrifice one makes may be in terms of wealth, property, or forgiveness. For example, to reconcile differences with each other is at the pinnacle of jihad.

Man in his struggle is often confronted with opposition. Disputes or fights may result. A Muslim who is struck a blow is entitled to return a similar blow to his attacker. With jihad, one reaches patience (sabr) by turning the other cheek, restraining himself by setting an example of the highest form of conduct and behavior. He walks away from the dispute or fight, or he tries to console his adversary with kind words or gestures. With patience (sabr) and dhikr (remembrance) of God, he will find the way to resolve the conflict peacefully. By resolving any conflict, patience is the panacea as it brings about the dhikr and closeness between God and mankind.

Chapter 5

Types and Praises of Dhikr

There is a sense of mutual relationship between God and mankind:

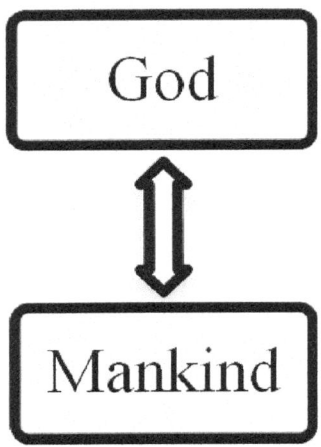

Through the language of nature, God relates Himself to mankind. God has enabled mankind to acknowledge His existence via Prophets and holy scriptures as well as the wonders of creation of the universe. In addition to the Oneness of God (Tawhid), there is a relationship between God and mankind, between mankind and fellow beings, and between mankind and its environment. It is remembrance of God that binds all of these relationships.

People forgetting God results in God forgetting them (Qur'an 9:67). It is in the awareness, or remembrance, that we perform the many rites, such as prayer, fasting, charity, pilgrimage, and jihad (struggle), in order to self-actualize our inner selves into a state of genuine piety. To constantly think of God and to retain Him in our memory is to bring our inner self into conformity with our dhikr of God.

The meaning and significance of remembrance is consistent with the verses in the Qur'an that state God does not forget anything (19:64; 20:52) and that He forever is aware of all that you do (4:94), meaning He remembers everything. By remembering God, He in turn remembers us with His mercy and forgiveness. Otherwise, God forgets those who do not remember Him, thereby withholding from them His mercy and forgiveness. Remembrance of God brings us closer to Him and also brings us closer to our own selves (59:19).

Basically, there are four types of dhikr: (a) remembrance of God, (b) prescribed prayers, (c) supplications (du'as), and (d) recitation of Qur'an and hadiths:

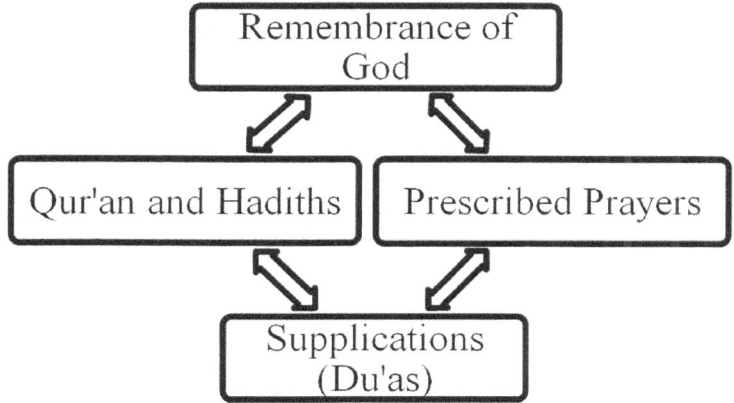

Practicing Dhikr (Remembrance) of God

In dhikr, there is a transformation of the consciousness of mind and heart from outward external thoughts to inward self of intention, meditation, awareness, and recitation of the Qur'an, prayer, supplications (du'a), and attributes of God. Following are selected examples of praising God (appendix D):

- There is no God but God (*La ilaha illallah*).
- O God (*Ya Allah*).
- Glory be to God, and praise Him (*Subhan Allahi wa bi Hamdihi*).
- Glory be to God, the Supreme, and praise Him (*Subhan Allahi 'l-adheem wa bi Hamdihi*).
- Glory be to God (*Subhan Allah*).
- There is no might or power except with God (*La Hawla wa la Quwata illa Billah*).
- All praise is for God (*Al-Hamdulillah*).
- I seek refuge in God (*A'udhu billah*).
- In the name of God, the Beneficent, the Merciful (*Bismillahi Al-Rahmani Al-Rahim*).
- I seek forgiveness from God (*Astaghfir Allah*).
- Praise be to God, the Lord of the Worlds (*Al-Hamdu lillahi rabbil 'alamin*).
- God is the greatest (*Allahu Akbar*).
- In the protection of God (*Fi Aman Allah*).
- For the sake of God (*Fi Sabil Allah*).
- This is by the grace of my Lord (*Hadha min fadl rabbi*).
- To God we belong, and to Him is our return (*Inna lillahi wa inna ilaihi raji'un*).
- If God wills (*Insha Allah*).

Easy Steps to Dhikr (Remembrance) of God

Following is a guideline of selected praises of God to be recited and the number of times repeated. Other praises of God can also be recited. In the beginning, recite one praise or two praises each day. Thereafter, the number of praises recited can be increased. Praising God is a blessing before, during, and after prayer; before going to sleep or when arising from sleep; sitting; standing; before or after eating; or any other daily activity:

Praise (Transliteration)	Translation	Recitation
Allahu Akbar	God is the greatest	34 times
Al-Hamdulillah	All praise is for God	33 times
Subhan Allah	Glory to God	33 times

After each of the five daily prayers, one should recite the above praises for a combined total of one hundred praises. This dhikr was taught by Prophet Muhammad to his daughter Fatima as a way to cope with the day-to-day hardships and is therefore known as Tasbih Fatima (Fatima's remembrance of God). One can also recite a fourth praise: there is no God but God (*La ilah illallah*). While not mandatory to recite these praises after each prayer, it is highly recommended to do so.

Another praise that is frequently recited is the Qur'anic verse Ayat al-Kursi:

> Allahu la ilaha illa Huwa Al-Haiyul-Qaiyum
> La ta'khudhuhu sinatun wa la nawm
> Lahu ma fi as-samawati wa ma fil-'ard
> Man dhal ladhi yashfa'u 'indahu illa bi-idhnihi
> Ya'lamu ma bayna aydihim wa ma khalfahum
> Wa la yuhituna bi shai'in min 'ilmihi illa bima sha'a
> Wasi'a kursiyuhus-samawati wal ard
> Wa lay ya'uduhu hifdhuhuma
> Wa Huwal 'Aliyul-Adheem

> God! There is no God but He—the Living, the Self-Subsisting, Eternal. No slumber can seize Him nor sleep. His are all things in the heavens and on earth.

> Who is there can intercede in His presence except as He permits? He knows what (appears to His creatures as) before or after or behind them. Nor shall they compass aught of His Knowledge except as He wills. His Throne does extend over the heavens and on earth, and He feels no fatigue in guarding and preserving them, for He is the Most High, the Supreme (in glory). (Qur'an 2:255)

While not mandatory, this verse is highly recommended to be recited once every morning and evening, after each of the five daily prayers, before going to bed at night, in our homes, and when leaving home. The benefits for reciting this verse is that we will be under God's protection, an angel will safeguard us, and no harmful thing will come close to us. The Kursi (Throne or Seat) is a name that denotes God's knowledge and power, and it includes all creation of the heavens and the earth.

Remembrance (Dhikr) of the Ninety-Nine Beautiful Names of God

When one has mastered the praises of God and is consistent in the daily recitation of these praises, it would further enlighten one's soul to become familiar with the Ninety-Nine Beautiful Names of God (appendix C):

> The most beautiful names belong to God: so call on Him by them. (Qur'an 7:180)

God has described Himself in the Qur'an through His names and attributes. Each name or attribute is an institution that speaks volumes about God. These noble names and attributes are guides for us to be just, wise, trustworthy, forgiving, kind, noble, compassionate, and patient. Each name and attribute nourishes our consciousness and humility in order to better our attitude and behavior. When praising God, one can call Him by one of His names or attributes. For example, if one is seeking forgiveness, he can call upon God as Al-Ghaffar (the All-Forgiving).

Prescribed Prayers

When of sound mind, every Muslim is required to pray five times a day. In addition, there are other types of prayer that are optional. Prayer is dhikr in that it is performed in remembrance of God. Prayer is the highest form of worship, as it establishes closeness with God:

> And establish regular prayers at the two ends of the day and at the approaches of the night: for those things that are good remove those that are evil: be that the word of remembrance to those who remember (their Lord). (Qur'an 11:114)

There are five daily prayers, which are obligatory and incumbent upon every Muslim to observe and perform. Each prayer has its required number of parts (rik'ats):

1. Dawn prayer (al-fajr) — two parts
2. Noon prayer (al-zuhr) — four parts
3. Afternoon prayer (al-'asr) — four parts
4. Evening prayer (al-maghrib) — three parts
5. Night prayer (al-'isha) — four parts

The combined number of parts (rik'ats) in the five daily prayers is seventeen. In addition to these, there are several other prayers, among which are prayers for the dead, for holidays, and even prayers for late into the night. We must be active in our search for truth through prayer. With patience (sabr), we can reach a higher level of understanding in our prayer, thereby setting us on the path of truth as we confront the tumultuous world that is full of discord and disenchantment.

Once each week, we meet at a mosque to perform the Friday Prayer. This Friday gathering of Muslims at a mosque further strengthens their unity via steadfastness in their prayer. At that Friday gathering, one can readily see how patient the Muslims are as they stand side by side, in unity, and prostrate in prayer. Even at the prayers during the pilgrimage, notice how patiently the millions of Muslims stand in prayer.

It is patience that makes the unity prayer or individual prayer a success. In addition, there are other congregational prayers that are emphasized—for example, the holidays celebrating the completion of fasting during the month of Ramadan and the completion of the pilgrimage (haj).

Before, during, and after prayer, there are salutations made in the remembrance (dhikr) of God. Some of these salutations are saying the praise of God, such as *La ilaha illallah* (there is no God but God) or *Allahu Akbar* (God is the greatest). The daily prayers, Friday prayers and the accompanying sermons, congregational prayers, and all other additional prayers are forms of dhikr (remembrance) of God.

Supplications (Du'as)

Supplication is additional dhikr (remembrance):

> And when My servants ask thee about Me, then (say unto them), verily I am nigh; I answer the prayer of the supplicant when he beseeches unto Me, so let them hearken unto Me and believe in Me, so that they may be led aright. (Qur'an 2:186)

Du'a means the act of remembering God and calling upon Him. As such, we call upon God for His guidance and forgiveness. While we can make our own personal supplications to God, there are, however, recommended examples from the Qur'an and hadiths (traditions). Supplications can be recited aloud or silently, and we are encouraged to recite them daily. Some of the supplications are already mentioned above. There are numerous additional supplications, some of which are the following:

Praise (Transliteration)	Translation
Allahumma bismeka amootu wa ahiya.	O God, with Your name I die and live.
Allahumma aftah li abwaba rahmatik.	O God! Open for me the gates of Your mercy.
Allahumma inee as aluka min fadlik.	O God! I beg of You of Your grace.
Allahumma inta salam, wa minka assalam tebaraekta yathel jelal wel ekram.	O God! You are peace, and peace comes from You. Blessed You are, O Possessor of Glory and Honor.
Allahumma a'innee ala thikrika wa shukrika wa husnee ibadatika.	O God, help me in remembering You, in offering thanks to You, and in worshipping You properly.
Allahumma ajirnee minannar.	O God, protect me from hell.

Supplication (du'a) and remembrance (dhikr) are closely connected. Supplication, or calling upon God, is to address Him with praise (dhikr). Both du'a and dhikr relate to the straight path. While du'a leads one to the straight path, dhikr helps one walk the straight path. The more du'a with dhikr, the further down the straight path one walks.

Additional supplications are listed in appendix G. While not mandatory, these supplications are recommended before and after eating meals, before sleeping and after waking up, before entering and after leaving the restroom, beginning and ending of *wudu* (ablution), entering and leaving the house, and entering and leaving the mosque.

Qur'an

The Arabic word *dhikr*, which translates into English as "to remember," "to remind," "remembrance," or "reminder," occurs in more than 150 verses in the Qur'an (appendix A). It is the most important virtue in earning God's pleasure. Appendix B cites selected Qur'anic verses on dhikr, some of which are listed below:

> Then do you remember Me. I will remember you. Be grateful to Me, and do not reject Faith. (2:152)
>
> Men who celebrate the praises of God standing, sitting, and lying down on their sides. (3:191)
>
> Those who believe, and whose hearts find satisfaction in the remembrance of God. For without doubt in the remembrance of God do hearts find satisfaction. (13:28)
>
> Men and women who engage much in God's praise—for them has God prepared forgiveness and great reward. (33:35)
>
> O you who believe! Let not your riches or your children divert you from the remembrance of God. If any act thus, the loss is their own. (63:9)
>
> That We might try them by that (means). But if any turns away from the remembrance of his Lord, He will cause him to undergo a severe Penalty. (72:17)
>
> But keep in remembrance the name of thy Lord and devote thyself to Him wholeheartedly. (73:8)

Hadiths (Traditions)

Appendix E cites selected Shi'a hadiths on the dhikr (remembrance) of God, some of which are listed below:

> Imam Ali said, "O God, I verily seek nearness to You through remembrance of You, and I seek Your intercession by Yourself, and, I ask You, through Your Munificence, to draw me nearer to Yourself, and to

motivate me to be grateful to You, and to inspire me with Your remembrance." (*Nahjul Balagha*, Du'a Kumayl)

Narrated from Imam as-Sadiq, God Almighty said, "O son of Adam, remember Me within yourself and I will remember you within Myself. O son of Adam, remember Me in secret and I will remember you when (you are) in secret. O son of Adam, remember Me when in an assembly and I will remember you in an assembly which is better than your assembly." (*Bihar al-Anwar*, Vol. 93, No. 31, p. 158)

God said to Prophet Musa said, "Under no circumstance (should you) abandon My remembrance." (*Bihar al-Anwar*, Vol. 13, p. 342)

Imam Ali said, "Remembrance is a source of great pleasure for the lovers (of God)." (*Ghurar al-Hikam* [Exalted Aphorisms and Pearls of Speech], No. 670)

The Holy Prophet said, "I urge you to recite the Qur'an and remember God frequently, for verily it (will result in) a remembrance for you in the heavens and a light for you in the earth." (*al-Khisal*, No. 13, p. 525)

According to Imam Ali, "The one who occupies himself with the remembrance of God, God beautifies his remembrance (among people)." (*Ghurar al-Hikam*, No. 5235)

Imam Ali said, "One who remembers God extensively is safe from hypocrisy; remembrance of God throws Satan away." (*Ghurar al-Hikam*)

Imam as-Sadiq said, "Verily the one who remembers God will never be struck by lightning." (*Amali al-Saduq*, No. 3, p. 375)

Appendix F cites selected Sunni hadiths on the dhikr (remembrance) of God, some of which are listed below:

Abu Musa reported that the Messenger of God said, "If one man has some dirhams in the possession which he divides and another remembers God, the one who remembers God is better." One variant has, "There is no sadaqa better than remembrance of God." (*at-Tabarani*)

Jabir reported that the Prophet said, "The best dhikr is 'La ilaha illa'llah,' and the best supplication is 'al-hamdu lillah.'" (*an-Nasa'i* and *Ibn Majah*)

'Ubada ibn as-Samit reported that the Prophet said, "If someone wakes up at night and says, 'There is no god but God alone with no partner. The Kingdom is His and His is the praise. He has power over everything. Praise belongs to God. Glory be to God. There is no god but God. God is greater. There is no strength or power except by God,' and then says, 'O God, forgive me or makes supplication to God,' it will be answered. If he does wudu', then his prayer will be accepted." (*al-Bukhari*)

Abu Dharr reported that the Messenger of God said, "If, after the Fajr prayer, anyone says while his feet are still folded before speaking, 'There is no god but God alone with no partner. His is the Kingdom and praise is His. He gives life and makes death, and He has power over everything' ten times, God will write for him ten good deeds, efface ten evil deeds from him, and raise him ten degrees, and that day he is protected from every very disliked thing, guarded against Shaytan, and no sin will overtake him in that day unless it is associating with God." (*at-Tirmidhi*)

Anas ibn Malik reported that the Messenger of God said, "If, when a man leaves his house, he says, 'In the name of God, I have relied on God and there is no power or strength except by God,' he will be told, 'It is enough for you. You have been guided, spared, and protected,' and Shaytan will be kept far from him." (*at-Tirmidhi*, *an-Nasa'i*, and *Ibn Hibban*)

Remembrance (Dhikr) of Ahl al-Bayt

Appendix E also lists Shi'a hadiths collected and recorded by Muhammad ibn Ya'qub al-Kulayni in his book entitled *Kitab Al-Kafi*. A couple of these hadiths on the dhikr (remembrance) of the Imams of Ahl al-Bayt are listed below:

> H 543, Ch. 20, h 1: Al-Husayn ibn Muhammad from Mu'alla ibn Muhammad from al-Washsha' from 'Abdallah ibn 'Ajlan from abu Ja'far who has said the following about the words of God, the Most Holy, the Most High. "Ask the people of Dhikr if you do not know" (Qur'an 16:43, 21:7). The Holy Prophet has said, "I am the Dhikr and the Imams are the people of Dhikr." About the words of God, the Most Holy, the Most High, says, "It is a Dhikr for you and for your people and you all will be asked questions" (43:44). The Imams said, "We are his people and we will be questioned."

> H 545, Ch. 20, h 3: Al-Husayn ibn Muhammad has narrated from Mu'alla ibn

Muhammad from al-Washsha' who has said that Imam al-Rida, "May God take my soul in service for your cause, what is the meaning of the words of God, 'ask the people of Dhikr if you do not know'"? (Qur'an 16:43, 21:7) The Imams said, "Dhikr is Prophet Muhammad and we are his family (people) about whom questions will be asked." I further asked about, "Are you the ones to be questioned and we will be the ones to question?" The Imams said, "Yes, that is true." I then asked, "Will it be right on us to ask you?" The Imams said, "Yes, it is so." I then asked, "Will it be a right on you to answer us?" The Imams said, "No, we will decide. We may or may not answer. Have you not heard the words of God, the Most Holy, the Most High that say, 'This is a gift from us. You may (give to others and) oblige or keep without being held accountable'?" (38:39)

These hadiths underscore the importance of Ahl al-Bayt, as they are instructional for understanding the virtues, effects, and benefits of dhikr.

Chapter 6

Virtues, Effects, and Benefits of Dhikr

Turning to virtues, effects, and benefits, we will explore these concepts as to how they impact the concept of dhikr (remembrance) in our daily lives.

Virtues: The virtue of dhikr necessitates us to be responsible for our actions. The dhikr of God carries immense rewards and blessings. The peace of mind from dhikr results in the serenity of the heart and elevates our spirituality. The more we invoke the remembrance of God, the greater our nearness to Him. The more we neglect His remembrance, the greater we distance ourselves from Him. Remembrance embraces a myriad of other virtues, some of which are shown below:

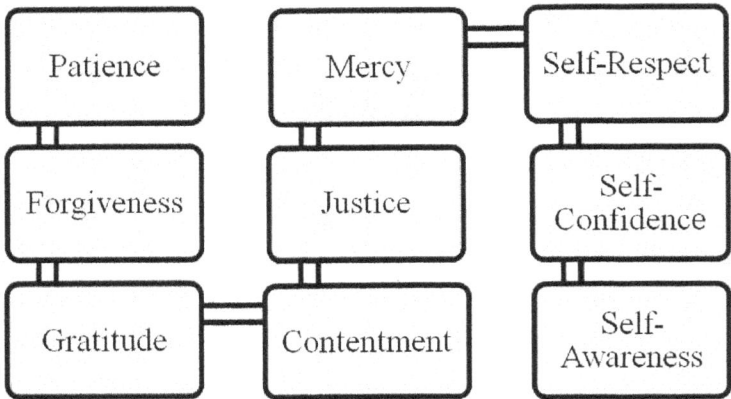

Let us examine the virtue of patience (sabr) as it relates to the virtue of dhikr (remembrance):

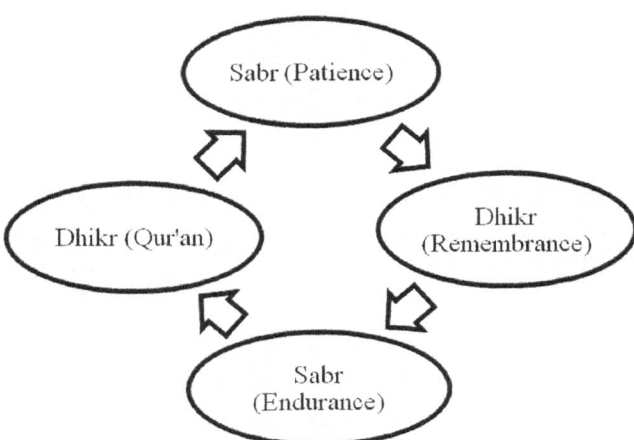

Sabr takes on many characteristics, some of which are patience, endurance, constancy, perseverance, self-restraint, forbearance, and steadfastness. Dhikr also takes on many meanings, some of which are remembrance, reminder, prayer, supplication (du'a), learning, teaching, and the Qur'an. Dhikr can also be depicted as to glorify, to exalt, to praise, to think, to mention, to recite, or to record.

While dhikr is the key to success (*miftah al-falah*), sabr is the key of relief (*miftah al-faraj*). Sabr transcends into what we call taqwah (consciousness of God). Thereafter, everything we do is *kurbatan illallah* (to become nearer to God). Without sabr, we are like ships lost at sea, never knowing which direction to turn. Sabr is the compass that directs and guides us to the dhikr of God in order to reach the sirat al-mustaqim (straight path). God is near those who have dhikr and sabr:

> Then you remember Me; I will remember you. Be grateful to Me, and do not reject faith. O you who believe! Seek help with patient perseverance and prayer: for God is with those who patiently persevere. (Qur'an 2:152–153)

The essential elements that bring about the tranquil and calm heart are dhikr (remembrance), shukr (gratitude), and sabr (patience). A heart that remains grateful (shukr) and patient (sabr) while in the remembrance (dhikr) of God will always be at peace. Sabr is mentioned before prayer because prayer cannot be firmly established without sabr. Our prayers also fill our hearts with the dhikr of God. After dhikr of God, shukr, and sabr, the Qur'an places love of God as an important resource. For only such love makes faith (iman) real and meaningful:

> And God loves those who are firm and steadfast (sabr). (Qur'an 3:146)

Sabr (patience or endurance) when coupled with, for example, recitation of Qur'an brings us even closer to God. Dhikr of God is stimulated exponentially by sabr (patience). When faced with hardships, calamities, or adversities, we need to attain patience in order to remain steadfast in our remembrance of God and in order to further strengthen that remembrance. Sabr (endurance) reinforces and ensures that dhikr of God is sustainable, thereby guiding us to firmly read and understand the Qur'an (dhikr), which leads us back to sabr (patience). This circular process enhances our faith (iman) by bringing us toward self-actualization in Islam, whereby we become in total harmony with belonging to God to Whom we shall return.

We now turn to the virtues of mercy, justice, and gratitude, as they interact with the virtue of dhikr (remembrance):

Mercy: In dhikr (remembrance) and love of God, we must be grateful for His benevolence and mercy, which are manifested in His creation and revelations. Here, mercy comes full circle, as it is a universal mercy that embraces everything. It is heightened when people live in peace and harmony with one another and are united in brotherhood and solidarity. In Islam, the spirit of mercy is manifested in two ways. First, the believers will love God, and God will love them. Second, the attitude of the believers will be one of mercy and humility as they strive for truth and justice. Remembrance (dhikr) is a virtue that softens our hearts and enables us to recall the mercy of God.

Justice: Because justice is the connection between peace and prosperity, it is the basis of the structure within mankind and the society. Muslims who truly submit to the remembrance of God are, in fact, resolute in justice because justice itself is what the society embraces. Muslims being drawn closer to the remembrance of God can also result in their justice becoming closer to all aspects of spirituality and moral principles.

Hence, justice and the remembrance of the worship of God must be firmly implanted to enable justice itself to be sanctified and valued. In a sense, justice and worship go hand in hand because justice emerges as a consequence of the remembrance of God. Here, the outcome of justice is based on spirituality that emanates from the remembrance of God. It is this remembrance that determines the true nature of justice.

Gratitude: Gratitude is an arousal of the virtue of remembrance (dhikr) that has become part of our spiritual practice. We give thanks for our remembrance of God because without gratitude we would be lost. Gratitude is considered central to the Islamic notion of dhikr. Gratitude flows from the remembrance of benefits received. In extending our gratitude in dhikr of God, we are at the same time inspiring ourselves with spiritual joy, thus making us embrace God with more energy and passion. The blessing that derives from this remembrance of God's kindness makes us put our hope and trust in Him more.

Gratitude is remembrance (dhikr) that softens our hearts, thereby awakening us to be thankful for God's blessings. With gratitude, we acknowledge the blessings of life that God has given us. Gratitude brings a sense of sufficiency, because we don't ask God for more but are thankful for whatever He has given us. Gratitude is the memory of the heart, a thankful remembrance of kindness received. We are grateful to God by thanking Him as we continue to fulfill our Islamic obligations, such as daily prayers, fasting, pilgrimage, alms, and jihad (struggle).

Effects: The effects of dhikr (remembrance) are immense. Dhikr cures our psychological disorders, purifies our hearts from pollution and tarnish, trains us in patience (sabr), and deters us from committing acts of disobedience to God. Because of the effects of self-purification, worshipping, and continuous recital of invocation, God hears our prayers, supplications, and dhikr. Although the effects are numerous, the following illustrates their importance:

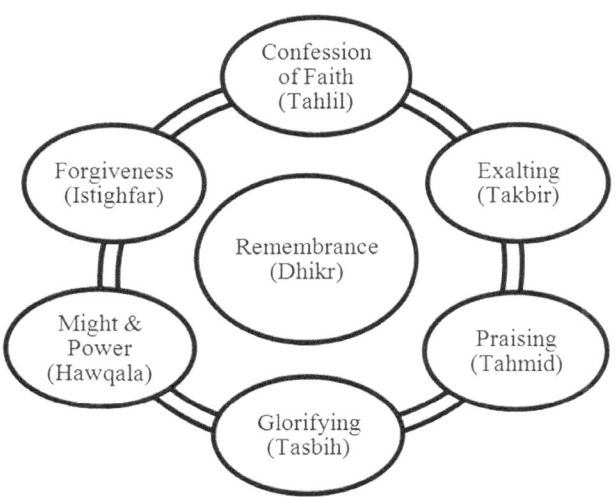

The praises from these effects of dhikr are many. A list of selected praises and their translation follows:

Dhikr	Meaning	Praise (Transliteration)	Translation
Tahlil	Confession of Faith	La ilaha illallah.	There is no God but God.
Takbir	Exalting	Allahu Akbar.	God is the greatest.
Tahmid	Praising	Al-Hamdulillah.	All praise is for God.
Tasbih	Glorifying	Subhan Allah.	Glory to God.
Hawqala	Might and Power	La Hawla Wa la Quwata illa Billah.	There is no might or power except with God.
Istighfar	Forgiveness	Astaghfir Allah.	I seek forgiveness from God.

Tahlil (Confession of Faith): *Tahlil* means to praise or acclaim and is verbalized by saying, "La ilaha illallah" (There is no God but God). Tahlil is part of the *shahada* (declaration of faith that declares belief in the oneness of God and the acceptance of Muhammad as God's Prophet) performed by Muslims in praise of God or by one converting to Islam. For Shi'as, the shahada is expanded with the addition of including Imam Ali ibn Abi Talib, "Wa 'aliyyun waliyyu-llah" (Ali is the wali [friend] of God).

Shahada is recited in each of the five daily prayers. The shahada softens the heart and eases the mind when declaring our faith. It provides us with a great deal of ease as we forget ourselves and remember to connect to God. Remembering God and honoring Prophet Muhammad have great merit in Islam, and they are not restricted to specific times or places (Al-Hakim 2011). The following verse underscores the importance of tahlil:

God (Himself) witnesses that there is no god but He, and (so do) the angels and those possessed of knowledge, standing firm for justice; (there is) no god but He, the Mighty, the Wise. (Qur'an 3:18)

Takbir (Exalting): *Takbir* exalts God that He is greater by uttering the words, "Allahu Akbar" (God is the greatest). Takbir inspires the reverence and magnificence of God. It is used in various contexts, such as in prayer and the call for prayer (*adhan*). Takbir can be said at any time or any place, for it is an expression of faith—for example, in happy or sad situations, in times of joy and gratitude, following births and deaths, empathizing with a distressed person, in war and peace, or when we ourselves are stressed (Al-Hakim 2011). Takbir is mentioned in the Qur'an a number of times:

> The month of Ramadan that in which was sent down the Qur'an a Guidance for mankind ... God desires ease for you and He desires not for you hardship that you shall complete the (prescribed) number (of days) and that you may glorify God for His guiding you and that you may be thankful (to Him). (Qur'an 2:185)

Takbir is repeated in the adhan (first call to prayer) and *iqama* (second call to prayer) several times. The prayer starts when takbir is pronounced.

Tahmid (Praising): *Tahmid* involves the beautiful names that denote God's benevolence and mercy by stating, "Al-Hamdulillah" (All praise is for God). Tahmid is the praise of God expressed right after saying "Bismillahi Al-Rhamani Al-Raheem" (In the name of God, the Beneficent, the Merciful) (Al-Hakim 2011). It is also the concluding part of our prayers:

> Their cry therein (will be), "Glory be to Thee O God!" and their greetings in it (will be), "Peace" and the last of

their cry (will be), that "God's is the praise, the Lord of the worlds." (Qur'an 10:10)

Tahmid establishes a distinct state of consciousness through which existence is viewed relative to its linkage with the universe (macrocosm) and with mankind (microcosm).

Tasbih (Glorifying): *Tasbih* exalts God by saying, "Subhan Allah" (Glory to God). Glorifying God includes all existence in the universe (Al-Hakim 2011). Everything in the universe is busy in the tasbih of God:

> Celebrate His glory the seven heavens and the earth, and (all) those in them; and there is not any thing but it glorifies Him, but you understand not their glorification; Verily, He is the Forbearing, the Oft-Forgiving. (Qur'an 17:44)

Tasbih involves repetitive recitations of short sentences in glorifying God. Muslims often carry a misbaha (string of prayer beads) to keep track of counting the praises referred to as Tasbih Fatima.

Hawqala (Might and Power): *Hawqala* praises God by saying, "La Hawla Wa la Quwata illa Billah" (There is no might or power except with God) (Al-Hakim 2011). The Qur'an cites the importance of reciting hawqala:

> Why did you not, as you went into your garden, say: God's Will (be done)! There is no power but with God! (Qur'an 18:39)

Hawqala is usually recited whenever an adversity, hardship, or calamity befalls a person. There are basically three descriptions of hawqala: (1) there is neither change nor power except by means of God, (2) there is no transformation or strength except through God, and (3) there is neither progress nor might except through God. Therefore, there is no movement from one position to another or strength to perform any affairs, except by God.

Istighfar (Forgiveness): *Istighfar* is recited by saying, "Astaghfir Allah" (I seek forgiveness from God). It is considered one of the essential parts of worship. When we abstain from doing wrong (e.g., envy, jealousy, and pride), we invoke the words "Astaghfir Allah" (Al-Hakim 2011). Even when we complete a prayer, we may ask God for forgiveness. Istighfar has been mentioned in the Qur'an:

> And (to preach unto you) that "Seek you the forgiveness of your Lord, then turn you unto Him repentant, He will provide you with a goodly provision to an appointed term and bestow on every gracious one endowed with grace; and if you turn back, then verily I fear for you in the torment of an awful day." (Qur'an 11:3)

A fountain of hope, istighfar always reminds us of our need of God's mercy. The main objective of istighfar is to beseech God's help to safeguard us against error or sin. The best road to seeking God's protection (*isti'adhah*) and support is through prayer.

Benefits: Dhikr of God has numerous benefits. Since dhikr is the remembrance of God, our invocations draw us nearer to the Creator. Therefore, we derive the benefits from this remembrance, some of which are the following:

- pleasure of God
- nearness to God
- God's mercy
- God's protection from and forgiveness of sins
- comfort and strengthening of heart
- intensified self-control
- sharpened insight and concentration
- the ability to ward off evil

- righteousness
- success and prosperity

We have a need to control our inner self and outer self. Remembrance (dhikr) helps immensely in this direction, whereupon God bestows upon us a reservoir of benefits. Following are some advantages of reciting dhikr and some disadvantages of not reciting dhikr.

Advantages of Reciting Dhikr

- Therefore, remember Me, I will remember you, and be thankful to Me and (be) not ungrateful. (Qur'an 2:152)
- O you who believe ... call God in remembrance much (and often); that you may prosper. (Qur'an 8:45)
- Those who believe, and whose hearts find satisfaction in the remembrance of God: for without doubt in the remembrance of God do hearts find satisfaction. (Qur'an 13:28)
- Recite what is sent of the Book by inspiration to you, and establish regular prayer ... and remembrance of God is the greatest (thing in life) without doubt. (Qur'an 29:45)
- For Muslim men and women ... who engage much in God's praise, for them God has prepared forgiveness and great reward. (Qur'an 33:35)
- God has revealed ... their skins and their hearts do soften to the celebration of God's praises. (Qur'an 39:23)

Disadvantages of Not Reciting Dhikr

- But whosoever turns away from My Message, verily for him is a life narrowed down, and We shall raise him up blind on the Day of Judgment. (Qur'an 20:124)
- Is one whose heart God has opened to Islam, so that he has received enlightenment from God (no better than one hard-hearted)? Woe to those whose hearts are hardened against

celebrating the praises of God! They are manifestly wandering (in error)! (Qur'an 39:22)

- And whosoever is blinded against the remembrance of the Beneficent (God), for him We appoint a satan and he shall be his close companion. (Qur'an 43:36)
- Satan has gained hold on them, so he makes them forget the remembrance of God; they are Satan's Party; Beware! Verily, the Party of Satan are the losers. (Qur'an 58:19)
- O you who believe! Let not your riches or your children divert you from the remembrance of God. If any act thus, the loss is their own. (Qur'an 63:9)
- That We might try them by that (means). But if any turns away from the remembrance of his Lord, He will cause him to undergo a severe penalty. (Qur'an 72:17)

There are at least seven doors of the human system that open in the remembrance (dhikr) of God:

Seven Doors of Dhikr

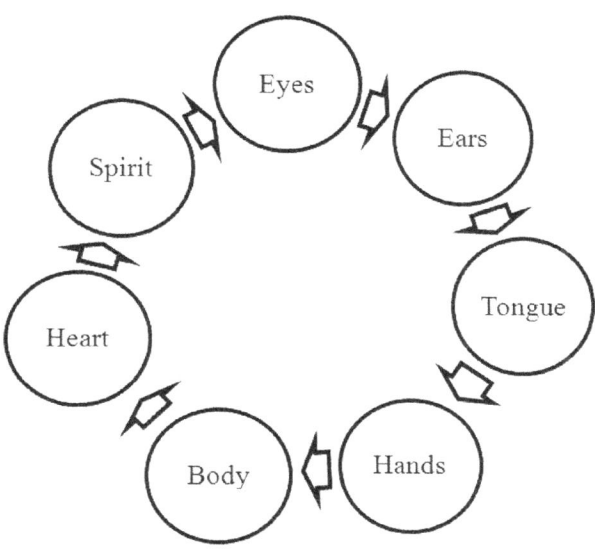

The dhikr of the eyes is weeping. The dhikr of the ears is listening. The dhikr of the tongue is praising and lauding. The dhikr of the hands is distribution and giving. The dhikr of the body is effort and accomplishment. The dhikr of the heart is fear and hope. The dhikr of the spirit is surrender and satisfaction of God (Renard 1996).

Dhikr is the foundation of good deeds. The more we remember God, the closer we are to reaching Him in the mind, heart, and soul.

Chapter 7

Dhikr: Memory, Brain, and Heart

How do we remember, and why do we forget?

Memory: Memory lapses are primarily caused by stress and overwork. Memory is impacted by an infinite number of variables that can lead to a wide range of outcomes depending upon the circumstances. Memories are the internal mental records that we maintain, which give us instant access to our personal past, complete with all of the facts that we know and the skills that we have cultivated. Encoding, storage, and retrieval are the three primary stages of the human memory process:

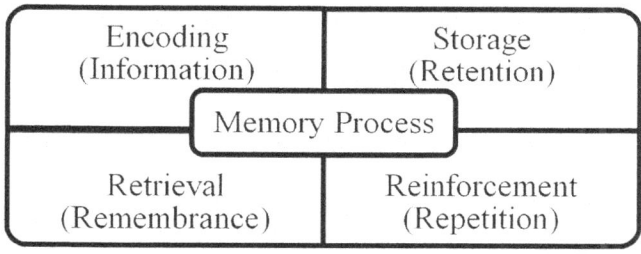

During the encoding stage, information is sent to the brain, where it is dissected into its most significant composing elements. An ensemble of brain cells processes incoming stimuli and translates that information into a specialized neural code. In the storage phase of memory formation, the brain must retain encoded data over extended periods of time. Retrieval constitutes the right of entry into the infinite world of stored information, where we bring old information out of permanent memory back into working memory, which can be mentally manipulated for usage (Wesson 2012).

Since Muslims need to invoke the dhikr (remembrance) repeatedly, the memory process necessitates a fourth stage: reinforcement. Reinforcement can come in the form of repetition or practice or through emotional arousal. Paying careful attention and consciously attempting to remember can reinforce memories. Reinforcement moves the memory relationship from being short-lived to longer-lasting ones. Continuous repetition of dhikr reinforces Muslims to self-actualize in the remembrance of God. Memory is quite fluid, and, over time, the brain continues to revisit and reorganize stored information with each subsequent experience. Our memory process enables us to recite dhikr either from the Qur'an, prayers, supplications (du'a), or God's attributes:

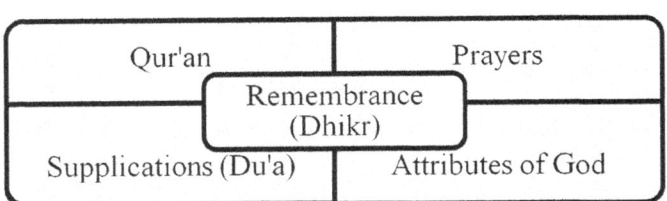

With an intense understanding of what these praises mean, Muslims begin to remember what they understand. Muslims are now able to recall from memory these praises, but equally important, they become proactive in the invocation of these praises. Hence, the memory process of dhikr becomes automatic. When extoling the virtues of God is determined to have long-term value, dhikr links the elements of encoding, storage, retrieval, and reinforcement, thereby forming a permanent memory.

Brain: Memory represents a change in what we are and, therefore, is predictive of what we will become. Neural activity in the brain is increased through the repetition of dhikr. When neurons are put to work, the brain becomes active, and its capacity begins to expand. As the brain capacity expands, the remembrance of God is established. Each time our brain's capability energizes, supplications (du'as) and brain transmission become effective. Hence, du'a itself is an action of directing brain waves. Repetition of dhikr creates familiarity, leads to understanding, and stimulates praises of God into longer-term memory. By constant repetition of praising God, dhikr allows us to remember these praises more easily by having been exposed to them before. So what we remember from the past has a lot to do with what we can remember, retain, and learn in the future. The brain controls many of our thought processes, some of which are comprehensive, imaginative, creative, and judgmental, as shown below:

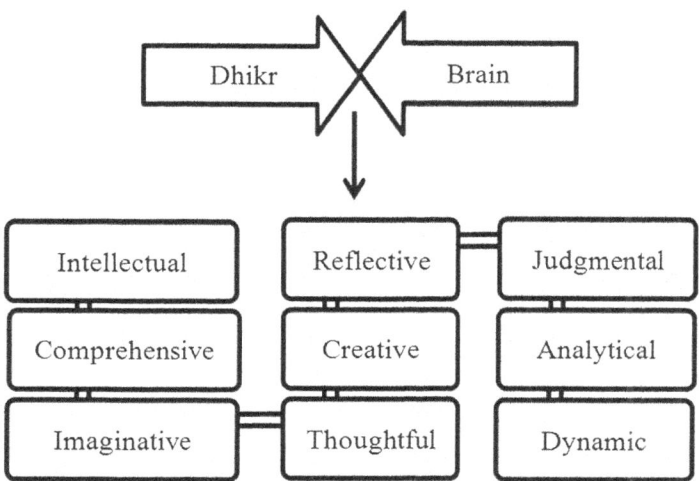

There are about one trillion brain cells. All of these cells keep on vibrating. If any discrepancy occurs in its vibration, we can become abnormal. However, these cells can be treated or fine-tuned with the help of sound waves. There is no sound as perfect, well structured, and rhythmic as the Qur'an. Reciting the Qur'an and saying the praises of dhikr (remembrance) of God to those who are ill can help in their cure. Dhikr transfers the wave energy generated by the brain to the person's soul (*ruh*). Our brain waves reveal our state of mind through the frequencies we choose to live by in the physical world. In addition, we defeat the wave of temptation by standing firm in our dhikr.

As brain waves are channeled through dhikr, the end result is that we experience a greater self-awareness and self-actualization of our prayers and supplications. The repetition of dhikr activates the dormant cells of the brain in order to revive and resurface the memory of the remembrance of God. The brain interacts with the heart to bring about the remembrance of God (dhikr):

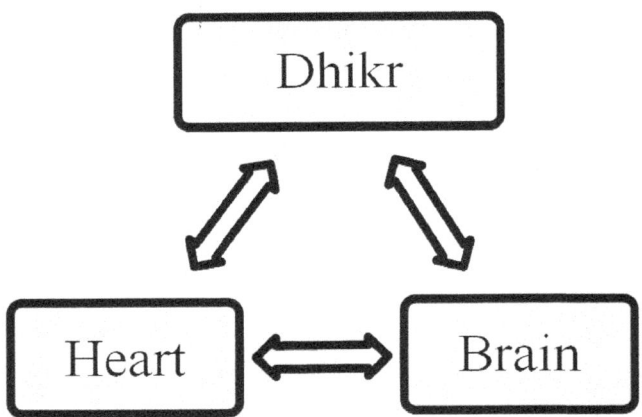

Heart: Research in neurocardiology shows that the heart is a sensory organ and a sophisticated center for receiving and processing information. The nervous system within the heart enables it to learn, remember, and make functional decisions independent of the brain's cerebral cortex. In addition, the heart communicates information to the brain and throughout the body via electromagnetic field interactions. Compared to the electromagnetic field produced by the brain, the electrical component of the heart's field is about sixty times greater in amplitude and permeates every cell in the body. Furthermore, the magnetic component is approximately five thousand times stronger than the brain's magnetic field and can be detected several feet away from the body with sensitive magnetometers (McCraty 2015).

The Qur'an has mentioned the importance of the heart relative to the dhikr (remembrance of God). Illnesses of the heart result from desires and doubts, and the Qur'an is a cure for both. The heart cures the diseases of desires and doubts that distort knowledge, understanding, and perception by enabling us to see things as they really are:

> O mankind! Indeed has come unto you an exhortation from your Lord, and a cure for (the diseases) what is in your breasts (hearts) and a guidance and mercy for the believers. (Qur'an 10:57)

> And those who believe and their hearts are set at rest by God's remembrance; Certainly! By God's remembrance (only) are the hearts set at rest. (Qur'an 13:28)

> What! Is he whose breast (heart) God has opened for Islam then he follows the Light from God (like unto the hardhearted one)? Nay! Woe unto those whose hearts are hard against the remembrance of God (dhikr); those are in a clear error. (Qur'an 39:22)

In the above verse, there is a linkage between dhikr and Islam. When there is dhikr of God, there is Islam, and where there is absence of dhikr, there is absence of Islam. When there is hardness in the heart, it can only be softened by dhikr. Dhikr is the remedy of the ills of the heart, thereby leading it to contentment. Praising God by words from the tongue is insufficient, as it must also be done in connection with remembrance of God (dhikr) in the heart:

> Imam Ali said, "Certainly, fear of God is the medicine for your hearts, sight for the blindness of your spirits, the cure for the ailments of your bodies, the rectifier of the evils of your breasts, the purifier of the pollution

of your minds, the light of the darkness of your eyes, the consolation for the fear of your hearts, and the brightness for the gloom of your ignorance." (*Nahjul Balagha*, Sermon 197)

Having "fear of God" means protecting oneself from God's punishment by carrying out what God has commanded and abstaining from what God has prohibited. Just as it is expected that the tongue and heart remain in a state of perpetual dhikr, so it is also imperative for the body as a whole to be engaged in dhikr. Some of the attributes of the heart are the following:

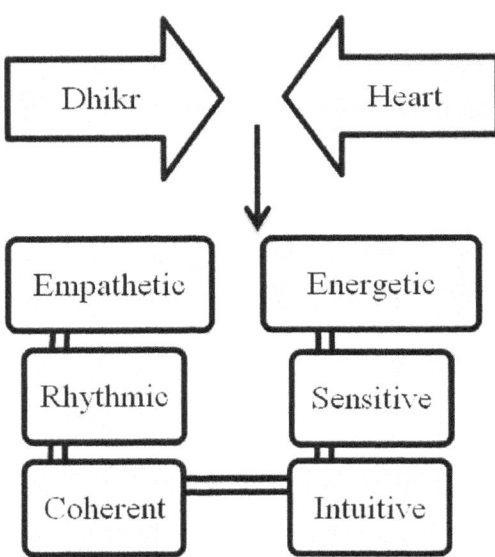

Inner performance of dhikr depends on the condition of the heart. What is important in dhikr is not just the action of the tongue but that of the heart as well. By just reciting God's name, the tongue helps dhikr settle deep in the heart, whereupon the heart participates in the dhikr. When dhikr takes the heart under its control, it enlightens all feelings of one with heavenly light. When the heart is deprived of dhikr, the soul is devoid of love. When the heart is rusted for not remembering God and goes astray from the divine path, its only cure is dhikr. Dhikr polishes the heart and surrounds the heart, shining with God's light. The most important outcome of dhikr is the purification of the heart (Tenik 2008).

Our emotional state is affected by vibrating energies that shape our personality whether we are, for example, happy or sad. Our mental and spiritual levels are affected by vibrating energies in that our conscience impacts the way we act and the way we think and feel. Through the dhikr vehicles of prayer and du'a, we are able to harmonize these weaved vibrating energies into a balanced state of energy that is physical, emotional, mental, and spiritual. These vibrating energies further enable us to understand the philosophical purpose of dhikr.

Chapter 8

Philosophy of Dhikr

The philosophy of dhikr brings into focus an understanding of our existence and the components that drive that existence. The basic foundation of life is a universal consciousness, which brings about all creation and their need for survival. All forms of energy are simply different manifestations of consciousness. Because we are part of this consciousness, our thoughts as well as our actions can influence anything and everything in existence. Consciousness itself is a kind of energy that has intelligence and organization, which is integrally related to the tiniest of creation (Kermalli 2008).

Cognition (*ma'rifah*) emanates from both the mind recognizing faith in God and the heart's devotion in remembrance (dhikr) of God:

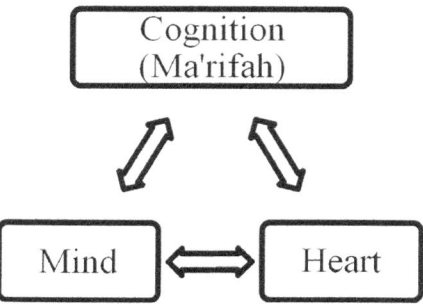

As faith and devotion increases, so does cognition (ma'rifah). As we remember (dhikr) God, He will remember us because He is aware of all that we do:

> It was We Who created man, and We know what dark suggestions his soul makes to him: for We are nearer to him than (his) jugular vein. (Qur'an 50:16)

Therefore, as ma'rifah nurtures over time, so does the act of worship in bringing into balance the heart with the mind. Remembrance of God affects consciousness of God in one's heart. We must invoke the remembrance of God to bring His revelation to our consciousness. Therefore, we not only live by the dhikr of revelation but also immerse in it as we glorify and obey God:

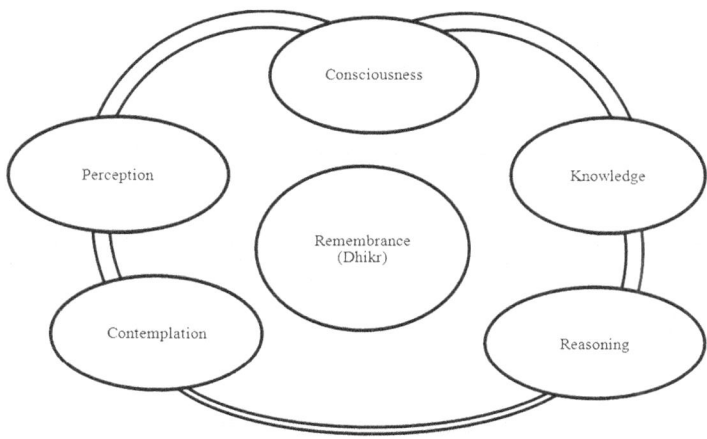

Consciousness: When dhikr is ignited by our consciousness, we are moving further ahead on the straight path of God. While we can remember God consciously and subconsciously, the zenith of dhikr intensifies when we remember God at the conscious level (e.g., prayer) (Qur'an 20:14). At this level, dhikr opens the door of the heart. Remembrance awakens a slumbering consciousness and transforms it to a higher level that ensures our nearness to God, thereby ensuring our success in the hereafter.

Conscience judges between right and wrong, between justice and injustice, between good and bad. Conscience can be the pure self (*nafs al-mutma'innah*) or the impure self (*nafs al-ammarah*). The pure self is the tranquil soul of the virtuous believer that will return to God. This is the stage when the soul of a person being delivered from all weaknesses is filled with spiritual powers and establishes a relationship with God. The impure self is the evil soul. The mind of man is ever ready to incite evil. This means that the human self urges man toward undesirable and evil ways, as it is opposed to his attainment of moral perfection. It is the voice of the pure conscience that awakens us to the remembrance of God and ultimately to our protection from the undesirable and evil.

Knowledge: Knowledge (*ilm*) of Islam and remembrance (dhikr) of God complement each other. Knowledge (ilm) makes remembrance effective, while remembrance makes the Qur'an, the book of knowledge (ilm), actionable. Knowledge is essential for us to learn and practice the faith of Islam in order to remember God. Without knowledge, remembrance is weakened. Without remembrance, knowledge is obscure. Remembrance of God purifies the heart, while knowledge of Islam enlightens us to the straight path. In increasing our knowledge of God's creation, we can, at the same time, perform dhikr in order to benefit from that knowledge and solidify our relationship with God as we draw nearer to Him.

The purpose of dhikr is that God's creation and the Qur'an are paths by which we can obtain knowledge in order to understand the essence of Islam. Through this knowledge, there are virtually an unlimited number of things that serve as dhikr for us to praise God and give thanks to Him. We often take knowledge for granted and don't consider the knowledge we learn to be part of our spiritual obligation to God. What we learn in school or in religious courses are both sources of knowledge that bring us closer to God. Prophet Muhammad made it clear as to the importance of knowledge when he said, "Seek knowledge from the cradle to the grave." To obtain knowledge is a primary responsibility of every Muslim. Remembrance of God through knowledge is a means by which we can become self-actualized as Muslims. We are reminded that the first word God revealed through Angel Gabriel to Prophet Muhammad was the word *read*:

> Read! (or Proclaim!) in the name of your Lord and Cherisher. (Qur'an 96:1)

Reasoning: Reasoning is the capacity for consciously making sense of things; applying logic; establishing and verifying facts; and changing or justifying practices, institutions, and beliefs based on new or existing information (Kompridis 2000). Reasoning is associated with thinking, cognition, and intellect. Like habit or intuition, reasoning is one of the ways by which thinking comes from one idea to a related idea. For example, it is the means by which rational beings understand how to think about cause and effect, truth and falsehood, and good and bad. It is also closely identified with the ability to self-consciously change beliefs, attitudes, traditions, and institutions and therefore closely identified with the capacity for freedom and self-determination (Foucault 2003).

Man was created with the faculty of reasoning (*ijtihad*). We are constantly called to think, to reason, to reflect when reciting the Qur'an. We are reminded of the dhikr, which is to remember God. God gifted us the faculty of reasoning, and the dhikr of His Qur'an reminds us to think and use our intellect to reason. For example, we can reason that there is a Creator by simply seeing the marvel of the universe and nature. Ijtihad (reasoning) is based upon the dhikr of the Qur'an, because the Qur'an itself is dhikr. In Islam, the whole significance of ijtihad is predicated on the verses of the Qur'an and the hadiths (traditions) of Prophet Muhammad. We derive an understanding from the ijtihad of the principles of Islamic jurisprudence.

In contemporary times, we are faced with issues that require ijtihad in order to reason how to deal with them. For example, the issue of why the Qur'an prohibits Muslims from indulging in intoxicants. This requires understanding of why Islam prohibits intoxicants and to reason whether or not drugs, such as Motrin, are acceptable when the patient is in extreme pain. Another issue deals with when to break one's fast during the month of Ramadan. In some areas of the world, the entire month is that of light (day) only or of dark (night) only. Here, reasoning (ijtihad), based on the jurisprudence of Islamic scholars, is done in order to determine how many hours in that day or night one should fast.

Contemplation: To effectively stimulate dhikr (remembrance) requires sabr (patience) to be channeled through the vehicle of *fikr* (contemplation). Dhikr is the key of success (miftah al-falah), while sabr is the key of relief (miftah al-faraj). Dhikr is the direct result of fikr (contemplation):

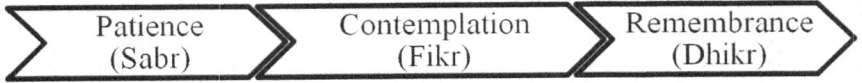

The expression of fikr (contemplation) derives from the concentration of sabr (patience). It is patience that brings about a steadfast and unwavering contemplation in order to be focused on the remembrance of God. Contemplation or reflection (fikr) is the search for something, while remembrance (dhikr) is the attainment of something. The strength and perfection of remembrance is dependent on the strength and perfection of contemplation and vice versa. Fikr and dhikr are indispensable to each other in that contemplation of the marvels of creation is linked with the remembrance of God. Hence, dhikr should be synthesized with fikr so that our praises of God are a reflection of our gratitude (shukr) to Him.

Relative to fikr, it must be understood that wisdom belongs to contemplation; knowledge to action. When Prophet Job suffered many adversities, such as losing his children, servants, and cattle as well as being inflicted with a form of lupus, he remained steadfast in his patience (sabr) and obedience to God. In the solitude of his contemplation, Prophet

Job's piety was cemented by his wisdom. His knowledge was motivated by his action of not complaining about anything bad that happened to him. His constant dhikr (remembrance) of praising God during his afflictions is symbolic of what we, too, have to do when we face difficulty or hardship. It is contemplation that steers us in the right direction to understand how wisdom and knowledge can illuminate the dhikr (remembrance) of God.

As we are in deep thought and reflection during the month of Ramadan, we perform remembrance (dhikr) and contemplation (fikr) of God. The difficulty of fasting without food and drink heightens our remembrance and contemplation. We overcome this difficulty by increasing our spiritual nourishment in order to ease the necessity of nourishment and sustenance of the body. Reading the Qur'an and reciting the praises of God each day of Ramadan is nourishment for the soul. As we reflect and contemplate (fikr) on the remembrance (dhikr) of God, our minds are released from the difficulty of hunger.

However, the reason as to why we read the Qur'an and praise God in Ramadan or at any other time needs to be understood. We should not be reciting the Qur'an or praying at the same time that we are also listening to conversations taking place nearby or the dialogue on a television program. Reciting the Qur'an and praying take precedence over everything else that may cause distractions. Truly, we have to contemplate, reflect, and concentrate on the Qur'an and prayer. What we utter by the tongue must be in consonance with what we feel in the mind and heart.

Whether in times of prosperity or hardship, dhikr and fiqr must be continuous and actionable. Fikr and dhikr take place in the mind as well as the heart. Without reflection, the heart is darkened. The heart determines what is thought, felt, or contemplated, while the mind can influence the emotions of the heart. During a religious sermon, the listener needs to contemplate or reflect (fiqr) on what is being said. Otherwise, the meaning and significance of that sermon falls on deaf ears. It is important to reflect on one's self:

> Do they not reflect (fiqr) in their own minds? Not but for just ends and for a term appointed, did God create the heavens and the earth, and all between them: yet there are truly many among men who deny the meeting with their Lord (at the Resurrection)! (Qur'an 30:8)

Fiqr is a necessary requisite that leads to guidance. While people who pray and fast have faith, it is dhikr and fiqr that act as guides to empower them to the proper way of remembrance and contemplation. It is the binding tie of sabr, fikr, and dhikr that generates the true meaning and significance of worship (*ibadat*). As a result, Muslims need to develop an attitude of contemplation that guides them to truly understand the message of Prophet Muhammad and the Qur'an. Even when we reflect on the design of the universe, we are reminded of the Creator.

Perception: Contemplation necessitates perception of oneself in order to avoid the mind from diverting elsewhere. Practicing dhikr requires self-perception, the light of spiritual advancement. Once dhikr is established in the heart, it moves through the center of perception. By not remembering God, the heart will become rusty and begin to lose perception of reality (Qur'an 83:14). Rust darkens and confuses the heart's perception, thereby rendering it unable to recognize things for what they really are. The more the heart gets rusty, the more it loses perception and recognition of things.

Perception is produced by God's dhikr. While the human intellect of the brain cannot perceive God, the perception of God is rendered clear and present to the heart by way of faith. The inner aspect of human consciousness via faith in the heart perceives the presence of the Creator. God enters into human actions through the dhikr of perception, as He is known through our senses of sight, sound, taste, touch, and smell:

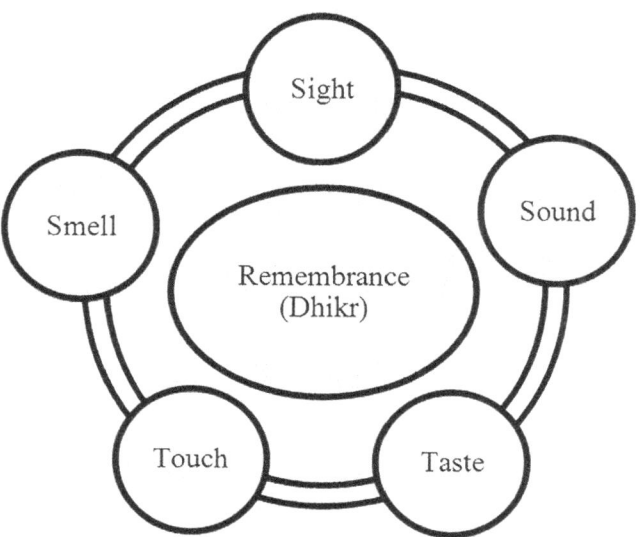

As the heart is polished and purified by the dhikr, it can interpret these senses, thereby perceiving the presence of God everywhere:

> He (God) is with everything but not in physical nearness. He is different from everything but not in physical separation. (*Nahjul Balagha*, Sermon 1)

The heart transforms perception into contemplation and everyday experiences. A unified perception is the gateway to the remembrance of God:

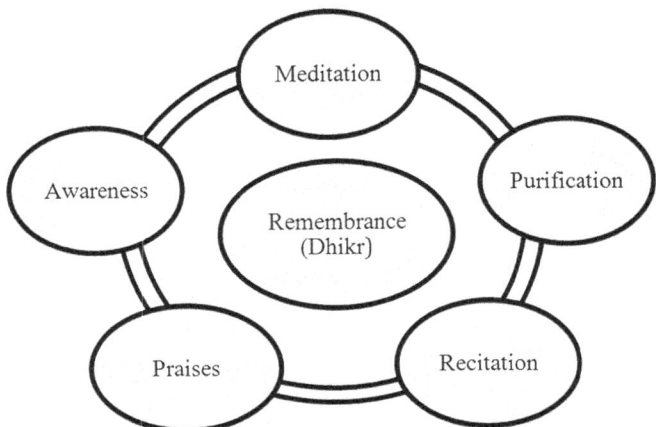

Dhikr is the gateway to God and the life of the heart. It is meditation that reaches the state of *ihsan* (perfection). The purpose of dhikr is the purification of hearts and souls to awaken the human conscience. Dhikr is recitation of the Qur'an and greeting God with His praises. One should do dhikr as often as possible until continual awareness of the divine presence of God is established.

Chapter 9

Dhikr: Books of God, Prophets, and Imams

Dhikr is enhanced through the remembrance of God's books as well as the prophets and imams who taught mankind how to achieve the straight path.

Books of God: Basically, there are four books of God: (1) Torah, (2) Psalms, (3) Gospel, and (4) Qur'an. God revealed each of these books to the prophets as a reminder (dhikr) to mankind.

Dhikr Only in the Originality of the Books of God

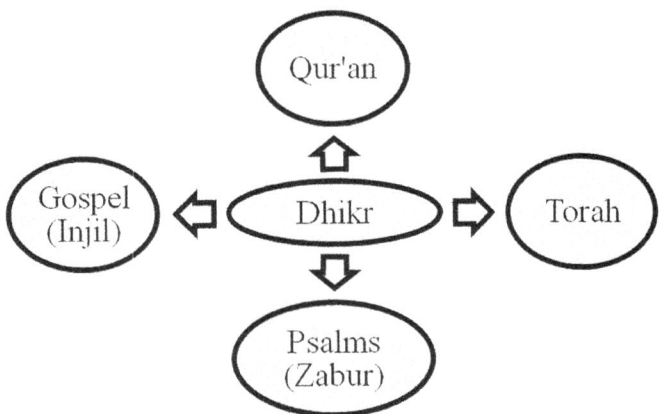

God revealed the Torah to Prophet Moses, the Psalms to Prophet David, the Gospel to Prophet Jesus, and the Qur'an to Prophet Muhammad. The Qur'an is referred to as dhikr:

> This, We recite unto thee of the signs and the Wise Reminder. (Qur'an 3:58)

> Verily We have sent down the Reminder (the Qur'an), and verily We (Ourself) unto it will certainly be the Guardian. (Qur'an 15:9)

> With clear proofs (miracles) and scriptures; and We sent down unto thee the Dhikr (the Reminder, i.e., Qur'an) that you may make clear unto mankind what has been sent down unto them, that they may reflect. (Qur'an 16:44)

> And this (Qur'an) is a Reminder full of blessings that We have sent it own (Unto Our Apostle Muhammad) Do you then deny it? (Qur'an 21:50)

The Qur'an is a reminder of the Creator, the purpose of our existence, articles and principles of faith, and the afterlife. Here, dhikr is a means by which to gain spiritual enlightenment and remembrance of God. The dhikr is an attribute of the Qur'an, and it is from the Qur'an that all forms of dhikr are derived.

It can be said that the Qur'an is the highest level of dhikr over the books of the Torah, Psalms, and Gospel. However, the Qur'an does not refer to the books of the Torah, Psalms, and Gospel as dhikr, because portions of these books have been changed over time by human errors, revisions, and interpretations, thereby rendering them as no longer completely reliable. However, since the originality of these books is preserved with God, then they can be considered as an attribute of dhikr.

The Qur'an (85:21–22) is referred to as *lawh al-mahfuz* (preserved tablet), which means that the Qur'an is the anchor and final revelation from God that is fully guarded and preserved in paradise. While all the books of God are reminders and preserved in paradise, it is the Qur'an that was revealed to supplant the other books of God that had been corrupted by mankind. Since its revelation to Prophet Muhammad, the Qur'an remains intact without revision for over fourteen centuries, and it will remain preserved for eternity.

Every verse in the Qur'an is a sign from God. The Qur'an is the greatest reminder (dhikr) and miracle that God has bestowed upon mankind. Even recent discoveries of scientific information, using modern technologies and advanced equipment, were already mentioned in the Qur'an fourteen centuries ago. Among these scientific wonders mentioned in the Qur'an are (a) human embryonic development, (b) mountains supported by pegs, (c) the origin of the universe, (d) functions of the cerebrum, (e) the barrier or partition between two different seas and between fresh water and saltwater that meet, (f) darkness in deep seas covered by waves, and (g) how clouds are formed.

Prophets: The prophets were instructed by God to act as reminders (dhikr) of His revelations:

> Recite thou that which has been revealed unto thee of the Book and establish prayer; verily prayer restrains (one) from filth and evil; and certainly the remembrance (dhikr) of God is the greatest (duty of the believers); and God knows what you do. (Qur'an 29:45)

God instructs Prophet Muhammad to recite the dhikr of the Qur'an and the importance of establishing the dhikr of prayer in remembrance of God. Two key sources of dhikr, Qur'an and prayer, are linked together as providing spiritual guidance, knowledge, wisdom, and enlightenment of the heart in order to direct us to the straight path (sirat al mustaqim). Prayer (Qur'an 20:14) and supplication are the means by which we can invoke the praises of God (e.g., Allahu Akbar—God is the greatest).

By the grace of God, there were numerous miracles performed by Prophet Muhammad that were witnessed by many people, two of which are recorded in the Qur'an:

Miracle	Qur'anic Verse
Splitting of the Moon	"The Hour is nigh and the moon is split asunder" (54:1).
Prophet's Night Journey to Jerusalem (Isra') and Ascent to the Heavens (Mi'raj)	"Glory to (God) Who took His servant for a Journey by night from the Sacred Mosque (Mecca) to the Farthest Mosque (Jerusalem), whose precincts We did bless, in order that We might show him some of Our Signs: for He is the One Who hears and sees (all things)" (17:1).

In Islam, miracles occur by way of God's intervention and act as reminders (dhikr) of God's presence. Prophets can perform miracles only by the permission of God. It was by the grace of God that Prophet Muhammad performed these two miracles.

The praises that Prophet Muhammad said regarding the remembrance of God are numerous. For example, Prophet Muhammad said in his farewell sermon at Ghadir Khumm on March 10, AD 632(18 Dhu-l-Hijja, AH 10):

> All praise is due to God Who is Exalted in His Unity, Near in His Uniqueness, Sublime in His Authority, and Magnanimous in His Dominance. He knows everything; He subdues all creation through His might and evidence. He is Praised always and forever, Glorified and has no end. He begins and He repeats, and to Him every matter is referred. God is the Creator of everything; He dominates with His power the earth and the heavens. Holy, He is, and Praised, the Lord of the angels and of the spirits. His favors overwhelm whatever He creates, and He is the Mighty over whatever He initiates. He observes all eyes while no eye can observe Him. He is Generous, Clement, and Patient. His mercy encompasses everything, and so is His giving. He never rushes His revenge, nor does He hasten the retribution they deserve. He comprehends what the breast conceals and what the conscience hides. No inner thought can be concealed from Him, nor does He confuse one with another. He encompasses everything, dominates everything, and subdues everything. Nothing is like Him. He initiates the creation from nothing; He is everlasting, living, sustaining in the truth; there is no god but He, the Omnipotent, the Wise One.

Earlier Prophets also explained and demonstrated to their communities the importance in remembering God. For example, we are reminded about Prophet Abraham, who was old but did not have any children, until God granted him Ishmael and Isaac:

> Praise is God's, Who has granted unto me in old age, Ishmael and Isaac: Verily my Lord is the Hearer of Prayer. O my Lord! Make me establish prayer and (also) some from my offspring (to do the same); O Our Lord! Accept thou my prayer! O Our Lord! Forgive me and my parents and the believers on the day when the reckoning shall be established! (Qur'an 14:39–41)

Abraham requested from God to grant him children, and his prayer was answered. Abraham thanks God for bestowing Ishmael and Isaac on him in his old age. In another experience in his life, Abraham had complete trust in God, even while he was about to be thrown into the fire. His faith and contentment at heart defied all those who placed him in the pit of fire for his destruction of the idols (Qur'an 21:58–67), but instead God made the fire cold to comfort him (Qur'an 21:68–69). Never did Abraham waver from his commitment to and remembrance of God, as he continually praised Him.

The remembrance of God by Prophet Moses is illustrated in detail in the Qur'an. A snapshot of the dialogue between God and Moses culminates in the dhikr of Moses praising God:

> Said he, "O My Lord! Expand for me my breast, and make easy for me my task, and loosen the knot of my tongue, (that) they may understand my speech, and appoint for me an aider from my family, Aaron my brother, strengthen my back by him, and associate him (with me) in my affair, that we may glorify Thee much, and remember Thee much, verily Thou art ever seeing of us." (Qur'an 20:25–35)

God revealed to Moses the importance of dhikr, particularly in special prayers, because it instills deep sincerity in the heart of the believer. The short dialogue between God and Moses changed his life and should change ours. Moses learned the inner meaning of his self, humanity, the world, and the nature of God. The essence of this exchange of dialogue teaches us that God can change one's character and outlook on life by replacing weakness with strength, failure with success, and providing the means necessary to support those who are righteous and are in constant remembrance of God. Despite the many trials and tribulations that came his way, Moses submitted himself completely to the remembrance (dhikr) of God. Moses followed God's commandments with purpose and resolve, and he was sincere in pleasing God.

Often, Prophet David engaged in dhikr of God in harmony with the nature around him. God blessed David when he revealed to him the Psalms:

> And thy Lord knows best (all) those who are in the heavens and the earth; and indeed We have exalted some apostles to some (other apostles): and gave We unto David, 'Zabur" (the Psalter). (Qur'an 17:55)

David's Psalms (Zabur) invoke praises of God when we are happy or miserable, wealthy or poor, healthy or ill, married or divorced, or in any other situation in our lives. It is one thing to praise God when we are having a nice day. It is quite another to praise God when the bottom appears to have fallen out of life, perhaps due to adversity, calamity, hardship, or deep despair. During our darkest hours, we find comfort and consolation in our praises of God. The Psalms provide us not only with a passage to ponder and to pray but also with a pattern for our prayer and worship. Hence, the Psalms help us to better worship God and to be more faithful than we would have been otherwise, both in prayer and in praise.

Inside the stomach of the whale, Prophet Jonah (Yunus), panic-stricken and distraught, called out to God:

> Then he cried out from the depths of darkness: "There is no god but Thou (O my Lord!), Glory be to Thee, verily I was of the unjust ones." (Qur'an 21:87)

> Then responded We unto him and delivered him from
> the grief, thus do We deliver the believers. (Qur'an 21:88)

Jonah realized that nothing in all creation could save him, except the remembrance (dhikr) of God. When Jonah remembered that it is God who created everything, he utters the dhikr that "There is no god but Thou (O my Lord)!" Jonah affirms the unity of God and that all causes and effects emanate from God. In addition, with the dhikr of "Glory be to Thee," he also affirms that all of God's creation is for a purpose. When Jonah says that he was of the "unjust ones," he admits he has done wrong. God accepts Jonah's plea and casts him on the shore for protection. God also forgives him for his impatience in deserting his people. Like Jonah, we too learn the lesson that forgetfulness of God leads us into the "depths of darkness," and we find ourselves in the stormy sea that submerges our souls into the abyss of emptiness. Yet the cure for being delivered from this emptiness and despair is the connection in the remembrance of the mercy of God.

Another example of dhikr is when Prophet Zachariah and his wife grew old in age but still were without a child:

> Then responded We unto him and gifted unto him John
> (Yahya), and adjusted his wife (of her barrenness) for
> him; verily, they did vie in goodness and did call unto
> Us, with love and reverence, and were unto Us humbled.
> (Qur'an 21:90)

God gave Zachariah the gift of knowledge and wisdom and engaged him to preach to his people about the straight path and worshipping only God. As Zachariah grew older, he prayed to God to bless him with a son who would follow in his footsteps in preaching about God. God listened to the cry of his humble and obedient servant by giving him the news of the pregnancy of his wife and telling him that a son, Yahya (John), would be born to continue the mission of spreading the message of God (Qur'an 19:7).

We are reminded (dhikr) in the Qur'an that the miracles of Jesus occur only by the grace of God:

> And (appoint him) an Apostle to the children of Israel (and who will declare) "that now I have come unto you with a sign from your Lord; Out of clay will I make for you like the figure of a bird, and I will breathe into it, and it shall become a flying bird by God's permission; and I shall heal the blind and the leper and will raise the dead to life by God's permission; and I will declare to you what you eat and what you store up in your houses; Verily, in this will be a sign for you if you (indeed) be believers." (Qur'an 3:49)

According to the Qur'an, Jesus never proclaimed to be the Holy Trinity (Qur'an 4:171) but only a servant of God. The Qur'an rejects the multiplicity of God and does not tolerate anything else besides the oneness of God:

> Verily God (alone) is my Lord and your Lord, so serve you (only) Him; This is the right path. (Qur'an 43:64)

Imams: The supplications (du'a) of the Imams of Ahl al-Bayt are numerous. Following are quotes from Imam Ali ibn Abi Talib, Imam Hussein ibn Ali, and Imam Ali ibn Hussein relative to dhikr (remembrance) of God.

Imam Ali ibn Abi Talib: Imam Ali stood on the shoulders of Prophet Muhammad and destroyed the biggest idols in the vicinity of the Ka'bah. Undoubtedly, as Imam Ali destroyed each of these idols, he would utter the remembrance (dhikr) of God by saying, "*La ilaha illallah*" (There is no God but God). Prophet Muhammad was the vehicle by which Imam Ali was able to accomplish this noble achievement. Following is one of many sermons Imam Ali gave in praising God:

> Praise is due to God whose worth cannot be described by speakers, whose bounties cannot be counted by calculators and whose claim (to obedience) cannot be satisfied by those who attempt to do so, whom the height of intellectual courage cannot appreciate, and the divings of understanding cannot reach; He for whose description no limit has been laid down, no eulogy exists, no time is ordained and no duration is fixed. He brought forth creation through His Omnipotence, dispersed winds through His Compassion, and made firm the shaking earth with rocks. The foremost in religion is the acknowledgement of Him, the perfection of acknowledging Him is to testify Him, the perfection of testifying Him is to believe in His Oneness, the perfection of believing in His Oneness is to regard Him Pure, and the perfection of His purity is to deny Him attributes, because every attribute is a proof that it is different from that to which it is attributed and everything to which something is attributed is different from the attribute. (*Nahjul Balagha*, Sermon 1)

Imam Hussein ibn Ali: The sacrifice of Imam Hussein, his progeny, and his followers at Karbala was the pinnacle of not only saving Islam but also displaying the true essence of remembering (dhikr) God. It was in the remembrance of God that they fought against injustice and tyranny, irrespective of the consequences. The following is Imam Hussein's *Sermon on the Night of Ashura at Karbala*:

> I thank God to the best of my ability and praise Him during the time of weal and woe. Lord! I thank You because You have honored us by means of Prophets (e.g. Prophet Muhammad), taught us the Qur'an, made us comprehend the religion and its commandments, granted us eyes, ears and hearts; kept us free from the

pollution of polytheism and then enabled us to thank You for Your blessings. (Ayati 1985)

Imam Ali ibn Hussein: Following the tragedy at Karbala, Imam Ali had the most difficult task of saving Islam. One of his numerous supplications and whispered prayers in the remembrance (dhikr) of God follows:

> In the Name of God, the All Merciful, the All Compassionate. My God, the uninterrupted flow of Thy graciousness has distracted me from thanking Thee! The flood of Thy bounty has rendered me incapable of counting Thy praises! The succession of Thy kind acts has diverted me from mentioning Thee in laudation! The continuous rush of Thy benefits has thwarted me from spreading the news of Thy gentle favours! This is the station of him who confesses to the lavishness of favours, meets them with shortcomings, and witnesses to his own disregard and negligence. Thou art the Clement, the Compassionate, the Good, and the Generous, who does not disappoint those who aim for Him, nor cast out from His courtyard those who expect from Him! In Thy yard are put down the saddlebags of the hopeful and in Thy plain stand the hopes of the help-seekers! So meet not our hopes by disappointing and disheartening and clothe us not in the shirt of despair and despondency! (*Al-Sahifah Al-Sajjadiyyah Al-Kamilah*)

The importance of the members of Ahl al-Bayt is part and parcel of our further understanding the straight path of Islam. Following is a hadith from a notable Sunni scholar relative to the importance of Ahl al-Bayt:

> Prophet Muhammad said: "I am leaving among you two weighty things, the first of which is the Book of God (Qur'an) in which is guidance and light. Follow the Book

of God and hold fast to it." And he encouraged us to adhere to the Book of God, then he said: "And the people of my Household, I remind you of God with regard to the people of my Household, I remind you of God with regard to the people of my Household." He said: "They are the family of Ali, the family of Aqil, the family of Ja'far, and the family of Abbas." (*Sahih Muslim*, Vol. 6, Book 44, Hadith 6225)

Let us take a look as to how Prophet Muhammad is inspired by the story of Prophet Joseph.

Chapter 10

Dhikr: Prophet Muhammad Inspired by the Story of Joseph

There are a number of events in which Prophet Joseph and Prophet Muhammad invoked the dhikr (remembrance) of God:

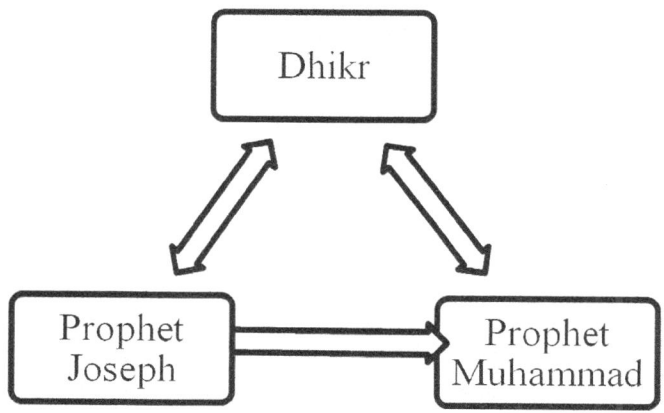

However, it was the dhikr of Prophet Joseph's story that inspired Prophet Muhammad to overcome the anxieties, stress, persecutions, hardships, and threats inflicted upon him by his enemies. The following is a recounting on why Prophet Muhammad needed that inspiration.

The story of Prophet Joseph was revealed to Prophet Muhammad as an inspiration and comfort, following the deaths of Prophet Muhammad's uncle, Abu Talib, and wife, Khadijah. Abu Talib and Khadijah were the greatest supporters of Prophet Mohammad from the onset of his mission until their death. Abu Talib was his external protector in the society, while Khadijah was his internal comforter at home. The dhikr (remembrance) of Abu Talib and Khadijah was always in the heart of Prophet Muhammad, and he was grateful to God for having been blessed with an empathetic and understanding uncle and wife.

Abu Talib sacrificed his own reputation and prestige in order to protect his nephew. By protecting him, Abu Talib, in fact, protected Islam, especially during the turbulent times of the Prophet's early mission and the tyranny of the tribal leaders and disbelievers of Quraysh. Furthermore, by encouraging his sons to follow and pray behind the Prophet indicates his strong conviction and belief in Islam.

It was the patience of Khadijah that comforted him when he was frightened upon receiving his first revelation from Angel Gabriel. Steadfastly, she stood by her husband and believed in him at the onset of his mission, even though others in the Meccan society rejected him. Her loyalty never wavered, as she even spent all her wealth in order for her husband to perpetuate the faith of Islam. It was she who lightened his heavy burden from the constant abuse and persecution by the people of Quraysh.

With the deaths of his uncle and wife, Prophet Muhammad became stricken with grief and sadness. God sent Gabriel to reveal the story of Prophet Joseph to Prophet Muhammad in order to comfort his soul. As a result, Prophet Muhammad began to realize that his problems were no different from those of Prophet Joseph. Through their patience amid the hardships emerged success and triumph in the name of God.

Unlike other stories in the Qur'an, the story of Joseph was revealed all at once in its entirety. While the stories of other prophets are meant to serve as a lesson or to highlight a certain event, the story of Joseph is meant to comfort Prophet Muhammad. Chronologically, the story describes the betrayal of Joseph by his brothers, his rise to prominence in Egypt, and the reunion with his family. In summation, the story unfolds as Joseph receives glad tidings from his father, Jacob, that he is a prophet. Afterward, Joseph is beset and tormented with a series of tragic trials and tribulations. Finally, Joseph achieves success and glory, as he becomes a ruler in Egypt. While he did not initially understand the meaning of his first dream (Qur'an 12:4), whereby he envisioned eleven stars, the sun, and the moon bowing to him, the story ends with his interpretation of that dream (Qur'an 12:100). All through his life, Joseph was in constant remembrance of God as well as his father and brothers. This was his true success. Moreover, Jacob never lost hope that his son was still alive, as he placed his reliance in the remembrance of God for his safety.

The story of Joseph was revealed in the Qur'an at the time when the first converts to Islam were brutally excommunicated or killed by members of the Meccan society. As with Joseph, God promises Prophet Muhammad that those who are patient and persistent in their faith will be victorious. Moreover, since God has unequivocal control over everything, He will provide Prophet Muhammad and his followers the means by which to overcome the malicious actions of those against them. We are reminded that Joseph reunited with his family, reconciled with his brothers who plotted to kill him, and forgave them. A similar parallelism can be drawn with Prophet Muhammad who, after being persecuted by the Meccans and driven out, reentered Mecca years later by winning the war, forgave his enemies, and declared a general amnesty.

Although Joseph had endured poor treatment from his brothers, he did not insult them nor was he revengeful. In addition, rather than reminding his brothers of the ill will they inflicted on him, he educated them and attributed their spiritual weakness to being tempted by Satan. Joseph's main objective was to direct them to piety and goodness. Likewise, Prophet Muhammad pursued a similar path, as he did not rebuke or take revenge against his former enemies. Rather, he pursued the course of educating the community about Islam and the Qur'an, establishing a system of ethics, virtues, and justice and bringing about a spiritual and cultural transformation of the society. Prophet Muhammad forgave his enemies by saying:

"Today is the day of open forgiveness." Then he asked his enemies, "How should I treat you today?" They replied, "We expect you to treat us just like Prophet Joseph treated his wrongdoing brothers." Prophet Muhammad replied, "There is no questioning from you today and you are all free." (*Fath ul Bari*, Vol. 8, p. 18)

The experiences in the lives of both Prophet Joseph and Prophet Muhammad are characterized by the polar opposites of hatred and forgiveness, jealousy and mercy, and difficulty and relief, accompanied by the guidance of God:

Verily, with every difficulty there is relief. (Qur'an 94:6)

Prophet Joseph extended his gratitude in the remembrance of God as follows:

Prophet Joseph said, "O my Lord! You have indeed bestowed on me some power, and taught me something of the interpretation of dreams and events. O You Creator of the heavens and the earth! You are my Protector in this world and in the Hereafter. You take my soul (at death) as one submitting to Your Will (as a Muslim), and unite me with the righteous." (Qur'an 12:101)

Prophet Muhammad also extended his gratitude, as evidenced by the following excerpt from his farewell sermon at Ghadir Khumm on March 10, AD 632 (18 Dhu-l-Hijja, AH 10):

Prophet Muhammad said, "I testify that He is God, the One Who has filled time with His Holiness, the One Whose Light overwhelms eternity, Who effects His will without consulting anyone; there is no partner with Him in His decisions, nor is He assisted in running His affairs. He shaped what He made without following a preexisting model, and He created whatever He created without receiving help from anyone, nor did doing so exhaust Him nor frustrated His designs. He created, and so it was, and He initiated, and it became visible. So He is God, the One and Only God, the One Who does whatever He does extremely well. He is the Just One Who never oppresses, the most Holy to Whom all affairs are referred."

It was their steadfast reliance through the dhikr of God that molded their Islamic personalities into ones of patience, sincerity, character, knowledge, wisdom, forgiveness, and truthfulness in which the masses of people were drawn to them.

The dhikr of Prophet Joseph and Prophet Muhammad relative to their trials and tribulations is further manifested in the dhikr of the tragedy of Imam Hussein ibn Ali.

AHL AL-BAYT

Chapter 11

Dhikr of Tragedy at Karbala

The tragedy at Karbala is an event that has been commemorated over the centuries. The commemoration is the remembrance (dhikr) of the suffering endured by the followers of Ahl al-Bayt. It is the dhikr of Imam Hussein ibn Ali and his fight against tyranny and injustice. Imam Hussein endured the chicanery and insidiousness of the despotic caliph, Yazid, until he could tolerate it no more. Yazid was the very essence of oppression and corruption that wreaked havoc throughout the Muslim world. A drunkard, gambler, pervert, tyrant, and oppressor, Yazid had no respect for Islam or mankind. He tainted the sanctity of dhikr (remembrance) of God by leading congregational prayers while drunk.

Yazid appointed governors with the major responsibility of terrorizing, oppressing, and torturing anyone who was loyal to Imam Hussein. These governors and officials were influenced by Yazid's corruption, including those in Kufa who reneged on their treaty with Imam Hussein. Therefore, Imam Hussein and his small contingent of less than one hundred followers were all alone in Karbala to face thousands of the enemy's soldiers.

Throughout the centuries, the dhikr of the tragedy at Karbala has been revisited and retold over and over again. Imam Hussein and his faithful and courageous Muslims were martyred at Karbala in their stand against tyranny and injustice. Their memories have not been forgotten, as this annual remembrance and reenactment of the tragedy during the ten days of Ashura in the month of Muharram has become a tradition.

Knowledge without dhikr is merely information. We attain the light in knowledge by the dhikr of God, and we need to be steadfast in the remembrance of God. Dhikr is the core, the essence, of knowledge. With knowledge, we know the meaning of what took place at Karbala, but dhikr helps connect this knowledge of the tragedy at Karbala to our hearts. Dhikr softens the heart, thereby enabling us to do more service. Dhikr makes the heart have more gentleness (*hilm*). Only by the dhikr of God will the spiritual heart attain tranquility, serenity, and happiness.

Along with chanting and reciting du'a (supplication) during the ten days of Ashura, we must transform our hearts and minds to be conscious in order to truly feel the meaning of what took place at Karbala. We recollect (dhikr) on Imam Hussein facing his enemies on the slaughter field of Karbala while wearing the dhikr of the *kisa* (cloak) and the turban of Prophet Muhammad and carrying Prophet Muhammad's personal copy of the Qur'an, itself being a dhikr, in his hand. He wasn't looking for sympathy but wanted his enemies to empathize that by attacking him, they attack the very sanctity of Islam, the Qur'an, Prophet Muhammad, and Ahl al-Bayt. Imam Hussein carried Ali al-Asghar in his arm within the kisa (cloak) of Prophet Muhammad, whereupon the enemies shot arrows at the kisa, piercing the neck of Ali al-Asghar. They shot the arrows in the very heart of Islam. Earlier on that tenth day, Imam Hussein was in total submission in the remembrance of God while leading the prayers of his followers. In his dhikr of God, Imam Hussein said,

> O God, You are my only trust in every calamity. You are my only hope in every hardship. You are the only promise in anxiety and distress in which the hearts become weak and human actions become feeble, in

which one is deserted and forsaken by his friends, and in which the enemies take malicious pleasure and rejoice at his misfortunes. O God, I submit myself to You. My complaint is to You alone against my enemies, and to You alone is my desire and request. Who else other than You can relieve me from grief. You alone are the custodian of every blessing and the Master of every excellence and the last resort for every desire. (Al-Tabari 1990)

However, Umar ibn Sa'ad, the head of Yazid's army at Karbala, was in complete disregard of dhikr while leading the prayers of his followers, the enemies of Imam Hussein. Umar ibn Sa'ad was ruthless, barbaric, and greedy and had total disregard for human life, making him succumb into the abyss of depravity. All of this was manifested in his prayers, totally devoid of the character and morality that embrace dhikr. Even more barbaric than Umar ibn Sa'ad was Ubaid Allah ibn Ziyad, the imposed governor of Kufa, who pressed Umar ibn Sa'ad to commit the treacherous acts:

> I did not send you to Hussein to hold off from fighting him, to give him time, to promise him peace and preservation, or to be an intercessor on his behalf with me. Therefore, see that, if Hussein and his followers submit to my authority and surrender, you can send them to me in peace. If they refuse, then march against them to kill and disfigure them, for they deserve that. If Hussein is killed, make the horses trample on his chest and back, for he is a disobedient rebel, an evil man who splits the community. Not that I think he would feel any harm once he is dead, but I vowed to do this if I killed him. If you carry out our order concerning him, we will give you the reward due to he who heeds and obeys. If you refuse, then withdraw from our command and our army. Leave the army to Shimr ibn Dhi al-Jawshan. We have given him our authority. (Al-Tabari 1990)

We commemorate and remember (dhikr) the tragedy at Karbala, because it was this stand of Imam Hussein that saved the faith of Islam. We remember that Imam Hussein said, "No!" to the evils of Yazid and his ilk. Even when Yazid was presented with Imam Hussein's head, he began to poke at the mouth of Imam Hussein with a cane. Abu Barzah al-Aslami, a companion, was nearby and cried out to Yazid,

> Take your cane away! By God! How often have I seen the Messenger of God kiss that mouth! (Al-Tabari 1990)

Prophet Jesus reminds us of the sanctity of Imam Hussein in the following narration:

> Imam Ali (AS) said to Ibn Abbas: Once when he happened to pass by Karbala, Isa Jesus (AS) sat down and began to weep. His disciples, who were observing him, followed suit and began weeping too, but not comprehending the reason for this behavior; they asked him: "O Spirit of God! What is it that makes you weep?" Isa Jesus (AS) said: "Do you know what land this is?" The disciples replied: "No." He then said: "This is the land on which the son (grandson, Imam Hussein) of the Prophet Ahmad (Prophet Muhammad) (p.b.u.h) shall be killed." (*Bihar al-Anwar*, Vol. 44, p. 252)

We find that Sunni hadiths also embrace the memory of Imam Hassan and Imam Hussein:

> Narrated Ibn 'Abbas: The Prophet used to seek refuge with God for Al-Hassan and Al-Hussein and say: "Your forefather (i.e., Prophet Abraham) used to seek refuge with God for Ishmael and Isaac by reciting the following: 'O God! I seek refuge with Your Perfect Words from every devil and from poisonous pests and from every evil,

harmful, envious eye.'" (*Sahih Bukhari*, Vol. 4, Book 60, Hadith 3371)

Narrated Ibn Abu Nu'um: I was present when a man asked Ibn 'Umar about the blood of mosquitoes. Ibn 'Umar said, "From where are you?" The man replied. "From Iraq." Ibn 'Umar said, "Look at that! He asked me about the blood of mosquitoes while they (the Iraqis) have killed the (grand) son of the Prophet." (Ibn 'Umar added): "I have heard the Prophet saying, 'They (Hassan and Hussein) are my two sweet-smelling flowers in this world.'" (*Sahih Bukhari*, Vol. 8, Book 78, Hadith 5994)

It was narrated that Abu Hurairah said: "The Messenger of God said: 'Whoever loves Hassan and Hussein, loves me; and whoever hates them, hates me.'" (*Sunan Ibn Majah*, Vol. 1, Book 1, Hadith 143)

Abu Sa'eed narrated that the Messenger of God said: "Al-Hassan and Al-Hussein are the chiefs of the youths of Paradise." (*Jami' at-Tirmidhi*, Vol. 6, Book 46, Hadith 3768)

Ya'la bin Murrah narrated that the Messenger of God said, "Hussein is from me, and I am from Hussein. God loves whoever loves Hussein." (*Jami' at-Tirmidhi*, Vol. 6, Book 46, Hadith 3775)

There are numerous Shi'a hadiths recollecting the tragedy at Karbala, some of which follow:

> Abu Baseer narrates that Imam Baqir (AS) said: "The humans, the jinn, the birds, and the wild beasts (all) mourned and wept over (the tragedy which befell) Hussein ibn Ali (AS)." (*Kaamil al-Ziyaraat*, p. 79)

Imam as-Sadiq (AS) said: "As for Ali Ibn al-Hussein (AS), he cried over Hussein (AS) for twenty years (after the tragedy of Karbala); never would any food be placed before him except that he would begin to weep." (*Bihar al-Anwar*, Vol. 46, p. 108)

Imam Reza (AS) said: "O Son of Shabib! Should you weep for Hussein (AS) in the measure that tears roll down your cheeks, God would forgive all of the sins committed by you, whether great sins or small sins and whether they be meager or immense." (*Amaali al-Saduq*, p. 112)

The tragedy at Karbala is a reminder not only for Muslims but also for mankind to rise up to seek positive reform in the face of resignation. The tragedy illustrates that numerical superiority does not count when it comes to truth and falsehood. Karbala signifies a lesson that human beings should never submit to tyranny, oppression, and falsehood, regardless of the consequences. Silence in the face of transgression is synonymous to the acceptance of injustice.

Mourning or grieving the day of Ashura at Karbala is not contradictory to commemorating the day of Ashura, when Prophet Moses freed his people:

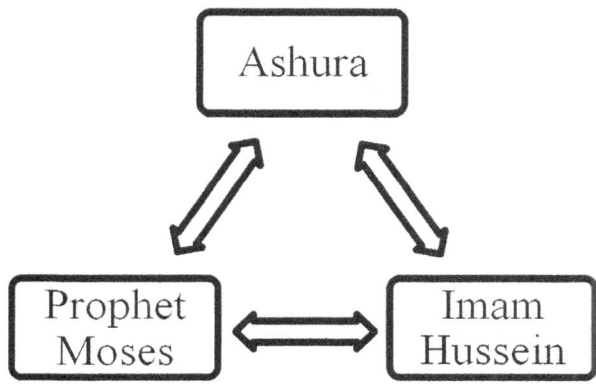

Both Prophet Moses and Imam Hussein refused to give allegiance to tyrannical rulers, while one (Pharaoh) considered himself God, and the other (Yazid) claimed to be a *khalifa* (representative) of God. We learn from the remembrance (dhikr) of both Prophet Moses and Imam Hussein that speaking truth to power is one of the qualities of people of tawhid (oneness of God), who believe that true power belongs to God alone. We also learn that desire and greed for material wealth and power corrupted the human soul to such an intense degree that human beings spilled the blessed blood of the progeny of Prophet Muhammad, committed the most heinous of crimes under the illusion of safeguarding their leadership, and inflated their status to such heights as to claim divinity.

If we deny or try to justify the event at Karbala or downplay the awful magnanimity of what occurred, we commit the same terrible treachery of the people of Kufa, who abandoned Ahl al-Bayt after giving them their allegiance. Like Prophet Moses freed his people from Pharaoh, Imam Hussein was also victorious as he parted the oceans of truth and falsehood to free his people, the progeny and followers of Ahl al-Bayt.

Pharaoh, who had earlier denied the existence of God, finally submitted to Him when he witnessed the drowning of his soldiers:

> We took the Children of Israel across the sea; Pharaoh and his hosts followed them in insolence and spite. At length, when overwhelmed with the flood, he said: "I believe that there is no god except Him Whom the Children of Israel believe in: I am of those who submit (to God in Islam)." (It was said to him:) "Ah now! But a little while before, you were in rebellion! And you did mischief (and violence)! This day shall We save you in your body, that you may be a Sign to those who come after you! But verily, many among mankind are heedless of our Signs!" (Qur'an 10:90–92)

As can be noted, Pharaoh truly pronounces the dhikr (remembrance of God) by stating, "There is no god except Him." Pharaoh had drowned with all of his soldiers (Qur'an 17:103), but God saved his dead body as a sign for those who would follow the Pharaoh to rule over the Egyptian empire. As to the preservation of a lifeless body, it was customary in ancient times to embalm one's body, particularly the Pharaohs and their families.

A group of scientists in Paris, led by Dr. Maurice Bucaille, examined the mummy of Ramses II, a Pharaoh who reigned during the time of Moses. Dr. Bucaille concluded that it was indeed the body of Pharaoh who had drowned in the Red Sea and then was cast ashore. The remains of the salt stuck in the mummy's body was shining evidence that he had drowned and that his body was retrieved from the sea swiftly after he drowned. It was also obvious that the body was immediately mummified so that it would remain intact. One of the scientists told Dr. Bucaille that the Qur'an, written fourteen centuries earlier, discusses how Pharaoh drowned and how his lifeless body was swept ashore. Curious, Dr. Bucaille read verses 90–92 of the tenth chapter of the Qur'an and was convinced that this was the conclusive evidence needed to substantiate his theory. Shortly thereafter, Dr. Bucaille converted from Christianity to Islam (Bucaille 1990).

Revolution for Imam Hussein was not to enhance his stature in the Islamic world but, rather, to establish justice and release the community from oppression and tyranny. In essence, Imam Hussein wanted to restore the people back to the straight path of Islam. His objective was not for glory or for power but, rather, for the supreme sacrifice to save Islam. Imam Hussein wanted to restore to the people their dignity and self-respect and to instill the true meaning of brotherhood. Imam Hussein did not revolt until all options had been exhausted. He came to the realization that the only way to transform the community back to the Islam his grandfather, Prophet Mohammad, had preached was to sacrifice his own life toward that cause. In essence, Imam Hussein's revolt was a struggle (jihad) only in defense of Islam, as he had to rise against the tyrannical regime of Yazid.

Imam Hussein revolted to restore Islamic law. He stepped up to the challenge, and with his bravery and courageous spirit, he was victorious. For in this victory, he reawakened the consciousness of the people. Following in the footsteps of his father, Imam Ali, he took upon himself the social responsibility of the community (Ummah), for that community was the community of his father and grandfather. As such, he fulfilled his responsibility and obligation with determination and sincerity, as he sacrificed his life and that of the members of his family and close followers, so that he could restore freedom, truth, and justice as well as Qur'anic law to the community.

The most important factor for which Imam Hussein undertook his revolt was to clean up the corruption of the Islamic caliphate under the control of Yazid. Islam considers the institution of caliphate as an important agency for spreading truth and justice among the people. Therefore, if the caliphate is righteous, the entire nation shall also be righteous. If the caliphate deviates from its responsibility, the community shall fall into terrible turmoil and calamities. Hence, Imam Hussein rose up so that he might restore to the Islamic caliphate a just and illuminated existence.

The martyrdom of Imam Hussein and his followers was the changing point in the history of Muslims and their lives. Suddenly, there was a complete change in them, as they became armed with determination and resolve. All the obstacles that had restrained them were removed, as the clouds of fear and submission that had imprisoned them changed into one of revolution and confrontation. In the dhikr (remembrance) of Imam Hussein, Mahatma Gandhi, the renowned former political and spiritual leader of India, stated, "I learned from Hussein how to achieve victory while being oppressed."

Truly, Imam Hussein's tragedy lives through the ages as a reminder that we should embrace his dhikr and those of Ahl al-Bayt. Nelson Mandela, Charles Dickens, Victor Hugo, Edward Gibbon, and several other renowned intellectuals, leaders, authors, and historians have similar quotes on their lessons learned from studying Imam Hussein and the tragedy at Karbala.

Creatures and inanimate objects also invoke the dhikr of God.

Chapter 12

Dhikr: Creatures and Inanimate Objects

All creatures (including mankind, angels, and jinn) seen and unseen on earth and in the heavens as well as inanimate objects, elements of earth, water, air, and fire, and everything else in existence make *tasbih* (glorification) in remembrance (dhikr) of God:

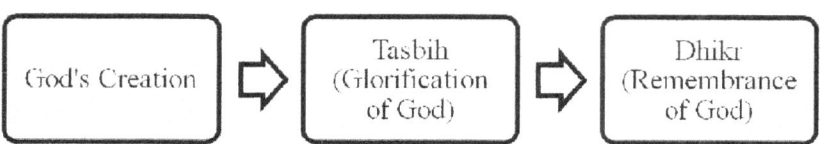

> Nay, thunder repeats His praises, and so do the angels, with awe: He flings the loud-voiced thunderbolts, and therewith He strikes whomsoever He will. Yet these (are the men) who (dare to) dispute about God, with the strength of His power (supreme)! (Qur'an 13:13)

> The seven heavens and the earth, and all beings therein, declare His glory: there is not a thing but celebrates His praise; and yet you do not understand how they declare His glory? Verily He is Oft-Forbearing, Most Forgiving! (Qur'an 17:44)

> To Solomon We inspired the (right) understanding of the matter: to each (of them) We gave Judgment and Knowledge; it was Our power that made the mountains and the birds celebrate Our praises, with David: it was We Who did (all these things). (Qur'an 21:79)

> Don't you see that it is God Whose praises all things in the heavens and on earth do celebrate, and the birds (of the air) with wings outspread? Each one knows its own (mode of) prayer and praise. And God knows well all that they do. (Qur'an 24:41)

> Whatever is in the heavens and on earth, declares the Praises and Glory of God, the Sovereign, the Holy One, the Exalted in Might, the Wise. (Qur'an 62:1)

Dhikr flows through each of these as a sign of obedience in praising God for bringing them into existence. Relative to the tasbih of the angels, Prophet Muhammad said,

> There is not a single layer of the heavens except that therein is an angel in the state of prayer and tasbih (glorifying). (Qara'ati 2014 [*Tafsir al-Qurtubi*, Vol. 8, p. 5581])

Imam Ja'far as-Sadiq said,

> Whenever Hadrat David would read the Zabur (Psalms), there was no mountain, stone and bird that

did not recite it with him. (Qara'ati 2014 [*Tafsir Nur ath-Thaqalayn*, Vol. 3, p. 444])

Whether mankind, animals, birds, trees, stones, mountains, or anything else, all are invoking the remembrance (dhikr) of God with *La ilaha illallah* (There is no God but God). As dhikr enters and strengthens each of these, they will ascend until they reach the level in which they perceive the dhikr of everything else in creation. At that time, they will understand that everything is reciting the same dhikr. All creation glorifies God. Just as mankind, angels, and jinn worship God, so do plants, animals, and inanimate objects:

> Do they not look at God's creation, (even) among (inanimate) things, how their (very) shadows turn round, from the right and the left, prostrating themselves to God, and that in the humblest manner? And to God does obeisance all that is in the heavens and on earth, whether moving (living) creatures or the angels: for none are arrogant (before their Lord). They all revere their Lord, high above them, and they do all that they are commanded. (Qur'an 16:48–50)

We move closer to God when we prostrate in prayer. In a sense, all of creation prostrates to God. While dhikr is a form of prayer, the more dhikr we invoke outside of prayer increases our closeness to God. This dhikr can result in glorifying God either consciously or unconsciously. Even the unconscious, lifeless things, such as stones, may glorify God through the intercession of angels.

Moreover, the Qur'an (38:17–19) indicates that glorification by inanimate objects and creatures is verbal, as the mountains and birds accompanied Prophet David with "hymns of their Lord" in glorifying God throughout the day. Relative to the sands speaking in Prophet Muhammad's hand, Ayatullah Murtada Mutahhari says Prophet Muhammad's miracle was not to make the sands glorify, but his miracle was to open people's ears to the sound of those sands. Those sands would glorify all the time, but the holy Prophet's miracle was to make ears hear the sound, not to make the sands produce the sound (Mutahhari 2014).

There are those who turn away from the dhikr of God. For them, we are reminded by the following verse from the Qur'an:

> If anyone withdraws himself from remembrance of (God) Most Gracious, we appoint for him an evil one, to be an intimate companion to him. Such (evil ones) really hinder them from the Path, but they think that they are being guided aright! At length, when (such a one) comes to Us, he says (to his evil companion): "Oh, I wish there was between me and you the distance between the east and west!" Ah! Evil is the companion (indeed)! (Qur'an 43:36–38)

For those who deliberately abandon true guidance, God will send them the jinn (evil one) to lead them astray and show them the path to hell. The evil one is the Shaytan (devil). Abu'l-Faraj ibn al-Jawzi of the twelfth century describes how the devil enters into the heart and corrupts it:

> The heart is like a fort that is surrounded by a wall and the wall has gates from which it can be torn down. In it lays the mind. The angels frequent that fort and next to that fort are places where the desires lie. And the devils enter into this surrounding area without being prevented from doing so. And the war exists between the inhabitants of the fort and the inhabitants of the surrounding areas. The devils never stop circling the fort and looking for an opening where the guard is heedless and from where he can tear down the fort. It is obligatory for the guards to be completely aware of all of the gates of the fort that must be guarded as well as all of its weak points from which destruction can come. The guard cannot take a break because the enemy never takes a

break. The fort is lit by the remembrance of God and faith in Him. In it is a polished looking glass through which (the guardians) can then see anything that passes by. The first thing that Shaytan does is to blow smoke into the fort to make its wall black. This causes rust and damage in the fort. Sound thought repels Shaytan and remembrance of God cleans the looking glass. The enemy has carriages and sometimes they are able to enter the fort. The guards may come upon them and force them to leave. Perhaps they may enter due to the heedlessness or carelessness of the guards. Perhaps, due to the smoke and the rust, Shaytan enters through any way and he is not perceived. Perhaps the guard is injured by the heedlessness or is taken prisoner and led to the following of the desires. (al-Ashqar 2005)

Relative to the rust of the heart, the Qur'an reminds us of the following:

> Nay! Rather, has rusted their hearts, what they used to do. Nay! Verily that day they shall be shut out away from the mercy of their Lord; Verily, they shall be committed to the flaming fire, then shall it be said (unto them): "This is that which you belied!" (Qur'an 83:14–17)

The rust is the result of the evil that penetrates the heart. As such, those afflicted by the rust are responsible for their sufferings of which the end result leads to hell. However, the recovery from evil is to engage in the remembrance of God. The Fifth Infallible Imam, Mohammad al-Baqir said:

> On the heart of every believer there is a white dot and when he commits any sin, a black dot is created and when the individual repents the black dot disappears and if the individual does not repent and continues to sin, the

black dot spreads and gradually covers the whole heart and the white dot disappears and then the individual is totally lost to the evils and gets unwilling to any amount of admonition. (*Bihar al-Anwar*, Vol. 70, p. 51)

Angels seek out those who recite dhikr, and once they find them, they encircle them with protection. When the expressions of dhikr are uttered, God sends His mercy upon them so they can be serene and tranquil:

> Our Lord! (they say), Let not our hearts deviate now after You have guided us, but grant us mercy from Your Own Presence; for You are the Grantor of bounties without measure. (Qur'an 3:8)

> Whenever dhikr of God is uttered, it is the heart that must feel its impact:

> But only he (will prosper) that brings to God a sound heart. (Qur'an 26:89)

The heart needs to be purified in order to free it from the diseases, such as jealousy and envy, that have stained it. God gave us a heart so that we can understand, reflect, and reason:

> Do they not travel through the land, so that their hearts (and minds) may thus learn wisdom and their ears may thus learn to hear? Truly it is not their eyes that are blind, but their hearts that are in their breasts. (Qur'an 22:46)

While we can reason with the intellect of the mind, we can also reason with the intellect of the heart. Knowledge resides both in the mind and the heart. Toward this end, the heart brings about faith (*iman*), mercy (*rahmah*), and certainty (*yaqin*), because God intervenes between man and his heart (Qur'an 8:24). By understanding the psychology of dhikr, we enhance our Islamic personality by way of the heart.

AHL AL-BAYT

Chapter 13

Psychology of Dhikr

The more we practice dhikr, the more we become serene in our lives. Dhikr leads to happiness, and it is a remedy for stress. Dhikr washes away our fears and anxieties and improves our lifestyle. Dhikr enhances our Islamic personality, which makes us cherish our human dignity and accept our responsibilities as Muslims. In the dhikr (remembrance) of God, we improve our behavior and attitude and overcome our shortcomings. For example, cowardice can be overcome with courage, laziness can be overcome with chastity, and prejudice can be overcome with justice.

While trained psychologists are skillful and proficient in the use of treating character disorders, we find that dhikr is also a method that can be administered to those willing to change for the better. Toward this end, we have developed a simplified model that includes at least five phases of the psychology of dhikr: (a) preremembrance, (b) remembrance, (c) preparation, (d) action, and (e) constancy.

Psychology of Dhikr

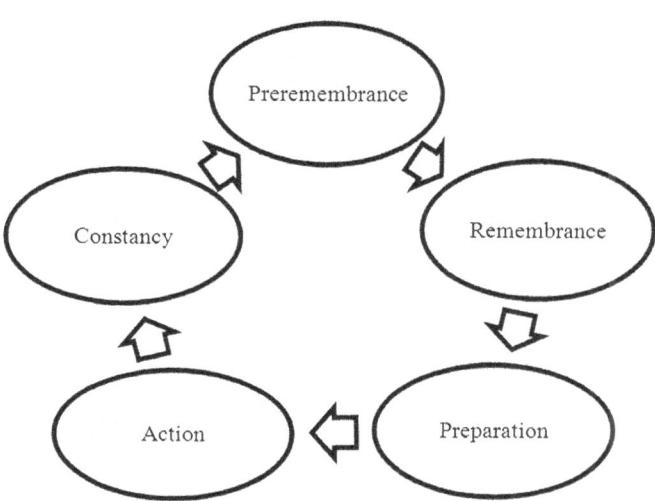

Preremembrance: An effective prescription for psychological disorders is the Qur'an, which is a guide and treatment that heals our mental attitudes and disciplines our minds. The Qur'an rehabilitates our well-being in order to improve the quality of our faith. It nourishes our souls and prepares us to be patient (sabr), which is the springboard toward contemplation (fikr), bringing us closer to the straight path (sirat al mustaqim) and remembrance (dhikr) of God. As a result, we improve upon our mental consciousness that energizes our Islamic personality.

Moreover, our mental consciousness will thereby reduce confusion, worry, stress, depression, and other psychological disorders. Throughout life, we are beset with a myriad of social and psychological problems that become more and more complex and difficult to solve. The Qur'an provides the means for preventive healing, constructive, and rehabilitative aspects that will improve our Islamic personality. Furthermore, the Qur'an brings into focus the body, mind, soul, and heart that are at peace in Islam, even with our trials and tribulations.

Remembrance: Following is one of the numerous verses in the Qur'an that refers to the necessity of the remembrance of God:

> Recite what is sent of the Book (Qur'an) by inspiration to you, and establish regular prayer; for prayer restrains from shameful and unjust deeds; and remembrance of God is the greatest (thing in life) without doubt. And God knows the deeds that you do. (Qu'ran 29:45)

Prayer is the dhikr (remembrance) of God. In prayer, our consciousness makes us aware of God. It is a reminder that performing good deeds and avoiding sin brings us closer to God. We must make our verbal declaration of dhikr. Hence, recitation of the Qur'an, purification of the heart, and prayer invoke the remembrance of God. When we become immersed in dhikr, every cell of our bodies repeats the dhikr. Once we invoke dhikr, then dhikr invokes us. It becomes part of our unconscious as it alters our mental, psychological, and physical bodies in positive ways. The effect of dhikr is more powerful than just an act of mental focusing. The end result of this process is that we are reprogrammed for God. Psychologically, dhikr frees us from the chains of forgetfulness by arousing, concentrating, and transforming the energies of our unconscious.

Preparation: There are those who pray and leave quickly, thereby gaining minimal benefit because of the lack of preparation. Others on the way to prayer and after prayer will utter dhikr in order to prepare the heart to obtain maximum benefit. After prayer, if our hearts remain unmoved and unaffected, then we have missed something. Concentration in prayer takes adequate psychological preparation. Daily activities should revolve around the five daily prayers, and we should make every effort to pray on time. Make our intention (niyyah) to pray and perform the proper ablution, which not only cleans us from any physical impurities but also helps clear our hearts and minds from our daily stresses as part of our mental preparation for prayer. This quiets our thoughts and focuses our energy on God and way from external interferences or distractions.

In addition, we need to find time for prayer. Undoubtedly, time spent on smartphones has enslaved us. As the average time spent on smartphones is almost five hours daily, we need to free some of that time to prepare and get ready for prayer. The combined total time of the five daily prayers only takes about one half hour to perform, which includes the ablution. In addition to prayer, we can make lists of dhikrs (remembrances) and begin reciting them, starting with short praises and gradually building up to longer praises over time. From those lists, we can decide how often we want to recite these praises. If necessary, we can record our daily dhikrs on Excel spreadsheets or in journals to measure how well we performed in accordance with our target levels.

Action: One's actions are judged by one's intentions. God will judge our actions based on the intentions behind those actions. The reward for one's action is according to his good intention, and the punishment for one's action is according to his evil intention. One cannot gain anything from his action, except what he intended. So if he intended good, he gets good. If he intended evil, he gets evil. If the action is sincere and incorrect, then it is not accepted. In addition, if the action is correct and not sincere, then it is not accepted. The action is only accepted when it is both sincere and correct. The action is sincere when it is done for the sake of God and correct when it is done according to the teachings of Islam. Hence, our actions are valued by the intention we hold and the consciousness of the importance in doing them.

Pray regularly. Pray with humility both in the mental state and physical manner. Pray with hope and reverence, asking God for His mercy and forgiveness. Commence prayer by seeking God's protection from the influences of Satan. Lower the gaze in prayer and avoid external distractions. Adopt a whispering technique in recitation. Display gratitude to God and invoke additional du'a (supplications). The following are hadiths on prayer:

> Prophet Muhammad said: "Say each of your prayers as if it were your last prayer." (*Bihar al-Anwar*, Vol. 69, p. 408)

> Imam Ali ibn Abi Talib said: "If a praying person knew to what extent he was surrounded by His Mercy, he would

never raise his head from (the state of) prostration."
(*Tasnif al-Ghurar-ul-Hikam*, p. 175)

Constancy: The blessing of constancy is achieved through frequent dhikr. Celebrate the remembrance of God by being constant in establishing regular prayers at the appointed times. Constancy in dhikr results in closeness with God, a feeling of inner peace and tranquility. By being constant in the action of prayer, the remembrance of God will come automatically. By being constant, dhikr will be habitual and durable, depending on the will of the believer. In dhikr, the will is dedicated to constancy of practice and the intellect to attention.

Energy and attention are complementary in that energy empowers attention while attention invokes energy. As emotions are energy and remembrance is attention, constancy brings about security from forgetfulness of God. Emotions rise and are transformed, once constancy is established and remains focused and free of distractions. By performing dhikr frequently, it is concentration that brings about its constancy. There is no better protection against Satan than constancy in dhikr. Therefore, make constancy by humbling ourselves before God and asking Him for His mercy and forgiveness.

We can achieve psychological and physical happiness by surrendering to the Qur'an, which is the greatest remembrance of God. Dhikr strengthens our faith, enlightens our hearts, and brings about spiritual awareness of who we are as Muslims. It is the inner performance of dhikr whereby the certainty (*al-yaqin*) of our faith transforms the tongue to utter praises of God from within the depths of the heart. When dhikr takes the heart under its control, it enlightens our psychological well-being and perfects our Islamic personality.

Fundamentally, there are three stages of the psychology of dhikr: (a) *dhikr al-lisan* (tongue), (b) *dhikr of al-yaqin* (certainty), and (c) *dhikr al-qalb* (heart):

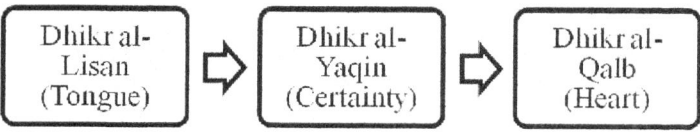

Let us examine the psychological impact of each of these three stages. Dhikr al-yaqin (remembrance of certainty) is the binding tie between dhikr al-lisan (tongue) and dhikr al-qalb (heart). Yaqin (certainty) has three levels:

(a) knowledge of certainty ('ilm al-yaqin)
(b) perception of certainty ('ayn al-yaqin)
(c) truth of certainty (haq al-yaqin)

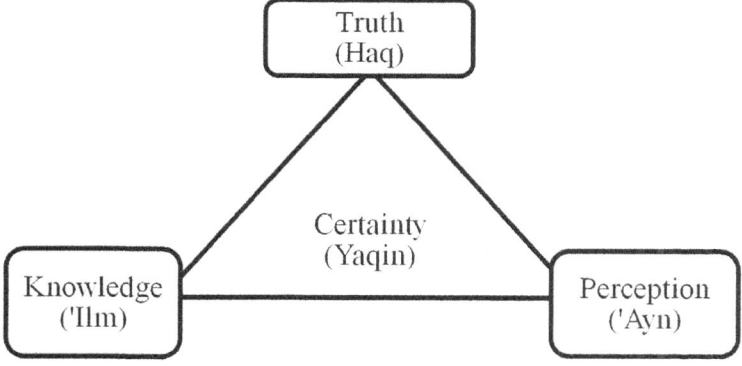

As an example of certainty, if we see smoke from afar, our knowledge of certainty tells us that the smoke must have emanated from a fire. Once we approach the area from where the smoke came, our perception of certainty reveals that the smoke indeed emanated from the fire. As we draw closer to the fire, the truth of certainty culminates in our feeling the intensity of the heat of the fire.

Another example is that of death. The knowledge of certainty is acquired by the study or observation of the body via the biological context of medicine. We know that life in this world is not perpetual but does, in fact, have an end. We know this to be fact through our own experiences of seeing our loved ones pass away. Some die at a young age; others die at an elderly age. In any event, death is inevitable. We see the angels who come to remove our souls as our loved ones weep and prepare our funerals. Once in our graves, we will witness the perception of certainty. In this regard, we have a direct perception of our temporary stay in the grave. From witnessing the phenomena of occurrences in the grave (i.e., experiencing happiness or sadness, depending on our past life's experiences), we now have reached the truth of certainty. Here, we actually experience that the process after death is real as we begin to feel the reality of our existence, demise, and rebirth in the hereafter:

> And worship thou thy Lord until there comes unto thee what is certain. (Qur'an 15:99)

The above verse reminds us that the greatest certainty is death. Though its hour is not known to us, its coming is definitely certain. We must always be aware of the closeness of death. We must always remember God and know that this life is temporary and that the next life in the hereafter is permanent. Many people do not remember God until it is time to sleep at night. Seemingly, the day goes by so quickly that they forget to remember God. Their lifestyles are such that they become immersed in the hustle and bustle of the day's events. They become occupied with words and thoughts that distract them from certainty. In addition, distractions will move them away from actions of certainty. Their minds are too cluttered dealing with the enormous amount of distractions, which render certainty as obscure. The end result is they become too tired or worn out to perform their daily prayers.

Forgetting dhikr is the result of mismanaging time. The time we waste is ours. Everything we have in life is from God, including the gift of time. When we don't allocate our time wisely, we become neglectful in our relationship with God. We pray every day to God so that He will give us peace in the mind and heart. However, to truly reap the benefit of peace is to be in constant remembrance (dhikr) of God throughout the day.

Certainty means that there is no doubt about the truth, once having the knowledge and perception through precise and accurate proof. Our tongue speaks, our eyes see, and our ears hear the truth. Our tongue speaks of the knowledge of the marvels of creation. Our eyes perceive the signs of creation, such as air, water, food, and shelter:

> Neither his eye did dazzle nor did it rebel. Indeed he did see of the greatest signs of his Lord. (Qur'an 53:17–18)

Our ears hear the sounds of the elements of nature, both inwardly and outwardly, as we repeatedly reflect on the creation. With the manifestation of the three levels of certainty, the end result is that we feel our purpose in life with our hearts.

The tongue is agile and quick. When dhikr (remembrance) of God is uttered, praises are vocalized in repetitive fashion. The gift of the tongue enables us to speak the praises of God in many languages. The power of the tongue enables us to partake in the power of words. In praising God, we need to control the tongue and be careful with our words in order to avoid falling and transgressing against God. We need to praise God and yield our tongues to the stirrings that rise up from our hearts. Hence, the gift of speaking with the tongue is a matter of the heart. Let our tongues get on with praising God with what is coming up from our hearts. The devotion of the heart, which includes all the feelings and intentions of the mind, is indeed absolutely necessary at all times and under all external experiences. For the numerous praises pronounced by the tongue would be but empty sounds without the devotional feelings of the heart.

Through the mind and conscience, we reach the level of awareness where we experience, through our senses, the signs of God's creation and purpose for our existence. For mankind, certainty is a gift from God, as it removes doubt, thereby causing our inner world to reach the level of *nafs al-mutma'innah* (tranquil self). We come to the realization that our life is but a test whereby we are firm in our faith, constantly perform good deeds, speak the truth, and practice patience (sabr) (Qur'an 103:1–3). We cling to our metaphysical relationship with God to overcome evil with good and refrain from complaining about the hardships, calamities, or adversities we experience. Hence, we will reach *idraq an-nafs* (self-realization), having passed the test of life preparing us for the eternal hereafter. Those who are in constant dhikr of God will embark on the straight path that leads to eternal bliss.

Dhikr can take place with the tongue, for once uttered, we receive its reward. When there is dhikr in the heart, then it is more complete. Dhikr by the tongue are the expressions that stand for tasbih, tahmid, and takbir—glorifying, praising, and exalting. As for the dhikr of the heart, it consists of reflections that point to God's essence and His attributes. The movement of the tongue is easier than the movement of any other part of the body. However, words of the tongue, unsupported by a willing heart, are of no benefit, potentially even sounding robotic. Dhikr of the tongue with the presence of the heart is preferable to dhikr of the tongue without the heart. When this connection is made, we feel it in our souls. We are all wired to worship, but it's up to us to exercise our free will on what to worship. Because of the ubiquity of technology, some find themselves following the every movement of entertainers, who target capturing share of mind and share of wallet. Their goal is to get us to remember them throughout the day; this leads to sales of their music, movies, perfumes, and so on. There is, of course, nothing wrong with making these purchases except when it penetrates every cell of our existence, possibly leading to missing prayers and losing out on the remembrance and worship of God.

Yet dhikr of the tongue, which combines sounds and letters, is not easy to perform, because the day-to-day activities divert our attention from such dhikr. The contrary is true of dhikr by the heart, which signifies its freedom from letters and sounds. In that way, nothing distracts one from his dhikr. With the heart, remembering God is the remembrance that is most preferred. Rather than just utilizing the tongue, dhikr manifests itself in the inner refuge of the heart in order to take firm hold of praising God. Imam Ja'far as-Sadiq captures the inner manifestation of dhikr in the following quotation, wherein he reminds us of the contrast between obedience and disobedience and between remembrance and forgetfulness:

He who truly remembers God is the one who obeys Him: whoever forgets is disobedient. Obedience is the mark of guidance, disobedience the sign of misguidance. The root of both states lies in remembrance (dhikr) and forgetfulness. Make your hearts the focal point of your tongues, which should not move unless the heart indicates, the intellect agrees, and the tongue accords with belief. Almighty God knows what you conceal and what you reveal. (As-Sadiq 1991)

When it is difficult to move from the tongue to the heart in dhikr, it may be that the door to the heart is locked through our forgetfulness. Forgetfulness of God is inexcusable negligence. Unlocking the door of forgetfulness is done through the dhikr (remembrance) of God by first putting in check some desires in this world that are essentially distractions and of no true benefit to us. We perceive a benefit to some of these harmful desires, but in reality, that benefit is a loss—a loss of proportion that will manifest itself when we are in the grave and beyond.

Knowing facts and remembering praises relative to dhikr need to be explored and understood relative to the psychological phenomenon of memory:

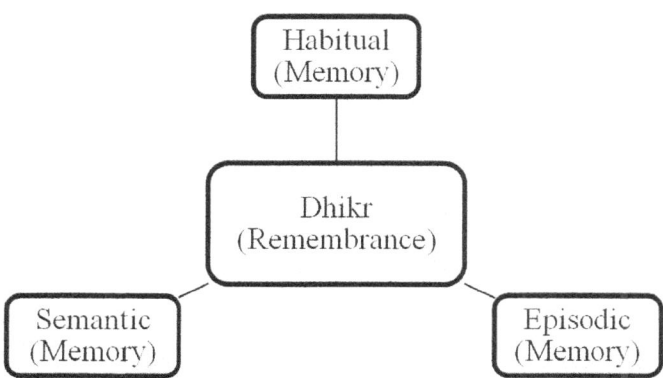

Dhikr (remembrance) can emanate from at least three levels: (a) semantic memory, (b) episodic memory, and (c) habitual memory

(Hass-Cohen 2015). Semantic memory is when we remember facts derived from knowledge throughout our lives that we share with others (e.g., Abraham Lincoln was the sixteenth president of the United States, or Prophet Muhammad was the final prophet). Episodic memory is when we remember specific events that we personally experienced (e.g., our first time driving an automobile or our first time memorizing a chapter from the Qur'an). Habitual memory is when we remember how to do something (e.g., using soap when taking a bath or performing ablution before prayer).

Semantic memory and episodic memory are two information processing systems that (a) selectively receive information from perceptual systems or other cognitive systems; (b) retain various aspects of this information; and (c) upon instructions, transmit specific retained information to other systems, including those responsible for translating it into behavior and conscious awareness. The two systems differ from one another in terms of (a) the nature of stored information, (b) autobiographical versus cognitive reference, (c) conditions and consequences of retrieval, (d) their vulnerability to interference resulting in transformation and erasure of stored information, and (e) their dependence upon each other (Tulving 1972).

Studies focusing on episodic and semantic memory systems assessed how participants respond while thinking about the source of a particular piece of information. Episodic memory was found to be more associated with "remember" responses, whereas semantic memory was found to be more associated with "know" responses. More specifically, when people report that they remember the specific moment at which they learned about a phenomenon, they use episodic memory system. When they report that they know the item but they do not remember a specific moment of learning it, they use semantic memory system (Tulving 1985). Therefore, remember/know paradigm corresponds to episodic and semantic memory systems.

When someone first chants tasbih (Subhan Allah [Glory to God]), tahmid (Al-Hamdulillah [All praise is for God]), takbir (Allahu Akbar [God is the greatest]), and tahlil (La ilaha illallah [There is no God but God]), these are associated with "know" responses and become stored in the semantic memory system. When "remembering" to chant these praises in the future, they become stored in the episodic memory system.

Semantic Memory: Semantic memory is stored in words, concepts, and meanings. In Islam, semantic memory is a record of abstract facts and knowledge we have learned about the religion (e.g., the 114 chapters in the Qur'an, Friday prayer, or fasting during the month of Ramadan). By eliciting the knowledge we have learned, we are giving special attention to that knowledge so as to habitually remember it for the future. For example, we first learned how to pray but now have acquired new knowledge to add supplication (du'a) to our daily prayers. After we have memorized the supplication (du'a), it will be fixed in memory. Repetition fixes the information in semantic memory so that we retain a constant knowledge of our Islam. When we perform dhikr (remembrance) of God, we retrieve this knowledge that remains in our semantic memory.

Episodic Memory: Episodic memory is in the form of sequences of events. Episodic memory records memorable events from our lives. It is our memory of experiences and life events tied to specific times and places. Every time we recall an episode (e.g., the holiday prayer event), we modify our episodic memory of that experience based on our current perspective. Remembering to recall the praises of God already stored in the semantic memory now becomes stored in the episodic memory system. Holiday prayers are events that we cherish and remember, and each event gives us added connection to the dhikr (remembrance) of God. Episodic memory is also linked to tragic events. Someone who is afflicted with cancer may call upon God for His help by activating what is already known in the semantic memory system. In this case, when that person constantly recites praises from both the tongue and the heart in remembrance of God for His help, God will provide comfort and serenity.

Performing a memory task repeatedly changes the nature of the task from episodic to habitual (Meier 2014). With semantic memory, we learned how to pray. With episodic memory, we can talk about the times we prayed. Similarly, from the first time we made our intention to perform dhikr of God to now repeating that praise is also an example of moving the memory from semantic to episodic.

Semantic memory and episodic memory are usually closely related to one another; that is, memory of facts (semantic) might be enhanced by interaction with memory about personal events (episodic) and vice versa. For example, the answer to a factual (semantic) question of whether people put ketchup on their chips might be answered positively by remembering the last time (episodic) you saw someone eating fish and chips. The other way around, semantic memory about certain things, such as football, can contribute to more detailed episodic memory of a particular personal event, like watching a football match. A person that barely knows the rules of that game will most probably have a less specific memory for the personal event of watching the game than that of a football expert (*Cognitive Psychology and Cognitive Neuroscience* 2013).

Habitual Memory: While habits may be formed without intention, there are situations in which we intentionally and deliberately want to form a habit (e.g., remembering to take medication on a regular basis or praying at the prescribed time). This situation is referred to as habitual prospective memory. Habitual prospective memory is the ability to remember to perform a previously formed intention at the appropriate occasion (e.g., keeping a doctor's appointment or complying with the regimented parts of prayer). Habit formation is the process by which a behavior, through regular repetition, becomes automatic or habitual (Lally 2010). A habit may initially be triggered by a goal, but over time that goal becomes less necessary and the habit becomes more automatic. Habits develop over time. Prayer seeks to develop habitual behavior that reinforces spiritual well-being. Memorization of prayers or supplications (du'a) results in habitual recitation.

Habitual memory of prayer, with patience (sabr), brings us closer to God. Through prayer, believers are able to express their faith in words. Memory tasks that are performed repeatedly become habitual. Remembering to pray is an example of an episodic memory task. After years of praying, it may be done without even thinking about it, in that prayer becomes automatic or habitual. When this happens, we need to ensure that we fully understand the prayer words by not losing concentration in our dhikr of God. We are reminded that the power of God remembers us as we remember Him.

AHL AL-BAYT

Chapter 14

Power of God's Dhikr

Dhikr takes on two primary characteristics: (a) remembrance of God by mankind and of mankind by God and (b) reminder that the Qur'an is from God and about God:

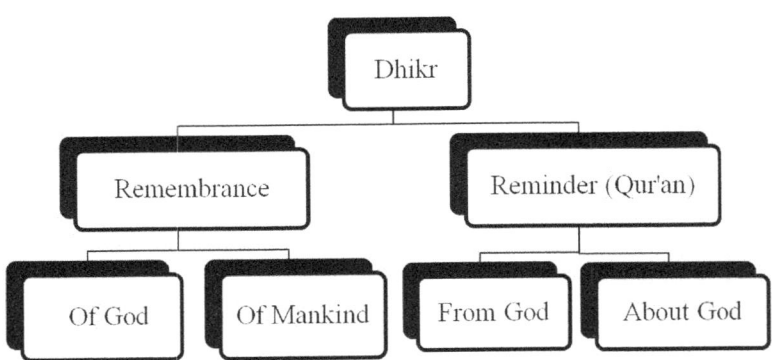

The preceding chapters have discussed the first characteristic of dhikr—that is, remembrance of God by mankind and of mankind by God. Following is a discussion of the second characteristic of dhikr—that is, that the reminder (Qur'an) is from God and about God. The Qur'an is the dhikr from God in that it is a reminder for mankind to declare that there is only one God. In addition, the Qur'an's message about God is that it is the true Word of God and that it represents the ultimate manifestation of His grace and mercy to mankind.

The Qur'an is from God and was revealed to Prophet Muhammad. The Qur'an is for mankind. The subject matter of the Qur'an essentially discusses our relationship to God, to each other, and to the rest of creation. A major theme of the Qur'an is the belief in the oneness of God and for us to have faith, perform righteous deeds, spread the truth, and practice patience (Qur'an 103:1–3). Since the aim of the Qur'an is to guide mankind, this theme permeates throughout the Qur'an over and over again:

> Verily We have sent down the Reminder (the Qur'an),
> and verily We unto it will certainly be the Guardian.
> (Qur'an 15:9)

The Arabic term for "reminder" in this verse is *dhikr*. The preservation of the Qur'an, "Lawh al-Mahfuz" (inscribed in a tablet preserved) means that the Qur'an was originally inscribed and has always existed in heaven (Qur'an 85:22). It is also associated with another description of the divine model of revelation, "Umm al-Kitab" (Mother of the Book), which is also stated in the Qur'an (Qur'an 13:39; 43:4). Its preservation also means the preservation of Islam in its final form.

The Qur'an is also about God:

> And your God (Allah) is One God (Allah): there is no god but He, Most Gracious, Most Merciful. Behold! In the creation of the heavens and the earth; in the alternation of the night and the day; in the sailing of the ships through the ocean for the profit of mankind; in the rain which God sends down from the skies, and the life which He gives therewith to an earth that is dead; in the beasts of all kinds that He scatters through the earth; in the change of the winds, and the clouds

which they trail like their slaves between the sky and the earth; (here) indeed are Signs for a people that are wise. (Qur'an 2:163–164)

God is the all-powerful and all-knowing creator, sustainer, ordainer, and judge of everything in existence. According to the Qur'an:

No vision can grasp Him, but His grasp is over all vision: He is above all comprehension, yet is acquainted with all things. (Qur'an 6:103)

God is the one and only God (Qur'an 112:1–4). The unity of God means that He is not dependent on anything, and everything depends on Him. He is the Creator and the ultimate source of all existence. Since God is the cause of creation, this universe has only one source, one end, and one truth. The universe and everything in it are the reflections of absolute unity, coherence, and discipline. All of the components in the universe have a common origin, a common purpose, and a common end, as they are creations of God.

Everything in the universe invokes and is committed to the remembrance (dhikr) of God. Everything in it is engaged in the glorification of God. Witnessing the grand and complex design of the universe reminds us of the One who created and keeps it expanding. The more we reflect on its perfection, the more we are reminded of God. However, God needs no designs to create the universe. His creation takes place instantaneously. The universe is truly vast, and as we use our high-powered telescopes or spacecraft to explore and navigate through it, we can further appreciate the Creator who put it all in place.

God has many attributes, all of which are linked together as one. There can be no pluralism in God's essence. Everything is dependent on Him. God has no partners and no associates in His divine essence. The Qur'an instructs us to remember God by His most beautiful names (Qur'an 7:180; 17:110; 20:8; 59:24). The Ninety-Nine Beautiful Names of God are listed in appendix C. Furthermore, the Qur'an is also a guide for mankind toward remembering God:

> And this (Qur'an) is a Reminder full of blessings that
> We have sent it down (unto our Apostle Muhammad);
> do you then deny it? (Qur'an 21:50)

All creatures and things that God created are in constant praise of Him, even if we cannot comprehend how they praise Him:

> The seven heavens and the earth, and all beings therein, declare His glory: there is not a thing but celebrates His praise; and yet you do not understand how they declare His glory! Verily He is Oft-Forbearing, Most Forgiving! (Qur'an 17:44)

The sun, moon, stars, planets, galaxies, animals, trees, mountains, stones, and everything in existence constantly glorify God. While mankind glorifies God, they are often forgetful and negligent in their praises. Nonetheless, God gives them the means by which they can remember Him, whether it is the marvels of the universe, the Qur'an, the Prophets and Imams, or countless other opportunities.

When we gaze at the sky, we marvel at the myriad stars that light up the heavens. Reflecting on this awesome display of creation, we cannot help but appreciate not only the energy that drives this spectacle but, more importantly, the Creator who shaped it. Even to ponder on just one star, the sun, and how it provides sustenance to maintain the earth's existence is amazing. How we come to understand our Creator and His creation is through our consciousness of Him. We are born with that consciousness, which allows us to distinguish between two polar opposites, such as right and wrong, good and evil, happiness and unhappiness, knowledge and ignorance, and love and hate.

How we move from consciousness that is mind based to one that is heart based is through our remembrance of God, entreating the power of His dhkir (reminder) upon us. God's dhikr brings about a transformation from total reliance on the mind to one that is heart driven, which then gives proper direction to the mind (e.g., relative to knowledge, peace, and security). The danger we face is that those who are strictly mind conscious will fall prey to the external world by satiating their appetite and maximizing on pleasures that go counter to the Qur'an, which is God's dhikr and gift to mankind.

Forgetfulness of God's dhikr leads to a myriad of problems, such as the destruction of the self by the ego. How we overcome the negative energy of the ego in order to safeguard the soul is to embrace virtues such as tolerance, kindness, love, and gratitude. These virtues are embedded in the heart, which truly defines and drives our consciousness. Hence, there is a shift from the consciousness of the external world of the mind to the consciousness of the inner world of the heart. Therefore, this shift will allow us to be more focused on moving from the fangs of materialism to the enlightenment of spirituality, thereby bringing us to the straight path and nearness of God:

> Behold! ... no change can there be in the Words of God ... for all power and honor belong to God: it is He Who hears and knows (all things). (Qur'an 10:62–65)

> Then you remember Me; I will remember you. Be grateful to Me, and do not reject faith. (Qur'an 2:152)

God's beautiful names reflect His powers, and the continuous remembrance of God's names can be felt in the innermost section of the heart. These beautiful names of God are the highest ideals of Islam, and dhikr will invite them to the heart that, in turn, will respond with unity, humility, and harmony. When the remembrance of and contemplation of God begins to resonate in the heart, that resonance will bring about peace in the heart. Those whose hearts are always in constant remembrance of God, it is God who will strengthen them with His own Spirit (Power), making them His helpers and true believers:

> You will not find any people who believe in God and the Last Day, loving those who resist God and His Messenger, even though they were their fathers or their sons, or their brothers, or their kindred. For such He

has written faith in their hearts and strengthened them with a Spirit from Himself. And He will admit them to Gardens beneath which rivers flow, to dwell therein (forever). God will be well pleased with them and they with Him. They are the Party of God. Truly it is the Party of God that will achieve felicity. (Qur'an 58:22)

O you who believe! You be helpers of God: as said Jesus the son of Mary to the Disciples, "Who will be my helpers to (the work of) God?" Said the Disciples, "We are God's helpers!" Then a portion of the children of Israel believed, and a portion disbelieved: but We gave power to those who believed, against their enemies, and they became the ones that prevailed. (Qur'an 61:14)

Verily, when He intends a thing, His Command is, "Be" and it is! (Qur'an 36:82)

Whenever God wills (*mash'iah*) a thing, it becomes a reality. For example, when the heart beats with the love of God, it is a love that brings about one's gratitude for God's remembrance. Love of God is the highest love of all! Love of God is greater than one's love for anyone or anything. Nothing can replace the love of God in one's heart:

God has not made for any man two hearts in his (one) body. (Qur'an 33:4)

It is because love for anyone else (e.g., parents or children) derives from the love of God in one's heart. God should always have first place in one's heart, and no other love may prevail over one's love of God:

Yet there are men who take (for worship) others besides God, as equal (with God); they love them as they should love God. But those of faith are overflowing in their love for God. If only the unrighteous could see, behold they would see the penalty: that to God belongs all power, and God will strongly enforce the penalty. (Qur'an 2:165)

> O God, I have left the entire world for the sake of You. And I have orphaned my children so that I be with You. My heart could not divert towards anyone but You. So, if they cut my body to a thousand pieces each piece would call out its love for you. (Imam Hussein ibn Ali)

One of God's beautiful names is the Loving. The significance and meaning of this name is that God is even more loving than a mother for her child, a husband for his wife, or a child for his or her parent or sibling. God does care for and love his creation, even to extend His mercy and forgiveness when man transgresses:

> Whatever good (O man!) happens to you, is from God; but whatever evil happens to you, is from your (own) soul. And We have sent you as a Messenger to (instruct) mankind. And enough is God for a Witness. (Qur'an 4:79)

God has prescribed His remembrance (dhikr) and other acts of worship for our benefit. All forms of remembrance and worship serve to remind us of God and keep us always mindful of Him. Consciousness of God holds us from sinning, committing injustices, and oppression, as it motivates us to fulfill His commandments. Dhikr is a step in the way of love. When somebody loves someone, they like to repeat their name and constantly remember them. Therefore, the heart in which the love of God has been implanted will become a dwelling place of constant dhikr (Mufti 2012).

God gave the trust to man to fulfill the religious obligations and not to be unjust in using it in the wrong way:

> We did indeed offer the Trust to the Heavens and the Earth and the Mountains; but they refused to undertake

it, being afraid thereof: but man undertook it; he was indeed unjust and foolish. (Qur'an 33:72)

In fulfilling the trust that God has bestowed on us, our hearts become larger in magnitude than the heavens, wider in expanse than the earth, and greater in strength than the mountains. When we fulfill the trust, then God expresses His spirit (i.e., power) in our hearts. We fulfill that trust through dhikr, which manifests itself in many facets (e.g., reciting the Qur'an, praying, performing supplication [du'a], and remembering God by praising Him). As such, our existence has to pass the test toward fulfilling that trust.

We need to get to know God, have faith, perform righteous deeds, speak the truth, and practice patience (Qur'an 103:1–3), which is the real purpose of our creation. In order to fulfill these obligations, a great deal of self-discipline is necessary. We must remember the trust that God has given us is a loan, as we will return (*istirja'*) back to God in the hereafter. Our actions in life are recorded, as we will be held accountable for everything we do in regard to that trust. As God has given us the trust (Qur'an 33:72), we must likewise have trust in God (Qur'an 3:159) with constant remembrance of Him. The essence of *tawakkul* (reliance) of the heart is built upon two important pillars: dependence upon God and trust in God. A benefit of tawakkul is that it helps us from the anxieties, worries, and depressions that we face in our daily lives. Reliance (tawakkul) on God helped Prophet Muhammad and his followers face and become victorious in many battles to safeguard Islam.

AHL AL-BAYT

Chapter 15

Dhikr: Islamic Battles

While there were a number of battles the Muslims were engaged in, following are the impact of the battles of Badr, Uhud, Khandaq, Khaybar, and Hunayn relative to dhikr:

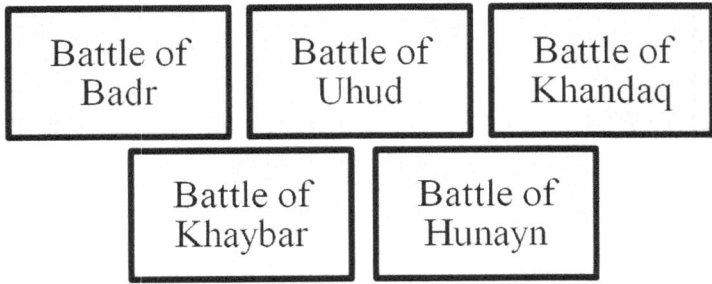

Battle of Badr (AD 624): The Battle of Badr is one of the greatest and most famous battles of Islam. Islam was still in its early stage, so this battle was a turning point in Prophet Muhammad's mission to perpetuate the faith of Islam. The battle began with champions from both armies emerging to engage in combat.

Imam Ali was the first person to fight the polytheists of Quraysh, who outnumbered the Muslims, and he defeated Walid ibn 'Utbah, the enemy's strongman (*Kashf al-Ghummah*, Vol. 1, p. 183).

Then Imam Ali defeated Sa'id ibn Al-'As ibn Sa'id, a man of horror (*Bihar al-Anwar*, Vol. 19, p. 338). Imam Ali was in the front line of the battle defeating the polytheists of Quraysh, and he killed seventy of their leaders (*Irshad*, Vol. 1, Part 2, p. 62).

The Muslims had only 313 soldiers against the polytheist Meccan army of 950 soldiers (Muir 1912). The Qur'an reveals that God helped the Muslims at Badr to maintain firm discipline:

> God has helped you at Badr, when you were a contemptible little force; then fear God; thus you may show your gratitude. Remember you said to the faithful: "Is it not enough for you that God should help you with three thousand angels (specially) sent down? Yes, if you remain firm, and act aright, even if the enemy should rush here on you in hot haste, your Lord would help you with five thousand angels making a terrific onslaught." (Qur'an 3:123–125)

> Prophet Muhammad is reminded of his request for God's help in the battle:

> Remember you implored the assistance of your Lord, and He answered you. "I will assist you with a thousand of the angels, ranks on ranks." (Qur'an 8:9)

> Remember (dhikr) when you were a small (band), despised through the land, and afraid that men might despoil and kidnap you; but He provided a safe asylum for you, strengthened you with His aid, and gave you good things for sustenance: that you might be grateful. (Qur'an 8:26)

> O God, accomplish for me what You have promised to me. O God, bring about what You have promised to me. O God, if this small band of Muslims is destroyed, You will not be worshipped on this earth. (*Sahih Muslim*, Vol. 5, Book 32, Hadith 4588)

The dhikr (remembrance of God) by the believers prevailed over the remembrance of Satan by the disbelievers:

> Remember He covered you with a sort of drowsiness, to give you calm as from Himself, and He caused rain to descend on you from heaven, to clean you therewith, to remove from you the stain of Satan, to strengthen your hearts, and to plant your feet firmly therewith. Remember your Lord inspired the angels (with the message): "I am with you: give firmness to the believers: I will instill terror into the hearts of the unbelievers: you smite above their necks and smite all their finger-tips off them." (Qur'an 8:11–12)

The Battle of Badr is a triumph over ignorance and a lesson that Muslims should always remember God by putting their "trust in Him" (Qur'an 8:2) in order for their "hearts to find satisfaction" (Qur'an 13:28) and not to be enticed by Satan, as the disbelievers were. The hearts of the believers soften to God's reminder, the celebration of His remembrance (dhikr), and the meaning of His mercy and generosity.

Battle of Uhud (AD 625): After the Muslims broke their promises to Prophet Muhammad by escaping from the battle scene, having taken shelter on the mountain, Imam Ali protected and defended the Prophet and was prepared to sacrifice himself from every side as the enemies attacked him. Imam Ali remained to repel the enemies (*Irshad*, Vol. 1, Part 2, p. 73). Those who escaped from the scene, though seeing the Prophet was being attacked, remained on the mountain, except fourteen of them, who returned (*Irshad*, Vol. 1, Part 2, p.74).

In this battle, Gabriel brought the deed of honor for Imam Ali:

> There is no man more valorous than Ali and there is no sword sharper than Dhu'l-Fiqar. (*Irshad*, Vol. 1, Part 2, p. 78)

During this battle, Imam Ali killed many of the enemy's soldiers. The Muslims' final victory and their returning to the Messenger of God was due to Imam Ali's steadfastness and courage in the battlefield (*Irshad*, Vol. 1, Part 2, p. 81).

Prophet Muhammad's army consisted of one thousand men versus three thousand men for the enemy. However, one-third of the Prophet's army returned back to Medina at the behest of Abdullah bin Ubay, who was a staunch critic of the Prophet in Medina (Al-Qasim 2012). God reminds the Prophet of the forthcoming battle:

> Remember that morning you left your household (early) to post the faithful at their stations for battle: and God hears and knows all things. (Qur'an 3:121)

> Remember two of your parties mediated cowardice; but God was their Protector, and in God the faithful should (ever) put their trust. (Qur'an 3:122)

The above verse is in remembrance (dhikr) of those whose morals had been undermined as a result of the withdrawal of Abdullah bin Ubay and his followers. The Muslims suffered a setback at the Battle of Uhud because of their lack of patience. During the Battle of Uhud, Prophet Muhammad's soldiers suffered a great loss because the archers disobeyed his orders by moving too soon from their strategic post on a hilltop in order to hurriedly collect the spoils of war that lay on the plains below. As a result, the Prophet's position was now defenseless, and so the Meccan cavalry attacked from the rear, eventually causing the Muslims to withdraw. The Muslims forgot that their goal was to defeat the aggressors and establish the truth. They learned a valuable lesson on the importance of obeying the Prophet at all times, including when our desires for booty, wealth, power, or other material gain in this world attempt to thrust us to do otherwise:

> Say: "Obey God and obey the Messenger: but if you turn away, he is only responsible for the duty placed on him and you for that placed on you. If you obey him, you shall be on right guidance. The Messenger's duty is only to preach the clear (Message)." (Qur'an 24:54)

> And obey God and the Messenger that you may obtain mercy. (Qur'an 3:132)

The Prophet had instructed his archers to remain in their post no matter what happens. However, they left their post, thinking that the enemy had turned away from the battlefield. Even when their commander reminded them of the Prophet's order not to leave their post, they did not listen. As a result, the Prophet was severely wounded and many of his companions were martyred. When the Prophet was injured, the following verses were revealed:

> "Yes, if you remain firm, and act aright, even if the enemy should rush here on you in hot haste, your Lord would help you with five thousand angels making a terrific onslaught." God made it but a message of hope for you, and an assurance to your hearts: (in any case) there is no help except from God, the Exalted, the Wise: That He might cut off a fringe of the unbelievers or expose them to infamy, and they should then be turned back, frustrated of their purpose. Not for you (but for God) is the decision: whether He turns in mercy to them, or punishes them; for they are indeed wrongdoers. To God belongs all that is in the heavens and on earth. He forgives whom He pleases and punishes whom

He pleases; but God is Oft-Forgiving, Most Merciful.
(Qur'an 3:125–129)

Behold! You were climbing up the high ground, without even casting a side-glance at any one, and the Messenger in your rear was calling you back. There did God give you one distress after another by way of requital, to teach you not to grieve for (the booty) that had escaped you and for (the ill) that had befallen you. For God is well aware of all that you do. (Qur'an 3:153)

God reminds (dhikr) His servants (Qur'an 3:154–155) of His favor when He sent down calm on those who were overcome with slumber while they were carrying their weapons and feeling distress and grief. God reminds (dhikr) His followers of the victory they had at the Battle of Badr while warning them not to be nearer to unbelief than to faith (Qur'an 3:165–167). Even though the Muslims were defeated at Uhud, the enemy came back to finish them off. However, God then commanded the Muslims to march and meet the enemy in order to bring fear to their hearts and to demonstrate that the Muslims still had strength to fight. Hence, the Muslims mobilized in obedience to God and His Messenger (Qur'an 3:172–173).

Battle of Khandaq (The Trench) (AD 627): Prophet Muhammad said,

> The killing of Amru by Ali is better than the worship of Jinn and human beings. (*Shawahid al-Tanzil*, Vol. 2, p. 5)

The horse riders of Quraysh dreamed of a quick victory. They asked for a challenger and declared a hand-to-hand fight. Among the Muslims, the first man who responded was Imam Ali, who defeated the giant warrior Amru ibn Abd Wid. Seeing Amru killed, the enemies found no benefit in continuing the fighting and thus were defeated (*Kashf al-Ghummah*, Vol. 1, p. 197). God revealed the following verse in honor of Imam Ali:

> And God turned back those who disbelieve in their rage, they achieved not any advantage; and God did suffice for the believers in fighting; for God is All-Strong, the Almighty. (Qur'an 33:25).

The Battle of Khandaq brings out the sincerest in faith to carry the banner of Islam. That sincere one was Imam Ali ibn Abi Talib, who defended Islam by fighting and beating the renowned giant warrior Amru ibn Abd Wid. God reminds us of such brave and courageous men:

> Of the believers are the men who are true to what they covenanted with God; of them is he who has fulfilled his vow and of them is he who awaits (its fulfillment); and they have changed not in the least, that God may recompense the truthful ones for their truth, and chastise the hypocrites if He wills or turn unto them (merciful); Verily God is Oft-Forgiving, the Most Merciful. And God turned back those who disbelieve in their rage, they achieved not any advantage; and God did suffice for the believers in fighting; for God is All-Strong, the Almighty. (Qur'an 33:23–25)

During the Battle of Khandaq (Trench), the number of soldiers of the enemy was ten thousand versus only three thousand for the Muslims (Rodinson 2002). Rather than immediately engage in battle, both sides agreed to have their champion duel each other. Imam Ali displayed his power and energy as he defeated Amru ibn Abd Wid, the champion of the enemy, who not only challenged but mocked the Muslims as well.

Imam Ali accepted the challenge and won the battle. As Imam Ali stood to thrust the sword into Amru, the latter spat in Imam Ali's face. Imam Ali was extremely angered by this act of insult. It took a great deal of self-control for Imam Ali to restrain his anger, so he momentarily postponed killing Amru until his anger was restrained. He waited to kill him because he didn't want his anger, or negative energy, to be the reason but, rather, his faith in God. Imam Ali's faith was active, and God moved him to face the danger and to rise to the level among the most faithful.

There is a significant difference between the person who is in control of his anger before finishing off his victim and one who is not in control of his anger as he punishes his victim without reflection. Imam Ali was a man in control of his emotions, and his electromagnetic energy waves sparked his temperament toward restraint in time of anger.

God reminds (dhikr) us in the above verses that the heroism of Imam Ali was the most decisive factor in the victory. The death of Amru proved to the enemy that they would not be able to pass through the moat (trench). The defeat of Amru struck terror in the hearts of the enemy so much that they abandoned the battlefield. This defeat was so devastating for the enemy that the disbelievers gave up their objective to advance to Medina. The death of Amru raised the morale of the Muslims as they regained their confidence.

During the Battle of Khandaq, Prophet Muhammad was reciting a poem in remembrance (dhikr) of God, recorded by Abdullah bin Rawahah ibn Tha'labah:

> O God, were it not for You,
> We would not have been guided,
> Nor would we have given charity, nor prayed.
> So bestow on us calmness, and when we meet the enemy,
> Then make our feet firm, for indeed,
> The enemy has revolted against us;
> Yet, if they want to afflict us,
> We oppose their affliction.
> (*Sahih Bukhari*, Vol. 5, Book 64, Hadith 4106)

The heroic feat of Imam Ali strengthened the hearts of the Muslims and made their faith in God even stronger. They were ready to sacrifice themselves, and the Qur'anic verses 33:23–25 tell us of the morale of these believers. While these verses do not reveal the number of those believers whose faith was increased, undoubtedly, the faith of many was increased once Imam Ali was victorious over Amru ibn Abd Wid.

Battle of Khaybar (AD 629): It was Imam Ali who achieved victory for Islam. Prophet Muhammad gave the banner of Islam to Imam Ali, who never abandoned the battlefield and defeated the enemy with his successive attacks:

> The Messenger of God said on the Day of Khaybar: "I shall give this flag to a man who loves God and His Messenger, and God and His Messenger love him, and God will grant him victory at his hands." Umar bin al-Khattab said: "I never desired leadership except on that day." He said, "I came before him in the hope that I might be called to it, but the Messenger called Ali bin Abi Talib. He gave it to him and said: march, and do not turn around until God grants you victory." (*Sahih Muslim*, Vol. 6, Book 44, Hadiths 6222–6224)

The enemy forces of the Jews numbered 10,000 (Haykal 2005), while the Muslims numbered between 1,400 and 1,800 (Nomani 2000). The Prophet was not in Khaybar to conquer land and wealth but rather to remove the threat to Islam from the Jews. Imam Ali defeated the two strongest warriors of the Jews. As a result of his bravery, the Muslim soldiers captured the forts. Thus, the battle ended, and the Muslims were victorious.

The importance regarding the bravery of Imam Ali is that there is a direct correlation between his physical strength and dhikr (remembrance) of God. His state of mind was constantly in dhikr of God, and it is this remembrance that became the source behind his physical strength. It was meditation and dhikr that caused a chemical change in his brain, thereby leading to strengthening his body. In the remembrance of God, Imam Ali was firmly focused in heart and valor, thereby paralyzing Satan in overcoming and gaining dominance over him. As a result, Imam Ali's strength of body and mind was the personification of his dhikr of God.

Battle of Hunayn (AD 630): After the conquest of Mecca, the Muslims had yet another battle, this time at Hunayn. Prophet Muhammad assembled a force of twelve thousand soldiers and marched to Hunayn to crush the Bedouin tribe of Hawazin and its subsection, the Thaqif, with an army of twenty thousand soldiers (IslamHouse 2006). When the Muslim army entered the narrow passes overlooking the valley, they were ambushed, causing the Muslims to panic and desert the Prophet. They were totally surprised and confused by the sudden attack, so they fled the battleground:

> Assuredly, God did help you in many battlefields and on the day of Hunayn: Behold! Your great numbers elated you, but they availed you nothing: the land, for all that it is wide, did constrain you, and you turned back in retreat. (Qur'an 9:25)

A small contingent, including Imam Ali, remained with the Prophet to protect him. Imam Ali, defending with his unsheathed sword in front of the Prophet, killed forty of the enemy troops (*Irshad*, Vol. 1, Part 2, p. 129). However, Ibn Abbas, who had a resounding voice, began to shout out to those who had fled to return. Once those who retreated returned, the tide turned in favor of the Muslims. As such, the enemy of disbelievers fled and dispersed:

> Then did send down God His tranquility upon His Apostle and upon the believers, and did send down hosts that you did not see, and chastised those who disbelieved; and that is the recompense of the infidels. Then will God turn merciful after this to whomsoever He wills; and verily God is the Oft-Forgiving, the Most Merciful. (Qur'an 9:26–27)

What we learn from the Battle of Hunayn is that numerical strength does not guarantee victory; rather, victory comes about because of our reliance on God. The reason for the Muslims experiencing defeat at the Battle of Hunayn is because they were overconfident that they would win. Given the taste of bitterness of defeat made them realize that it is the dhikr (remembrance) of God and the humbling of their hearts that culminates into being triumphant. Once they realized their error and became humble in their hearts, the path to receiving God's blessing and guidance was open. God then granted victory first and foremost to the small band of courageous and patient Muslims who remained steadfast and dedicated to the Prophet in their dhikr of God and also to the returning Muslims who realized their mistake.

All of these battles demonstrated a major lesson: conquering one's desires and love for this world was necessary before conquering the enemy on the battlefield. The path to doing so is the remembrance of God, even if the chaos we're experiencing is other than war, as we look to fulfill the obligation and trust that God has given us. The humble heart, when connected to God, conquers all fears.

AHL AL-BAYT

Chapter 16

Dhikr: Unity in Islam

While convergence of brotherhood has been met with some success, much more still needs to be done. To be sure, Muslims have made inroads into cooperation and collaboration with one another. Muslims have also been engaged in interfaith-based initiatives and dialogue with non-Muslims. More and more non-Muslims are beginning to understand Islam and its contributions to the world. Yet winning the intrafaith unity among Muslims has been met with obstacles. Some of these obstacles have severely impacted the understanding of the true nature of Islam, as rogues have distorted the faith with their blatant and dastardly objectives. These rogues have succeeded at the expense of a fragmented and ignorant Muslim society.

What is needed is a mechanism to effectively promote the unity between Sunnis and Shi'as. That mechanism is the dhikr (remembrance) of God. Toward this end, we must rely on the Qur'an and the traditions of Prophet Muhammad, whereby knowledge, wisdom, tolerance, mercy, flexibility, ease, and diversity are among the hallmarks of dhikr:

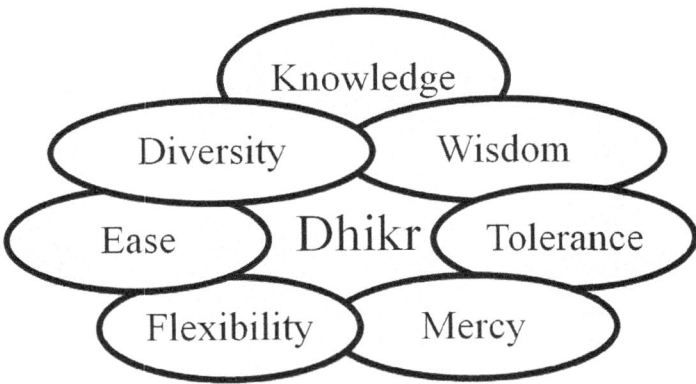

Knowledge: To promote unity is to promote knowledge, which is an inescapable duty imposed on every Muslim. Knowledge and ignorance are always at war with each other. Knowledge is the light and the means of reaching the threshold of unity. Knowledge is parallel with guidance, while ignorance is akin to torment. Knowledge gives rise to wisdom:

> He grants wisdom to whomsoever He wills, and he who has been granted wisdom has been given abundant good; and none shall remember it save those endowed with wisdom. (Qur'an 2:269)

Understanding Islam without knowledge is a mere formality, and without remembrance (dhikr), knowledge is obscure. Enlightenment emanates from the knowledge of the remembrance of God, and remembrance of God is increased when knowledge is present. Remembrance of God purifies our hearts and polishes it, while knowledge of Islam enlightens and enables us to follow the straight path (sirat al-mustaqim).

Wisdom: As experience results in knowledge, knowledge results in change. Knowledge being the forerunner of wisdom, the more we know, the more we become. Where there is wisdom, there is neither fear nor ignorance. Prejudice is a sign of ignorance and the lack of ethical sensitivity. We promote the unity by rebelling against the ignorance of intolerance and fanaticism. It is through the spirit of detachment that we experience the meaning of freedom to help influence change for the sake of unity.

Wisdom and discipline have been neglected, owing to the sectarian divisions that are in opposition to the unity in Islam. While the schools of thought started out as interpretations of Islamic jurisprudence, Muslim followers of these ideologies began to drift into ignorance, darkness, and despair. While Muslims speak of unity, and they make attempts to unify, the end result has been dismal. The reason is that over the centuries this enmity and hatred among each other has been inculcated and imbedded within the minds of Muslims. Their offspring carry on the dissention and, at times, even magnify the fragmentation to even greater heights of animosity. We are guided by the following Qur'anic verse:

> As for those who divide their religion and break up into sects, Thou has no part in them in the least: their affair is with God: He will in the end tell them the truth of all that they did. (Qur'an 6:159)

As we become weak in our dhikr of God, wisdom subsides, and the void is filled with negligence. We need to steadfastly adhere to the signs that God has sent us within the Qur'an, the wise dhikr:

This, We recite unto thee of the Signs and the Wise Reminder. (Qur'an 3:58)

The Wise Reminder is the hallmark of unity. Differences in jurisprudence should not deter Muslim unity, since all schools of thought have agreement, for the most part, on similar historical facts. Jurisprudence is a major criterion in Islam and is the means by which those scholars who are qualified are able to interpret and apply Islamic laws. Nonetheless, jurisprudence interpretation must not be infected by individual aspirations and arrogance. Muslim unity is one of the goals of the Muslim society and is an obligation on all Muslims.

Tolerance: To hold fast to the Rope of God means to uphold and comply with God's commands. We need to hold fast so as not to deviate from the straight path. While it is one's right to believe that the Islamic school of thought he follows is the best school of thought, it is not right to admonish the followers of other schools of thought. Here we should not put a wedge or barrier between the followers of different schools of thought. Rather, we should meet with the intent to find the solution of how to work together. Compulsion or force is unacceptable in Islam:

Let there be no compulsion in religion. (Qur'an 2:256)

In Islam, people are not compelled to change their faith. Forced faith is no faith by the imposed or the imposer. Faith is a moral achievement and as such mandates us to thwart off evil. As such, we must not be impatient or angry; rather, we should exercise tolerance. Tolerance is one of the greatest strengths of dhikr, because it is the remembrance and attitude of truth. In Islam, tolerance is a religious moral duty. Tolerance means to bear or put up with the convictions of other people and not to impose one's will upon the will of others. If one is intolerant and unable to enjoy dialogue with fellow Muslims or non-Muslims, such person's heart is certainly closed to the divine message of Islam, which is the practice of dhikr of both the tongue and the heart. As Muslims, we need to remember to be tolerant, whether we are Sunni or Shi'a.

Mercy: Prophet Muhammad's mission of mercy was one of a great number of duties and responsibilities:

We sent you not, but as a Mercy for all creatures. (Qur'an 21:107)

God sent Prophet Muhammad to be the best example of mercy for all mankind. We need to fill our hearts with mercy and to render mercy to others when needed. When we recite a surah (chapter) from the Qur'an, we start with the remembrance of God as the Beneficent, the Merciful. God's mercy descended upon Prophet Muhammad, who in turn taught mercy to others, and his teachings remain lessons for us today.

Brotherhood originates from mutual respect and emotional feelings for one another, whether it is Sunni or Shi'a. The enforcement of brotherhood is the greatest social ideal of Islam. Brotherhood is a notion based on faith and equality. It unites mankind on the basis of beliefs and principles. Brotherhood and mercy are inseparable. If we hold fast to the Rope of God, then we will attain brotherhood.

In our dhikr and love of God, we must be grateful for His benevolence and mercy. God's benevolence and mercy are manifested in His creation and revelations. Here, mercy comes full circle, as it is a universal mercy that embraces everything. God chose Prophet Muhammad to spread the message of universal mercy among all people and creatures, and it is the Qur'an, the Rope of God, that explains what this universal mercy is. This mercy is heightened when people live in harmony with one another and unify in the common cause of brotherhood and solidarity.

Flexibility: One of the main reasons why Islam as a faith survives to this day is because of its flexibility. The nature of Islam is such that it has a great deal of flexibility and practicability and can cope with any situation. Islam does not prevent the human mind from thinking, but instead it gives our minds guidance and assistance. Within this flexibility, we must use our minds to remember the guidance of the Qur'an. Islam encourages reasoning, thought, and personal opinion. It is this flexibility in having differences of opinion among the scholars that underscores the meaning of God's mercy.

The beauty of the *shari'a* (law) of Islam is its flexibility, as it is a framework appropriate for all times, all places, and all peoples. To ensure the eternal relevance of His revelation, God provided for inherent mobility and flexibility. By providing us with the shari'a, He established the legal boundaries within which the community can develop and flourish in concord with the requirements of the changing times. However, because there are so many facets and contingencies of life, and because the shari'a does not cover all these details in minuscule form, there is room for interpretation. In other words, there is room for flexibility. This flexibility transforms into *ijtihad*, or independent reasoning. Islam is a faith that endures over time and a faith that meets the requirements of any new era. As such, flexibility and adjustability to these requirements must be in compliance with the teachings of Islam.

Unity can be achieved only if Muslims are flexible in being tolerant of each other's school of thought. Undoubtedly, this flexibility necessitates that we remember to hold fast to the Rope of God and be not divided (Qur'an 3:103).

Ease: One of the criteria of Islam is the concept of ease:

> God intends every facility for you; He does not want to put you to difficulties. (Qur'an 2:185)
>
> And We will make it easy for you (to follow) the simple (path). (Qur'an 87:8)
>
> So, verily, with every difficulty, there is relief. Verily, with every difficulty there is relief. (Qur'an 94:5–6)

When we practice dhikr, our hearts feel at ease, and this is a sign that God has chosen for us. God does not make Islam or life more difficult than we are able to tolerate, nor does He make it entirely easy. As God provides us with ease and difficulty, He provides us more ease through this difficulty. While there are hardships in life, we persevere in overcoming these hardships within our capacity to do so. Ease is the sense of knowing how to overcome these hardships. When the inner self is unified with nature and its needs are fulfilled, then the path toward harmony will be one of ease.

Just as tolerance, mercy, flexibility, and ease are essential in Islam, so must they be essential to achieving brotherhood and solidarity. Sunnis and Shi'as must display tolerance and mercy for each other and at the same time exhibit ease and flexibility for the purpose of driving home the unity. Tolerance and mercy bring about not only forgiveness but also compassion. Flexibility and ease remove the difficulties for Muslims so that they can engage in constructive dialogue and seek windows of opportunities for more productive discussion.

Our challenge, therefore, is to bring about understanding and harmony with each other. Religious leaders and scholars have a responsibility of teaching dhikr to plant the seeds of religious tolerance, mercy, flexibility, and ease in the hearts and minds of their followers. These leaders and scholars must collaborate in the spirit of mutual understanding that will enable them to work together for the advancement of unity.

For constructive dialogue among the religious leaders and scholars of the Islamic schools of thought to be successful, essential requirements are necessary. First, in their quest for unity, they must place their reliance on God and remember Him constantly through their praises. They must be committed toward laying aside their prejudices so as to achieve unity. Reliance is the start of the journey, surrender is its end, and commitment is its result. This, of course, necessitates some of the following guidelines:

- Prepare for the dialogue by thinking ahead about group dynamics and the directions in which the discussion might go.
- Establish an atmosphere of trust and relaxation by focusing differences on ideas rather than on personalities.
- Institute clear guidelines for discussion by encouraging openness and respect for honest opinions.
- Share concerns and beliefs by listening carefully to others, and strive to understand the positions of those who disagree.

The objective of religious leaders and scholars should be one of unity, rather than the domination of one sect by another. There is mutual agreement among the sects that they all agree on obeying God and His Messenger, Prophet Muhammad. There is also mutual agreement that piety, adherence to the principles of the Qur'an, and striving for goodness in daily life are among the greatest virtues. In addition, they agree on the need for a strong ethical and moral code to regulate human behavior in all its manifestations. Since these agreements among Sunnis and Shi'as are already in effect, this sets the stage for pursuing unity on other issues in Islam.

With the objective being unity, disagreements as to interpretations of Islamic law can be harmonized. We must realize that the existing ambiance of conflict and discord pervasive among various Muslim sects is utterly ineffective and absurd. The Islamic civilization has now existed for over fourteen centuries, and each of these sects has been part and parcel of this great culture.

As it is futile, we need to cease and desist in spending enormous amounts of time, energies, and resources in promoting the dominance of one sect over the other. It is nothing more than a delusion that one faction can somehow eliminate the other. It is neither feasible nor practical to either ignore the existence of different sects in Islam or to try to remove their longstanding differences. With tolerance, mercy, flexibility, and ease, we can acknowledge the right of each to practice what it believes, while at the same time cooperate with each other toward the common goal of unity. This would be a more viable and workable alternative rather than trying to deal with the issue of Sunni versus Shi'a.

Many other Islamic values, such as patience, forbearance, kindness, temperance, and courage, can help immensely in the way of unity. If we are going to be successful in our pursuit for unity, we need to instill within our minds and hearts the dhikr of these virtues. We should consider the convergence of Muslim thoughts and discuss topics of interest in which there is common agreement. Accentuate the positive and eliminate the negative. Let us dwell on issues we can come to an agreement on and forego those issues that cause heated discussions and disputes. We have many things in common, so why not build an alliance on these agreements? Some of our common agreements are the following:

- We have the same Declaration of Faith—there is one God, and Muhammad is His Prophet.
- We perform similar obligations, such as prayer, fasting, charity, and pilgrimage.
- We are all part of the great Islamic culture and civilization.

What we need now is a strong sense of brotherhood, whereby Muslims tolerate and respect one another. It is important to familiarize and educate Muslims about holding dialogues in order to move forward and build a strong and cohesive Islamic society. To achieve this requires that we should no longer attack other Muslim sects publicly or verbally or by means of force. Otherwise, we open the door to the enemies of Islam who employ their vicious objectives to destroy Islam.

Unless we remove the aura of dominance of one sect over the other, it will be difficult to achieve the unity. Let us work for the future, even if unity is not in reach today. Let us confront the enemies of Islam who continue to promote despair so unity cannot be achieved. Only by achieving unity can we stop the oppression and the domination by the enemies of Islam. Henceforth, justice, security, and peace will become dominant facts of life.

Whenever we discuss a disputed matter, we must be civilized, open-minded, and kind to others. We should also acquire in-depth knowledge of the points of view of all parties. We should be positive and respectful toward other Muslims regardless of difference in opinions. We should not condemn each other. Rather, we should promote empathy so that we can understand each other's point of view.

Building lasting, cohesive relationships takes a great deal of time and energy. Community representatives would exercise responsibility and accountability while at the same time benefit from a rich and rewarding learning experience. Religious leaders get infusions of energy, enthusiasm, and credibility as well as great ideas. Imagination is a vital element in building a better future. The Muslim leadership must imagine and promote a more sustainable unity of Muslim brotherhood and solidarity. This will encourage the Muslim community to join in.

How we go about preserving the unity is by way of education. We must work to educate Muslims about the importance of unity. We can conduct educational seminars and invite leading scholars to speak about unity. Academic sessions will attract prominent scholars to engage in conversations about a variety of topics relative to unity. We can write books on the subject of unity and give our readers a workable plan of action in attaining the unity. Whether we hold seminars or write books, the participants or readers will experience euphoria. They will be excited and jubilant about winning the unity. Since a great number of our youth access the Internet, utilizing web-based videos relative to topics on unity can be very effective. Even the use of full-color video and audio streaming features can generate enthusiasm among the users. Let's use technology to celebrate our youth and let them drive the unity instead of some of the older generation clinging to negative emotions that drive toward disunity. Other suggestions for complementation deal with cooperation in the areas of global economics, science, technology, and culture. Possibly most important, we should do more to collaborate regarding dealing with social issues around drugs, alcohol, and pornography, issues that plague all our communities.

To generate enthusiasm among Muslims for the purpose of unity, religious leaders must maintain a congenial relationship with their constituents. Religious leaders must be role models. Psychology teaches that people repeat the behaviors that leaders call attention to, whether good or bad. It is not enough to keep the community informed; keeping the community involved is critical. When a community takes responsibility for its future, things happen. The best way for building enduring relationships and unity in the community is to offer opportunities to a wide range of people to get involved. Encouraging community involvement transcends beyond just involvement in education, business, government, and religion. It is a total effort encompassing all aspects of life.

Unity should be on the lips of every Muslim, and each Muslim must remember (dhikr) to do their best in fulfilling the obligation of a lasting and just unity. Unity must be pursued on all fronts, both with the highest level of religious leadership and equally with the entire Muslim community. The sum of the parts does equal the whole, and if each Muslim begins to preach unity, then it will help cement that unity. Unity leads to strength, and this strength is needed to address the ills of the society and those who wish to distort and destroy Islam.

Effective and workable communication among Muslims is necessary. Both Sunni and Shi'a senior religious leaders must make a joint declaration of unity. This is ambitious but necessary and may work from the grassroots up—from the communities demanding it of the senior scholars and key religious institutions. The joint declaration must further stipulate that religious leaders should not engage in profane language directed at other Muslims, whether historical or current. Muslims who engage in vulgar and profane language should be held accountable for their actions. Joint declarations must be issued to reproach those Muslims who are deviating from and tarnishing Islam for their own personal benefit.

Diversity: Islam teaches that human diversity is a sign of the richness of God's mercy. Continually remembering God and seeking His acceptance results in Muslims collaborating with each other in the diverse arena of various sects in Islam. Diversity is an effective tool in bridging the gap between those in dispute. Diversity in Islam is the awareness that divergent issues do exist among the various schools of thought, and these issues are fomented by distinctly different and significant views.

In Islam, diversity can pave the way for reconciliation among the various schools of thought. The first question that comes to mind is the nature of Islamic unity. Barriers toward achieving this unity have exacerbated meaningful dialogue. Muslim religious leaders and the community who intentionally propagate division on the basis of pride, suspicion, and self-interest are guilty. This disunity among Muslims has paved the way for outsiders to capitalize on this fragmentation. In the words of Grand Ayatollah Khomeini:

> The ones who separate Islamic World by making Shiite-Sunni division, are neither Sunni nor Shiite, they are impure. They are certainly the hands of oppressors who want to invade the lands of Islam.

Islam demands unity, and that an unwillingness to accept this is a sin against that unity. If our mission is to confront the moral, political, and social influences of each of the Islamic schools of thought, then surely there is sufficient basis for common cause. Apparently, the Sunni and Shi'a communities have been marked more by discord than by collaboration, more by hostility than by mercy, more by doubt than by trust, more by misinformation and lack of knowledge than by respect for the truth.

Moreover, we do not take the time to comprehend the issues but are simply satisfied to rudely pass along unnecessary insults in the place of frank and insightful reflection. In many instances, we have been motivated by pride and prejudice. It is not that disparities between Sunnis and Shi'as do not or should not matter. The issue in the minds of the Muslim community is whether these disparities should be allowed to restrain both groups from dealing with a greater common enemy: disunity.

There must be mutual support, irrespective of how profound our differences are with one another. As Sunnis and Shi'as have shared Islam's great history during the last fourteen centuries, they have no reason not to develop mutual partnerships and work together for the betterment of the Muslim community. Unity necessitates awareness, patience, concentration, and, above all, the dhikr of God.

Diversity must be respected, diversity must be valued, and diversity must be managed. How to respect diversity is to promote tolerance, mercy, flexibility, and ease among the Muslim community. How to value diversity is to understand and appreciate our Islamic heritage. How to manage diversity is to be goal oriented in order to achieve that unity. To respect diversity, we must be willing to listen to the points of view of others. To value diversity requires a qualitative sense of well-being that is based on ethics and ideals. To manage diversity necessitates that we be strategically driven, pragmatic, and synergistic.

By changing the current state of affairs, Muslim leaders may feel their leadership is threatened and thereby decide to polarize. The challenge for diversity is to convince all parties that mutual exchange is mandatory. For diversity to work, the process must be continuously evaluated for accountability and improvement. With diversity, perceptions and points of view change through recognizing individual prejudices and moral attitudes as well as confronting preconceptions and stereotypes.

Diversity focuses on distinctions among people with respect to ethnicity, religion, and other human differences. On the other hand, pluralism incorporates mutual respect, acceptance, and teamwork among people who are diverse in the dimensions of human differences. Pluralism holds to one's school of thought and at the same time engages other schools of thought to learn more about their path and how they want to be understood.

Pluralism and dialogue are the means for building bridges and relationships that create harmony and peace in the Muslim society. Pluralism does not mean just to tolerate religious differences but, rather, to understand the other's point of view albeit cultural, political, psychological, sociological, or philosophical disparities. Having a broader perspective can mean tolerance, and it can also mean understanding a variety of meanings. Pluralism is unity plus diversity. Despite diversity of opinion between various Islamic sects, Muslims need to come together on sacred occasions to revisit the past and reunite it with their daily lives.

Perhaps reasons why unified efforts in the past have failed were because the Muslim leadership did not have a clear and shared understanding of their purpose and the outcomes they wanted. In addition, political reasons may have been a deterrent to understanding each other. Or some Muslims may have put more emphasis on power and the necessity to be in control. Shared purpose, values, and vision provide the critical guidelines for weighing options and opportunities. They also provide the basis for evaluating if community efforts are making a difference.

In order to succeed in our vision of unity, all participants must share in that vision. One person can make a difference; collectively we can transform the community. People are naturally good and are motivated by their capacity to genuinely serve. Human relationships are venerated and interactive in nature. Successful decision making unites the efforts of both heart and mind and brings us within the realm of the dhikr (remembrance) of God. Each person is a unique and valued part of the whole. It is only through collaboration and teamwork that we can truly attain unity. We revere unity in all that we do. All our decisions and actions are as a result of our influence on the Muslim community. New ideas necessitate an atmosphere that cultivates diverse perspectives. A sustainable Muslim community can meet the future with self-assurance because it has a reliable and renewable supply of resources, a resilient social fabric, and a healthy environment.

We pray to God to continue to guide us in our quest for unity and a more peaceful and prosperous life. We need to restore Sunnis and Shi'as back to a healthy and vital state of cohesiveness. While our responsibility is to adhere to the basics of Islam, we must also be willing to recognize the following:

- There are disparities in the perceptions of how people think and administer their affairs.
- Diversity is the mechanism by which elements in Islamic society can understand each other and flourish.
- Intellectual development and cross-fertilization of ideas can be the vehicle by which to better understand the perspectives of each other.
- Divergent issues should be approached in a more balanced and collaborative posture so as to encompass the magnitude of these issues.
- Knowledge and ethics must be linked and strengthened with the aim of restoring unity.
- The gap between the ideals of Islam and the realities of the Muslim Ummah must be bridged.
- Muslim scholars must address contemporary issues and challenges in the direction of overcoming them.
- Brotherhood and solidarity must be preserved.
- We must maintain a deep consciousness and the dhikr of God as we seek His pleasure and guidance to unify us.

When the Muslim community becomes aware of its Islamic responsibilities, it will win back the unity and understand the true meaning of the dhikr (remembrance) of God. Each Muslim must search his or her conscience and bring it into harmony with the consciousness of other Muslims. This will bring about the unity, and the Ummah (Muslim community) will once again prosper and flourish as it did during the days of Prophet Muhammad. Reliance on God's remembrance (dhikr) must be integrated into the conscious of all who aspire to unify so that reconciliation becomes the driving force toward the realization of that unity.

It is the inner feeling that binds us together. Unless we have this feeling in our hearts, no appeals and no attempts will help! The feeling that binds us to God must draw us together as brothers and sisters in faith. We need to seek this feeling and strengthen it in our hearts. Otherwise, the unification of Muslims is unfeasible. This feeling must live in the heart of every *mu'min* (believer)—it comes from God; it is a gift from the Almighty. The key to this feeling is the dhikr (remembrance) of God.

The heart is the source of all our deeds. If the heart of a Muslim is empty, no good deeds will help. One of the greatest gifts that God has bestowed upon us is the affection in our hearts:

> And (moreover) He has put affection between their hearts: not if you had spent all that is in the Earth, could you have produced that affection, but God has done it: for He is Exalted in Might, Wise. (Qur'an 8:63)

The dhikr of God is the most important requirement of the Almighty. It is the essence and soul of Islam. If we mention the praises of God as often as possible, wherever we are and whatever we do, our hearts are pure. It radiates love that creates brotherhood among Muslims. The key to our unity is truly the remembrance of God. It is the transformation of the heart that brings about the genuine unity so as to hold fast to the Rope of God and be not divided (Qur'an 3:103).

Chapter 17

Transformation of Dhikr

The transformation of dhikr manifests itself by our performing dhikr, and then the dhikr of God reciprocates. In our unconscious, dhikr transforms the energies within our psychological framework so we can be aligned with the straight path of Islam. Whenever we praise God, the sound of our praises transforms our psychic energy so as to awaken the energies of the unconscious. Dhikr relieves us of the psychological impediments, such as envy, anxiety, and greed that have imprisoned us both consciously and unconsciously. The repetition of God's name helps us to detach from the poisonous fangs of these negative energies:

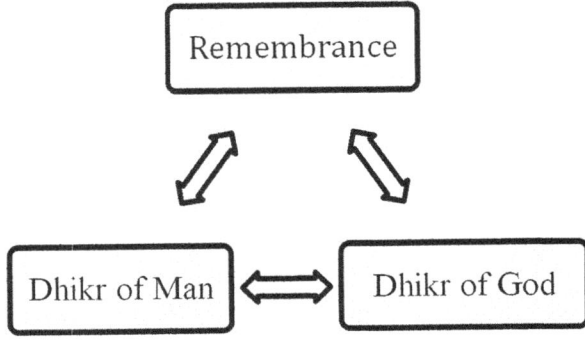

Dhikr implants the unconsciousness with the light of consciousness to remember God. Hence, the physical body becomes gradually aligned with the higher consciousness of the self, thereby purifying the heart (Vaughan-Lee 2012). We begin to feel the rhythmic beating of the heart that transforms the energy of the cells within our bodies. Thus, we embrace the remembrance of God, who in turn remembers us. It is through the consciousness of this mutual bond between God and man that embeds the unity in our hearts. Remembrance (dhikr) is a means of awakening a slumbering consciousness in order to strengthen our hearts in bringing us nearer to God:

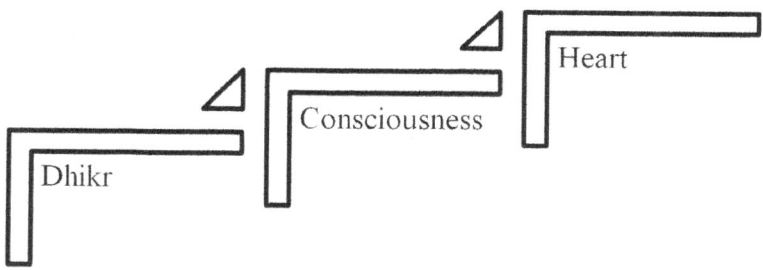

The essence of dhikr is when the transformation in the heart results in seeking God rather than just seeking from God, in serving God rather than just worshipping God, and in remembering God rather than just reminders about God. Based on the Qur'anic verse "Then you remember Me, I will remember you. Be grateful to Me, and do not reject faith" (Qur'an 2:152), our remembrance of God is necessary in order to receive God's remembrance. When we are overwhelmed with grief, are tearful, distressed, sleepless, and anxious, we pray constantly and hold fast to our spirituality. During this time of constant prayer and supplication, our dhikr does not abate, and our gratitude (shukr) for God's remembrance does not diminish:

A transformation takes place whereby our behavior is one of generosity, attentiveness, sincerity, compassion, and detachment, as life's struggles do not grieve or bother us as much as they would otherwise. Moreover, detachment from life's material things and desires in this world prepares us better for the difficulty of ultimately having to do so during and after death. From this transformation, the heart becomes strengthened by the certainty of truth (*haq al-yaqin*), as it has been purified of blemishes and sins (Shulman 2002). The goal of remembrance is to transform our being through absorbing the truth. The pure heart (*qalbun saleem*) is now motivated to love all that God loves and to detest all that God detests. Dhikr transforms the heart, for it brings ease and strength to attain the serene self (*nafs al-mutma'inna*):

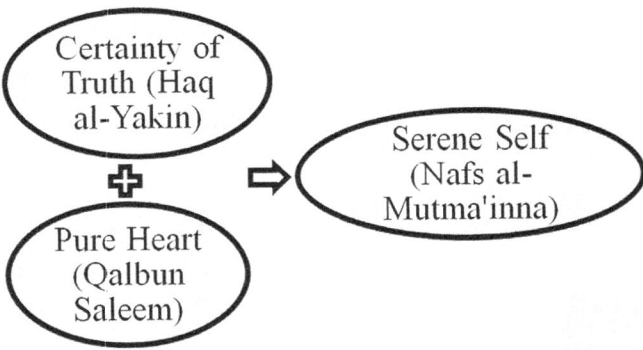

Remembrance of God has healing and therapeutic effects:

> Those who believe, and whose hearts find satisfaction in the remembrance of God: for without doubt in the remembrance of God do hearts find satisfaction. (Qur'an 13:28)

This verse reminds us of our moral obligations in order to abstain from lapses in moral judgment. If we transform our experiences into that of spirituality, we will find serenity:

> But those will prosper who purify themselves, and glorify the name of their Guardian-Lord, and (lift their hearts) in prayer. (Qur'an 87:14–15)

Transformation comes full circle once we achieve the freedom of the soul by strengthening its connection with God in remembrance of Him and empowering it with moral virtue.

The human heart is mentioned in the Qur'an 132 times, besides other notions under the term *fu'aad* (inner heart) that is mentioned sixteen times, and under the metaphoric term *al-sadr* (chest), which means the heart, that is mentioned forty-four times (El-Naggar). In our remembrance (dhikr) of God, and by His grace, the natural self and spiritual self will become transformed into the serene self (nafs al-mutma'inna). When the serene self enters our hearts, the end result is one of peace, harmony, and love. By remembering God, our actions become peaceful, harmonious, and loving.

When the tongue (lisan) and heart (qalb) become united as one in our dhikr (remembrance) of God, this constant practice enables us to strive toward reaching the level of perfection (ihsan) in our praises:

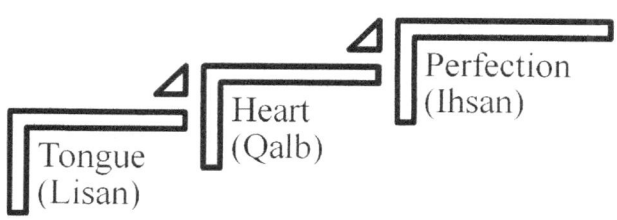

Ihsan means perfection in worship (*ibadat*). It results in the perfection of the inner faith (iman) to bring about our performance of both deed and action. However, to reach the level of ihsan requires making a genuine intention to do so, to be thankful (*shukr*) to God in the dhikr of Him and constantly seek God's help and guidance toward the straight path (sirat al-mustaqim). Other meanings of ihsan are supreme spiritual aspiration in worshipping God, good behavior that results in kindness, and excellence in our actions. In short, ihsan is a complete way of life.

Among the many attributes of ihsan, it is also referred to as beauty, balance, discipline, and goodness:

> Is there any reward for good (ihsan) except good (ihsan)?
> (Qur'an 55:60)

Nothing can explain good better than good, and the reward for having done good is the good in having done it. When this level of good is attained, we will feel ihsan in our hearts. Why? Because in ihsan, there is healing, there is forgiveness, there is love, and there is divine presence.

Good moral conduct is the basis for reaching ihsan. God has shown us the example of what perfection (ihsan) is through the example of Prophet Muhammad and his Ahl al-Bayt. God has established what the standard of perfection is in the Qur'an and how to achieve it:

> By the soul as it is perfected! And inspired unto it (against) its vices and (about) its piety! Indeed succeeds he who purifies it! And indeed fails he who pollutes it!
> (Qur'an 91:7–10)

What this verse means is that a perfected soul does exist in human creation, as God inspires the soul. God has created mankind with complete essentials, which include the soul, body, and mind and the ability to think and feel. Hence, it is necessary for us to understand the tools of maintaining and growing our spirit of perfection. Once we consider our negative actions and truly take the time to contemplate the ultimate consequences of our bad deeds, we come to realize what would have been a better moral choice. Negative actions or indulgence in worldly pastime can also lead to what God described in verse 83:14 of the Qur'an as "rust upon their hearts" (Kasmai-Nazeran 2008).

By holding strictly to the remembrance of God within both our tongues and hearts, we will gain the greatest gift in our lives, which is perfection (ihsan) in communication with Him. Whenever we sincerely and piously call upon God, we will be answered, and our requests will be granted. Praising God is also the hallmark of other religions.

Chapter 18

Monotheistic Aspects of Dhikr

Judaism, Christianity, and Islam command their followers to remember God whether sitting, standing, kneeling, lying down, or prostrating. Depending on the denomination, there are variations as to how Christians pray. For example, during worship, the Adventist church allows for praying sitting, standing, or kneeling (Rodriguez 2004).

Christians, Jews, and Muslims pray to God for numerous reasons. However, there is common ground and common principle in some of these reasons:

Prayer	Christians	Jews	Muslims
More than once daily	68%	37%	92%
God's forgiveness	76%	42%	92%
God's guidance	93%	74%	94%
Stronger faith	74%	44%	91%
Giving thanks	91%	84%	90%

| At home | 80% | 76% | 89% |
| Silently | 91% | 90% | 95% |

Source: 2004 Online Prayer Survey conducted by Beliefnet.com.

According to a 2004 online prayer survey conducted by Beliefnet.com, Muslims pray at a higher rate than Christians and Jews in a number of categories. Muslims sustain about a 90 percent positive response in each category (i.e., pray more than once daily; ask for God's forgiveness and guidance; seek a stronger faith; thank God; pray mostly at home; and pray silently). All three faiths have the same message, which is to submit to God and be in constant remembrance of Him by complying with His commands to perform good deeds and abstain from bad deeds.

The Hebrew word *zakar* is most often translated as "remember." Dhikr in Islam is also referred to as *zikr*, which corresponds closely to the pronunciation of the Hebrew *zakar*. All three faiths of Judaism, Christianity, and Islam emphasize that the heart brings out the innermost tranquil feelings for those who praise God and pray to Him.

Following are selected verses from the scriptures of the three faith traditions relative to how one prays, as well as the importance of the heart in the remembrance of God:

> Those who believe, and whose hearts find satisfaction in the remembrance of God: for without doubt in the remembrance of God do hearts find satisfaction. (Qur'an 13:28)

> Those who remember God standing, and sitting and reclining on their sides and think (seriously) in the creation of the heaven and the earth; saying "O Our Lord! Thou hast not created (all) this in vain! Glory be to Thee! Save us then from the torment of the (Hell) fire." (Qur'an 3:191)

And now, Israel, what does the Lord your God ask of you but to fear the Lord your God, to walk in obedience to Him, to love Him, and to serve the Lord your God with all your heart and with all your soul, and to observe the Lord's commands and decrees that I am giving you today for your own good. (Deuteronomy 10:12–13 NIV)

Hear, O Israel: The Lord is our God; the Lord is one. Love the Lord your God with all your heart and with all your soul and with all your strength. These commandments that I give you today are to be in your hearts. Impress them on your children. Talk about them when you sit at home and when you walk along the road, when you lie down and when you get up. Tie them as symbols on your hands and bind them on your foreheads. Write them on the doorframes of your houses and on your gates. (Deuteronomy 6:4–9 NIV)

Remember me for this, my God, and do not blot out what I have so faithfully done for the house of my God and its services. (Nehemiah 13:14 NIV)

I will praise you, Lord my God, with all my heart; I will glorify your name forever. (Psalm 86:12 NIV)

He (Jesus) answered, "Love the Lord your God with all your heart and with all your soul and with all your strength and with all your mind; and, love your neighbor as yourself." (Luke 10:27 NIV)

How great you are, Sovereign Lord! There is no one like you, and there is no God but you, as we have heard with our own ears. (2 Samuel 7:22 NIV)

Now when Daniel learned that the decree had been published, he went home to his upstairs room where the window opened toward Jerusalem. Three times a day he got down on his knees and prayed, giving thanks to his God, just as he had done before. (Daniel 6:10 NIV)

Come, let us bow down in worship; let us kneel before the Lord our Maker. (Psalm 95:6 NIV)

When he (David) was in the Desert of Judah. You, God, are my God, earnestly I seek You; I thirst for You, my whole being longs for You, in a dry and parched land where there is no water. I have seen You in the sanctuary and beheld Your power and Your glory. Because Your love is better than life, my lips will glorify You. I will praise You as long as I live, and in Your name I will lift up my hands. I will be fully satisfied, as with the richest of foods; with singing lips my mouth will praise You. On my bed I remember You; I think of You through the watches of the night. (Psalm 63:1–6 NIV)

Moses bowed to the ground at once and worshipped. (Exodus 34:8 NIV)

Praises in the remembrance of God are practiced by each of three monotheistic faiths. Praises relative to Muslims have already been discussed in the preceding chapters. What follows is the rationale as to why Jews and Christians praise God.

Jews are expected to recite the praise "Blessed are Thou Lord, our God, King of the Universe" after each meal. Bending the knee and bowing is done to indicate how blessed (*berakhah*) God is. As a practice, according to Jewish tradition, a person should recite one hundred *berakhot* (plural of berakhah) each day (www.jewfaq.org/prayer.htm). Following are the ten most prominent Hebrew praises (www.justworship.com):

- *Barak*: To kneel or bow, to give reverence to God as an act of adoration (Psalms 34:1; 100:4; 95:6).
- *Guwl*: To spin around, under the influence of any violent emotion (Psalms 32:11; 35:9; 118:24).
- *Hallal*: To praise, to make a show or rave about, to glory in or boast upon, to be clamorously foolish about your adoration of God (Psalms 22:23; 44:8; 63:5).
- *Ranan*: To creak, to emit a stridulous sound, to shout aloud for joy (Psalms 7:17; 33:1; 98:4).
- *Shachah*: To depress or prostrate in homage or loyalty to God, bow down, fall down flat (Psalms 29:2; 66:4; 95:6).
- *Shuwr*: Strolling minstrelsy, to sing, singer (man or woman) (Psalms 18:49; 33:3; 144:9).
- *Tehillah*: To sing hallal, a new song, a hymn of spontaneous praise glorifying God in song (Psalms 34:1; 40:3; 149:1).
- *Todah*: An extension of the hand, avowal, adoration, a choir of worshippers, confession, sacrifice of praise, thanksgiving (Psalms 50:14; 69:30; 100:4).
- *Yadah*: To use, hold out the hand, to throw (a stone or arrow) at or away, to revere or worship (with extended hands, praise thankful, thanksgiving) (Psalms 33:2; 61:8; 18:49).
- *Zamar*: To touch the strings or parts of a musical instrument (i.e., play upon it), to make music accompanied by the voice, to celebrate in song and music, give praise, sing forth praises, psalms (Psalms 66:2; 71:22; 144:9).

Judaism has a preoccupation with memory—remembrance through reenactment and ritualization is an inherent part of Judaism. It would be impossible to observe a Jewish holiday (e.g., Passover) without remembering a past event. Rosh Hashanah is also a day of remembrance, but it is also one meant for repentance. Jewish scripture commands Jews to remember (e.g., the Sabbath day) (Exodus 20:8) the Sabbath as a reminder of the creation (Exodus 20:11) and the Exodus (Deuteronomy 5:15). Today, remembering is more often discussed in conjunction with the Holocaust (Rosenbloom 2009).

The nature or praise in Christianity is an act of one's will that flows out of awe and reverence for the Creator. Praise gives glory to God and opens up a deeper union with Him. It turns attention off of people's problems and on the nature and character of God Himself. As Christians focus their minds on God and proclaim His goodness, they reflect His glory back to Him. Christians praise God because He is worthy of their praise. Praising God is simple obedience, and Christians discover benefits for their lives (CBN.com).

In Christianity, praising God is done for numerous reasons. As God deserves and is worthy of praise, Christians are reminded of the greatness of God; praising God strengthens one's faith, and God inhabits the atmosphere of praise. There are a number of ways in which praising is done (e.g., singing songs and hymns and clapping of hands) (www.allaboutgod.com):

> For great is the Lord and most worthy of praise; He is to be feared above all gods. (Psalm 96:4)

> Great is the Lord and most worthy of praise: His greatness no one can fathom. (Psalm 145:3)

> You are worthy, our Lord and God, to receive glory and honor and power, for You created all things, and by Your Will they were created and have their being. (Revelation 4:11)

> Praise the Lord, for the Lord is good; sing praise to His name, for that is pleasant. (Psalm 135:3)

> Let everything that has breath praise the Lord. Praise the Lord. (Psalm 150:6)

> I will extol the Lord at all times; His praise will always be on my lips. (Psalm 34:1)

> Because Your love is better than life, my lips will glorify
> You. I will praise You as long as I live, and in Your name
> I will lift up my hands. (Psalm 63:3–4)

Interreligious understanding seeks wisdom in four ways: (a) going deeper into the faiths of others, (b) going deeper into one's own faith, (c) going deeper into understanding the common good, and (d) going deeper into the relationship with others committed to interreligious understanding and engagement (Ford 2011). The hope is that Jews, Christians, and Muslims, who worship God and practice their faith differently, might be open to many forms of friendship with each other for the sake of God.

One of the common principles among the three faith traditions is an event that takes place in the future with the arrival of the Messiah by Jews and Christians and the arrival of the final Infallible Imam by the Muslims.

AHL AL-BAYT

Chapter 19

Eschatology of Dhikr

Eschatology is a branch of theology that addresses the final events of history or the end of the world. It is also a doctrine about death and the aftermath. In Islam, eschatology documents the hadiths (traditions) of Prophet Muhammad regarding the signs leading to the final destiny of mankind and the Day of Judgment. Particularly, it deals with the resurrection of the dead, the Second Coming, last judgment, heaven, and hell.

When Imam Muhammad al-Mahdi appears, he will prevail over evil in an apocalyptic battle against the enemies of God. Prophet Jesus will appear and join forces with Imam al-Mahdi. Both of them will put an end to injustice and tyranny and to mankind's immoral and depraved lifestyles as they establish a new world order. To comprehend the significance and importance of these two luminaries, we first need to understand how dhikr unfolds at the time of their arrival. Toward this end, we will examine the importance and significance of dhikr relative to the many attributes of the Qur'an, some of which are reminder, admonition, and explanation:

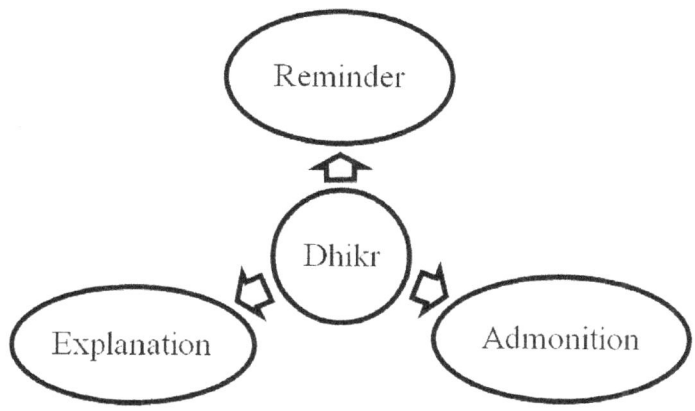

As a reminder (*tadhkeer*), the Qur'an reminds us of who we are, the purpose of our creation, the reality of life, our duties, and our obligations. As an admonition (*maw'idhah*), the Qur'an is advice for us not to be disobedient, which brings about God's punishment, but rather to be obedient in performing good deeds. As an explanation (*bayan*), the Qur'an is the clear manifestation that includes knowledge of what is to come in the future and what has occurred in the past.

God says the Qur'an is a reminder (Qur'an 80:11). The Qur'an reminds us to have faith, worship God, follow in the footsteps of Prophet Muhammad, perform righteous deeds, speak the truth, and practice patience (Qur'an 103:1–3). It is a reminder to read the Qur'an, listen to it, and learn from it. The Qur'an has the universal message for mankind leading them to the straight path, as it is a book of wisdom, guidance, and mercy unto the righteous ones (Qur'an 31:2–3).

The Qur'an is full of admonition (warning) (Qur'an 38:1). Prophet Muhammad came with the truth (Qur'an), yet many people rejected the truth. Even though God gave them an admonition, they still turned away from the truth (Qur'an 23:70–71). God makes it abundantly clear that the Qur'an is a guidance and admonition for the pious ones (Qur'an 3:138). As an admonition, God instructs mankind to follow the Qur'an in order to know the right course, thereby earning God's mercy and grace (Qur'an 73:19).

God sent the Qur'an as an explanation of the truth (Qur'an 25:33) and explanation of events for mankind (Qur'an 3:138). For example, the Qur'an explains a mystery that was unknown to the most renowned physicists for centuries. It reveals that in the beginning, the heavens and earth were joined together and then separated (Qur'an 21:30). Recent advancements in astronomy, especially the big bang theory, regarding the creation of the universe support this Qur'anic explanation.

We find these three attributes of the Qur'an (i.e., reminder, admonition, and explanation) demonstrated in the story of Prophet Joseph, which was revealed to Prophet Muhammad at a time when he lost his uncle, Abu Talib, and wife, Khadijah. An earlier chapter discusses the relationship between Prophet Joseph and Prophet Muhammad. The symbolic importance of Prophet Joseph also extends to Imam Hussein and Imam Muhammad al-Mahdi.

The people of Kufa reneged on their support by betraying Imam Hussein in his most dire need. Similarly, the sons of Prophet Jacob betrayed their father by lying to him that a wolf devoured their brother, Prophet Joseph (Qur'an 12:17). Although Prophet Joseph disappeared for a long time, he walked among his brothers and recognized them, but they did not recognize him (Qur'an 12:88). Relative to Imam al-Mahdi, when he first appears, the people will not recognize him. The imprisonment of Prophet Joseph for a number of years prevented him from seeing his family. Likewise, the occultation (Shi'a belief) of Imam al-Mahdi for centuries hid him from his community.

The tragedy of Imam Hussein was discussed in an earlier chapter. Annually, we remember (dhikr) that tragedy and reenact the events of the ten days leading up to Ashura. We will now focus on the eschatology of Imam al Mahdi.

We find commonalities on the signs of the end of the world as well as the signs preceding the arrival of Imam al-Mahdi and Prophet Jesus. Both Islam and Christianity hold that the world will come to an end. Cosmic signs, wars, the appearance of the Antichrist or false messiahs will mark the end, the resurrection of the departed, and their final judgment as to whether they go to final damnation or eternal reward in heaven. Such chaos will serve as a test of the purity of the faithful who will remain in the final stage of this process. Imam al-Mahdi and Prophet Jesus will usher in a new era of restoration and reconfirm the validity of God's revelation (Gilani 2014).

As Muslims, we become immersed in the dhikr (remembrance) of Imam al-Mahdi's longevity and creative energy that illuminates our hearts and minds by sustaining us within the sanctity of Islam and belief in God. Likewise, followers of the Jewish and Christian religions also adhere to the concept of the awaited Messiah, as depicted in the table below. Christians and Muslims believe that Jesus was the Messiah expected by the Jews, but the Jews reject this idea, alleging that Jesus was a false Messiah. However, the belief in the eventual coming of the Messiah (Moshiach, or Anointed One) is a basic fundamental part of traditional Judaism.

Dhikr (remembrance) of the Awaited One in the Abrahamic faiths

Criteria	*Judaism*	*Christianity*	*Islam*
Awaited One	Messiah ben David appears some time in the future after Messiah ben Joseph is killed	Jesus	Imam Muhammad al-Mahdi
Lineage	Prophet Abraham	Prophet Abraham	Prophet Abraham
Arrival	Messiah (Anointed One)	Second Coming of Jesus	Prophet Jesus governs with al-Mahdi
Enemy's objective	Conquer Jerusalem and persecute the Jews	Antichrist to abolish all religions	Dajjal to abolish all religions
Great war	Gog and Magog	Gog and Magog	Gog and Magog (Yajuj and Majuj)

Battle	Armilus (Anti-Messiah), or Gog and Magog, will slay Messiah ben Joseph	Jesus defeats the Antichrist and the False Prophet	Aided by al-Mahdi, Prophet Jesus slays Dajjal
Expected outcome	Political and spiritual redemption of Jews by restoring Jerusalem; establishment of a government in Israel as center of all world government, both for Jews and Gentiles; reconstruction of the temple and reestablishment of worship; restoration of the court system and establishment of Jewish law	Armageddon; complete destruction of non-Christians, who will all drown in a lake of fire burning with brimstone; the rule of Jesus	Victory over evil in an apocalyptic battle against the enemies of God; global government; institution of justice through the eradication of injustice by God; establishment of Islam as the only acceptable religion

Source: Wikipedia.

Before the arrival of Imam al-Mahdi, we have a great deal of preparation that needs to be done. Once we have prepared ourselves to attain the Islamic personality that sets us on the straight path, we will be better equipped to overcome biases and prejudices based on tribalism, culture, race, color, creed, and other obstacles that separate people and erode the unity of humanity. Preparation also takes on a social obligation insofar as we strive to rid ourselves of injustice and tyranny. We cannot be complacent about the inhumane treatment of people throughout the world, and we must take an active part in abolishing and eliminating unjust systems of government. Justice must prevail in all aspects of human life whether cultural, social, political, governmental, legal, ethical, or economical. It is justice that is a major symbol of Imam al-Mahdi's global government, as God will fill the earth with justice and eradicate injustice through him.

The foundation of justice is the inner self that seeks peace, harmony, and a sense of positive direction. In today's society, we seek instant gratification. However, self-fulfillment through one's perspective is not instant. Becoming who we want to be is not instant. We cannot do everything at once, but we can do something at once! Controlling the Islamic self is not an easy task. It requires control of one's inner thoughts and actions. Becoming enlightened in Islam is to invoke the dhikr (remembrance) of God in order to understand one's self-concept, control one's self-esteem, and attain self-fulfillment by way of patience. Control is achieved by way of order and harmony within the self.

Within our personality structure, we have individual selves. Each of these selves has a unique system. For example, the self has its own goals and priorities. Each has its own perceptions and motives. Each has its own style and development cycle. Each has its own limits of tolerance and emotional sensitivity. Dynamic and interactive, our subselves can communicate with each other to form a decision. When making decisions, the subselves condition our true basic self. We are not born with a personality. Our personality is formed, shaped, and developed in the framework of our relationships with our family and environment. We should strive to behave in a manner consistent within each of us through the invocation of the dhikr (remembrance) of God. It is the consistency of our behavior that defines the kind of personality we are associated with.

We need to develop unity within ourselves by holding fast to the Rope of God. The Islamic personality makes the believer cherish his human dignity and prestige and accept his responsibilities as a Muslim. The justification of Islamic morality promises the continuance of life in heaven in the hereafter for the morally good individuals. Faith, righteous deeds, truth, and patience are the basic virtues of Islamic morality. We gain eternal happiness through moral virtues and our constant remembrance (dhikr) of God. We must cleanse our thoughts and our hearts, which ultimately leads us to the straight path. We must free ourselves from the spiderweb of this frail world. We must walk the path of struggle against immoral tendencies.

As a safeguard, we must strive in the way of God by remembering to repeat constant praises of Him. With firmness of purpose, determination, and patience, we can attain the mercy of God. The ideal Islamic personality is one where faith leads to good deeds and good deeds lead to faith. By helping others, we are in effect helping ourselves to become better Muslims. We sincerely concentrate on every aspect of life as we continue to understand the beauty and wisdom of Islam. We must continue to remember God and to win the satisfaction of the Creator.

Development of the Islamic personality takes a great deal of preparation. We must prepare ourselves against the ego, which is the belief that self-interest is the just and proper motive for all human conduct. Ego is the excessive preoccupation with one's own well-being and interests, usually accompanied by an inflated sense of self-importance. It is the tendency to evaluate everything in relation to one's own interests—that is, self-centeredness. This self-centeredness and self-absorption within oneself immensely diminishes the chances of ever reaching moral fulfillment and self-respect. Keeping occupied with thoughts and actions of materialism, greed, center of attention, and conceit, the person continues to fall deeper and deeper into a spiral pit of which he cannot escape. The obedience to the self further erodes the soul, as the person commits every act of transgression, deception, and sedition in order to achieve superiority or authority over others. In a nutshell, he begins to worship himself, thereby becoming totally impervious to spirituality and the common good.

A Muslim fulfills his needs by devoting and preparing himself to spirituality and not to vanity and conceit. Dhikr (remembrance) of God brings about spirituality that helps mold one's personality and sets the individual on the right track. With humility and self-sacrifice, one can recover his sense of worth and regain his spirituality free of pride and complacency. Preparation to become better Muslims also includes self-forgiveness and self-criticism. The self-realization of forgiveness is when one is willing to forgive when he has the power to take revenge.

Forgiveness is an acknowledgment of a person's pledge to not inflict harm on anyone and to make a concerted effort to remedy his inner self toward one of peace and harmony. Toward this end, forgiveness benefits both the one who harms as well as the one who is harmed.

Self-criticism is a necessary requirement for one to bring his thoughts and actions in harmony with righteousness. A righteous Muslim constantly evaluates his actions and seeks improvement in order to bring him closer to the remembrance of God. The Muslim becomes unified within his self by overcoming his inner weakness of sins and deviant behavior. Through self-criticism, one can seek and discover his spirituality. Self-criticism brings us closer to God, as it intensifies and heightens our piety. It enjoins what is right and forbids what is wrong. It is the Islamic way and the straight path! It is the purpose and goal of Imam al-Mahdi!

Whether silently in the heart, verbally by the tongue, or consciously in the mind, the dhikr (remembrance) of Imam al-Mahdi must perpetuate through the ages awaiting his appearance. However, the best way to remember Imam al-Mahdi is in the heart, as we need to protect the heart from forgetting him. It is the sabr (patience) that will strengthen the dhikr of Imam al-Mahdi in our hearts. Remembering Imam al-Mahdi will strengthen our remembrance of God. According to Imam Muhammad al-Baqir:

> Surely our remembrance is from the remembrance of God. (*Al-Kafi*, Vol. 2, No. 2, p. 496)

The arrival of Imam al-Mahdi will occur. Until then, we should also be in constant remembrance of him. Toward this end, we should strive to seek the straight path, oppose injustice, and improve upon our Islamic personality.

Remembrance of God, the Prophets, and Imams also necessitates us to remember our parents and children as well as others that have an impact on our lives.

AHL AL-BAYT

Chapter 20

Dhikr: Remembering Others

Constant remembrance of God is the greatest goal and gift in our lives. In order for this remembrance (dhikr) to be fully realized and accepted by God, we need to also remember the true believers, male and female, and help them where we can as they set the example for others to follow. Further, we must also remember our parents, siblings, children, spouses, relatives, neighbors, community, and others. We live in a turbulent and unrestrained society that saddens our hearts. We witness the erosion of the family structure and the lack of control to help restore the dignity and importance of faith to unleash the rope of complacency that suffocates the inner soul. We feel a sense of emptiness and disconnect with one another.

But all hope is not lost. We have the tool to connect with each other, to empathize with each other, to help each other. That connection is dhikr (remembrance) of God, of family and relations, and of others. When we invoke the dhikr of God, we must truly feel it in our hearts. Once we have reached this level of remembrance of God, we will be able to bring about the panacea to help others regain their remembrance of God as well.

By remembering each other, we fulfill one of God's greatest gifts to mankind. The most effective start in this endeavor is to help others understand that God is waiting for their praises to Him and for them to ask for His guidance. We need to help them make their intention to begin praising God in order to lighten their own hearts and minds. By praising God, they will begin to feel His remembrance, thereby bringing them into focus of their purpose in life. They will then be more focused on the purpose of their prayers, supplications, fasting, charity, pilgrimage, and remembrance of others.

In reconnecting to our remembrance of God, we can energize ourselves to reconnect with others. Being interactive and empathetic with others will necessitate moving out of our comfort zone. In a nutshell, people care about big things, including their education, their careers, their money, and their entertainment. Have we ever had time to care about the feelings of others when they lost their jobs, or had a divorce, or became disabled, or had a death in the family, or were orphaned, or were hungry, or lost their faith? Have we ever had time to think of the elderly, who have difficulty in moving about, or parents who have grown old and need help, or friends who have become depressed and lonely? In this age of information technology and fast life, we rush to develop our minds and chase our success. We may feel that there is no time left to be aware of troubled waters, no time to be sensitive to others experiencing unhappiness, and no time to help others solve their problems. Oftentimes, we neglect to develop our empathy:

Empathy is identification with and understanding of another's situation, feelings, and motives. Empathy is being aware of, sensitive to, and experiencing the emotions and thoughts of others. It may be tacit in that one feels what others feel without oral communication. Empathy is synonymous with compassion, compatibility, congeniality, responsiveness, warmth, and understanding. The challenge is how to engage dhikr (remembrance) in developing empathy. There are many aspects of the word *empathy*. For example, empathy is the emotional response of shared understanding in which each person assumes the other's perspective and cultured values as much as possible.

Empathy requires mutual respect and goodwill between people to have an understanding for another person's beliefs and values. Empathy results in actually feeling the pain or the joy of the other person. Empathy is more than just awareness. We may be aware that our friends are feeling lonely; however, we are too busy to spend an afternoon with them listening to their troubles. We don't lack awareness; rather, we are actually well informed about their problems. However, if we don't remember their needs, share their feelings, even show how much we care about their troubles, then we lack empathy. Tenderness, comfort, and sacrificing our time are hallmarks of empathy.

We regard empathy as a value the family engenders and as a strength to be cultivated at home. Yet we see vast evidence of its absence in both children and adults. Ironically enough, there are a number of parents without much empathy for their children and vice versa. What really matters is that empathy can be taught, and it should be taught very early in childhood—at home and at school. It is not just a matter of family values; it is a matter of the values of society and civilization. There needs to be connectivity in the family, school, and society. Empathy can save a family; it can save lives from diving into despair and depression.

Simply said, empathy is the capacity to put oneself inside the soul of others and to see the world through their eyes. Empathy implies that we have trained ourselves to consider how other people perceive situations, how they perceive us, and how they would describe us. We are all born with the capacity of empathy. Empathy is like a muscle; if it is used, it develops.

Empathy is an active process; it must be put into action. It protects us, and it is really a guardian in that it allows us to move to a wider lens rather than a narrow vision. It means that we see into the minds, hearts, and souls of others. A lack of empathy is a sign of moral failure. To empathize is to find the way to cross the bridge with another who is suffering. Crossing the bridge to reach connectivity is a path to healing for them and sometimes for us.

Empathy is the springboard to sacrifice. Are we prepared to sacrifice what we love for the material things we treasure? For the believers, these treasures and possessions are meaningless and render worthless compared to their sacrifice to earn God's blessings (Qur'an 49:15). As all blessings come from God, we should open our hearts and share with others. The pinnacle of sacrifice is attained when we relinquish some of our own possessions by helping those in need. Hence, our spirituality is strengthened and reinforced with each act of charity, as it nourishes and increases our faith.

Sacrifice is an act of submission to God. Once we come to the realization that we must rely on God's provisions rather than the material aspects of life, the spiritual effect of sacrifice comes full circle. In effect, it is sacrifice itself that contributes to the success of our struggles in life, and in that way, it enhances our Islamic personality. Sacrifice energizes our sabr (patience) and vice versa, thereby strengthening our faith. With each sacrifice, faith becomes fulfilled within the depths of our sabr. This discipline of allowing for the interdependency of sacrifice and sabr in our lives is a hallmark of faith that catapults us closer to God.

Our experiences in life should enable us to understand what others are experiencing in similar situations. We find the remedies to solve our troubles in the Qur'an, the reminder (dhikr), as it has the answers. The Qur'an is the path of remembrance (dhikr), and it underscores the importance of empathy and sacrifice. For example, the Qur'an demonstrates the necessity of being kind to parents. We were taught by our parents that there is no easy way to get to where we want to be. They encourage and help us tackle obstacles and overcome our fears and weaknesses. They teach us to be ourselves and to be compassionate, honest, and peaceful. They teach us to remember to love our family and to be proud of our faith and culture.

Our parents teach us about a work ethic—that hard work is its own reward and is a form of faith. They set an example that life is more about giving than receiving. They have a strong, unshakeable faith that pulls our families through many trials, as they underscore the importance of worship in the remembrance of God. If our parents have passed away, we remember their influence; we build on such memories and share them with our children. We remember that our mothers carried us for nine difficult months in their wombs before we were born. Our parents nurtured and cultivated our upbringing for many years as they taught us, helped us, and provided us with food, clothing, shelter, education, and the purpose of prayer, supplication, and charity. As we get older, and if our parents are still living, we tend to forget that they are growing older as well. We must remember that God has commanded us to treat our parents with utmost respect and kindness and to ask God to have mercy on them (Qur'an 17:23–24), even if they are doing an injustice and even if they are disbelievers:

> O you who have believed, be persistently standing firm in justice, witnesses for God, even if it be against yourselves or parents and relatives. Whether one is rich or poor, God is more worthy of both. So follow not [personal] inclination, lest you not be just. And if you distort [your testimony] or refuse [to give it], then indeed God is ever, with what you do, acquainted. (Qur'an 4:135)

> But if they (your parents) endeavor to make you associate with Me that of which you have no knowledge, do not obey them but accompany them in (this) world with appropriate kindness and follow the way of those who turn back to Me (in repentance). Then to Me will be your return, and I will inform you about what you used to do. (Qur'an 31:15)

This is a call to action for parents to teach their children, and themselves if necessary, the dhikr (remembrance of God), so that they can absorb these praises, which will remain with them for the rest of their lives. Teaching our children dhikr of God is just as important as feeding, clothing, and sheltering them. This teaching process reinforces our own connection with God and, as a result, strengthens our faith and potential for success in the hereafter. The goal is to truly embrace praising God instead of it feeling like a chore or feeling robotic.

Although everything happens by the will of God, He has given us a free will to make our own choices, and we will be accountable for our actions. Had God not given us free will, we would not be able to do anything. While free will instills within us God's gift of independence, we need to strive for a unified sense of life by remembering (dhikr) and extending our gratitude to Him. Further, the remembrance of God also instills in our minds and hearts the importance of family unity. Sacrifice steers us in the right direction in achieving that unity. It frees us from the complacency of our irrational behavior and selfishness by driving home the importance of unity within our family and community to safeguard our children and their growth.

Children of the future must be the leaders and advocates of that vision of unity. As we spend time with children and truly open our hearts, we will find that they have something to teach us—their innocence and their trust. Children come into the world carrying the light of unity within them. They have a remarkable sense of empathy and gratitude. As we open ourselves to their teaching, they can show us how to be unified, how to be absorbed in the present, and even how to better practice our faith. We need to start them at an early age to invoke the remembrance (dhikr) of God. This will protect them even from our shortcomings and failures.

While education and parenting is a start in the right direction, are we up to the task? Are we clear about where we want to go and how to get there? Do we understand our responsibilities? It is not beneficial to let children be pulled in all different directions in the hope that they will sort out things for themselves. We must bring our children into focus by balancing the elements of knowledge, tolerance, collaboration, sacrifice, and empathy. We must bring our children to inculcate in their minds and hearts the importance and constant practice of prayer, supplication, and remembrance of God—all as a safeguard from temptations, indecency, and evil.

As parents, we should be loving, caring, understanding, and supportive of our children. We need to be good role models for them. We need to give our children inspiration and hope in order to keep their spirits up. We need to put our children first and foremost, to spend time with them, and to teach them the importance of our Islamic faith. Sometimes a parent is incapable of being a role model, but hopefully in this situation, neighbors, relatives, teachers, and friends will step up to the challenge.

> Verily your possessions and your children are only a trial and verily God it is (He) with Whom is a great recompense. (Qur'an 64:15)

Since our children are but a trial and the highest reward is with God, it is then our responsibility to guide our children to Islam. It is through Islam that they can become righteous and be of service to God. We pass God's trial once our children worship and please Him. Undeniably, we cannot become passive parents. While we have our own needs, we must remember to sacrifice our time to address the needs of our children by teaching them Islamic principles and morals. To starve our children from these needs paves the way for them to become complacent in their obligations to Islam, thereby distancing them from God. It is narrated as follows from Imam Ja'far as-Sadiq:

> Teach traditions to your children as soon as possible, before opposers (to your beliefs) reach them before you do. (*Al-Kafi*, Vol. 6, p. 47)

In order to have our children remember the importance of prayer, we influence their interest when we pray with them. We can begin early in the lives of our children to also teach them short praises in the remembrance (dhikr) of God. In the ensuing years, they can learn longer praises. However, we need to invoke these praises together with our children and explain their meaning and significance. Let us begin by teaching them to say the following:

> Remember Me, and I will remember you. (Qur'an 2:152)

Epilogue

Dhikr flows through our minds and hearts as we invoke the remembrance of God. Dhikr immerses us into deep meditation glorifying the name of God. It has a variety of expressions, including chanting God's names. Dhikr means praising God for His blessings on us by saying, *Subhan Allah wa bi Hamdihi* (Glory be to God, and praise Him); *La ilaha illallah* (There is no God but God); Allahu Akbar (God is the greatest); and countless other expressions.

When we have dhikr on our tongues, we have a constant connection with God in our hearts. Our gratitude to God never ceases, because we remember every one of His blessings. The more we think about God, the more we want to praise Him. Remembrance of God and blessings from God become full circle as they reinforce and strengthen each other.

Dhikr helps us become more in tune with our inner self by bringing into focus the essence of our Islamic personality:

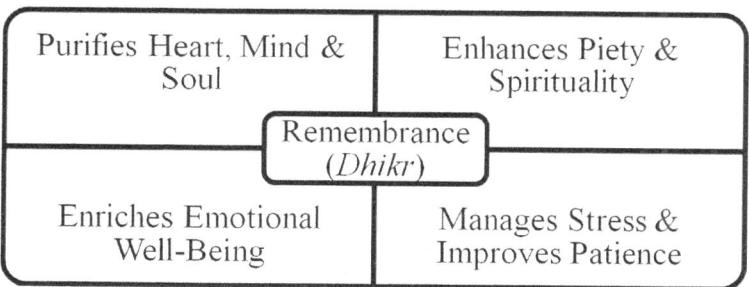

These criteria of the Islamic personality are intertwined with each other. As these criteria are dependent on each other, they cannot be separated. They comprise the Islamic personality. For example, managing stress and improving patience enhances our piety and spirituality. Likewise, when we purify our hearts, minds, and souls, we enrich our emotional well-being. From another perspective, piety results in the self-achievement of the straight path, righteous deeds, worship, and prosperity. Our happiness from dhikr emanates from self-satisfaction and occurs when we have freed ourselves from selfishness and basic desires. At the zenith of the fulfillment of our needs is self-realization through patience (sabr).

Moral judgment is applied to all activities of mankind, which results in a single undivided Islamic personality. Through dhikr, we can strengthen our Islamic personality in order to grapple with evil and overcome its dastardly venom. God provides sustenance for all, just and unjust, in this transient world, which ends almost as soon as it begins. So be prudent and wise in how we utilize that sustenance and exercise dhikr and sabr in the way of God by doing good and prohibiting evil.

While utterances of the tongue, recitation of Qur'anic verses, and feelings from the heart are important, it is their outcomes that matter to our development and ultimate success. With Dhikr, we are better positioned to have faith, perform righteous deeds, speak the truth, and practice patience (Qur'an 103:1–3). The one who engages in dhikr has the highest rank of all before God.

Death is inevitable, and in the end, we will return to God. What lies ahead in the afterlife is our reward or punishment for how we lived our lives on earth. As death is unavoidable, our return to God is prearranged and prescribed by Him. Whether we led a good life or a bad life, there is no escape in our return to God. However, it is because of the constant dhikr (remembrance) of God, in which our hearts are absorbed in His mercy and grace, that we willingly welcome our return to Him, even before our death. Once we have reached the straight path of perfection (ihsan) in this life, we hasten our return to God. Moreover, it is in this state of mind that our hearts freely and enthusiastically pursue the return to God.

Our soul's search for God gives meaning to everything we do in life. We have been created to know and love God, and our souls are transformed into the reflection of God's light through dhikr in remembrance of Him. This transformation comes about when we are able to understand spirituality with our experiences in life and ignite our hearts' passion for God. Summoning the heart through meditation induced by dhikr brings about the knowledge of God's purpose for our existence. By embracing dhikr both inwardly and outwardly—"Remember Me, and I will remember you" (Qur'an 2:152)—we become self-actualized as Muslims.

Dhikr is important because it not only inspires us to do good, but it also heals, energizes, and transforms our lives. When engaging in dhikr, we feel more forgiving and enthusiastic. Dhikr is the adhesive that binds the mind and heart together. It serves as a key link in the dynamic between praising God and receiving blessings from Him ("Remember Me, and I will remember you"). Dhikr requires mental discipline, as gratitude to God is about remembering God. If there is a crisis in our lives, it may be because we are forgetful of God's blessings, or it may be that God is testing us in order that we move closer to him. Dhikr helps us to look at calamities as blessings or, said differently, as opportunities to improve our patience and perseverance. In this is tremendous reward. Our gratitude to God is the memory of the heart, for it is the way the heart remembers. To be grateful to God, we must remember to remember!

> We surely belong to God and to Him we shall return.
> (*Inna lillahi wa inna ilayhi raji'un.*)
> (Qur'an 2:156)

Appendix A

Selected Occurrences of Dhikr in the Qur'an

2:40	10:3	25:29	46:21
2:47	10:71	25.50	47:18
2:63	11:114	25.62	50:8
2:122	11:120	25:73	50:37
2:152	12:45	26:5	50:45
2:198	12:85	26:209	51:55
2:200	12:104	26:227	53:29
2:203	13:28	27.62	54:15
2:231	14:5	29:45	54:17
2:239	14:6	29:51	54:22
2:269	14:25	33:9	54:25
2:282	15:6	33:21	54:32
3:41	15:9	33:34	54:40
3:58	16:13	33:35	54:51
3:103	16:17	33:41	56:73
3:135	16:43	35:3	57:16
3:191	16:44	35.37	58:19
4:103	18:24	36:11	62:9
4:142	18:28	36:69	62:10
5:7	18:83	37:3	63:9
5:11	18:101	37:13	65:10
5:20	19:2	37:168	68:51
5:91	19:67	38:1	68:52

5:110	20:14	38:8	69:12
6:69	20:34	38:17	69:48
6:70	20:42	38:32	72:17
6:90	20:99	38:43	73:8
6:152	20:113	38:46	73:19
7:2	20:124	38:49	74:31
7:3	21:2	38:87	74:49
7:26	21:7	39:21	74:54
7:63	21:24	39:22	76:25
7:69	21:42	39:23	76:29
7:74	21:48	40:44	77:5
7:86	21:50	40:54	79:35
7:130	21:84	41:41	80:4
7:171	23:71	43:5	80:11
7:201	23:85	43.13	80:12
7:205	23:110	43:36	81:27
8:2	24:36	43:44	87:9
8:26	24:37	44:13	87:15
8:45	25:18	45:23	89:23

Appendix B

Selected Qur'anic Verses on Dhikr

Then you remember Me; I will remember you. Be grateful to Me, and do not reject Faith. (2:152)

It is no crime in you if you seek of the bounty of your Lord (during pilgrimage). Then when you pour down from (Mount) Arafat, celebrate the praises of God at the Sacred Monument, and celebrate His praises as He has directed you, even though, before this, you went astray. (2:198)

So when you have accomplished your holy rites, celebrate the praises of God, as you used to celebrate the praises of your fathers,- yes, with far more heart and soul. There are men who say: "Our Lord! Give us (Thy bounties) in this world!" But they will have no portion in the Hereafter. (2:200)

Celebrate the praises of God during the Appointed Days. But if any one hastens to leave in two days, there is no blame on him, and if any one stays on, there is no blame on him, if his aim is to do right. Then fear God, and know that you will surely be gathered unto Him. (2:203)

When you divorce women, and they fulfill the term of their ('Iddat), either take them back on equitable terms or set them free on equitable terms; but do not take them back to injure them, (or) to take undue advantage; if any one does that; He wrongs his own soul. Do not treat God's Signs as a jest, but solemnly rehearse God's favors on you, and the fact that He sent down to you the Book and Wisdom, for your instruction. And fear God, and know that God is well acquainted with all things. (2:231)

If you fear (an enemy), pray on foot, or riding, (as may be most convenient), but when you are in security, celebrate God's praises in the manner He has taught you, which you knew not (before). (2:239)

He said: "O my Lord! Give me a Sign!" "Thy Sign," was the answer, "Shall be that thou shalt speak to no man for three days but with signals. Then celebrate the praises of thy Lord again and again, and glorify Him in the evening and in the morning." (3:41)

And hold fast, all together, by the rope which God (stretches out for you), and be not divided among yourselves; and remember with gratitude God's favor on you; for you were enemies and He joined your hearts in love, so that by His Grace, you became brethren; and you were on the brink of the pit of Fire, and He saved you from it. Thus doth God make His Signs clear to you: That you may be guided. (3:103)

And those who, having done something to be ashamed of, or wronged their own souls, earnestly bring God to mind, and ask for forgiveness for their sins,- and who can forgive sins except God.- and are never obstinate in persisting knowingly in (the wrong) they have done. (3:135)

Men who celebrate the praises of God, standing, sitting, and lying down on their sides, and contemplate the (wonders of) creation in the heavens and the earth, (With the thought): "Our Lord! Not for naught Has Thou created (all) this! Glory to Thee! Give us salvation from the penalty of the Fire." (3:191)

When you pass (Congregational) prayers, celebrate God's praises, standing, sitting down, or lying down on your sides; but when you are free from danger, set up Regular Prayers: For such prayers are enjoined on believers at stated times. (4:103)

The Hypocrites - they think they are over-reaching God, but He will over-reach them: When they stand up to prayer, they stand without earnestness, to be seen of men, but little do they hold God in remembrance. (4:142)

And call in remembrance the favor of God unto you, and His covenant, which He ratified with you, when you said: "We hear and we obey": And fear God, for God knows well the secrets of your hearts. (5:7)

O you who believe! Call in remembrance the favor of God unto you when certain men formed the design to stretch out their hands against you, but (God) held back their hands from you: so fear God. And on God let believers put (all) their trust. (5:11)

Remember Moses said to his people: "O my people! Call in remembrance the favor of God unto you, when He produced prophets among you, made you kings, and gave you what He had not given to any other among the peoples." (5:20)

Satan's plan is (but) to excite enmity and hatred between you, with intoxicants and gambling, and hinder you from the remembrance of God, and from prayer: will you not then abstain? (5:91)

Then will God say: "O Jesus the son of Mary! Recount My favor to thee and to thy mother. Behold! I strengthened thee with the Holy Spirit, so that thou did speak to the people in childhood and in maturity. Behold! I taught thee the Book and Wisdom, the Law and the Gospel and behold! Thou makes out of clay, as it were, the figure of a bird, by My leave, and thou breathes into it and it becomes a bird by My leave, and thou heals those born blind, and the lepers, by My leave. And behold! Thou brings forth the dead by My leave. And behold! I did restrain the Children of Israel from (violence to) thee when thou did show them the clear Signs, and the unbelievers among them said: 'This is nothing but evident magic.'" (5:110)

Follow (O men!) the revelation given unto you from your Lord, and follow not, as friends or protectors, other than Him; how little do you remember. (7:3)

Do you wonder that there hath come to you a message from your Lord through a man of your own people, to warn you? Call in remembrance that He made you inheritors after the people of Noah, and gave you a stature tall among the nations. Call in remembrance the benefits (you have received) from God. That so you may prosper. (7:69)

And remember how He made you inheritors after the 'Ad people and gave you habitations in the land: you build for yourselves palaces and castles in (open) plains, and carve out homes in the mountains; so bring to remembrance the benefits (you have received) from God, and refrain from evil and mischief on the earth. (7:74)

Those who fear God, when a thought of evil from Satan assaults them, bring God to remembrance, when lo! They see (aright)! (7:201)

And do thou (O reader!) Bring thy Lord to remembrance in thy (very) soul, with humility and in reverence, without loudness in words, in the mornings and evenings; and be not thou of those who are unheedful. (7:205)

O you who believe! When you meet a force, be firm, and call God in remembrance much (and often); that you may prosper. (8:45)

Those who believe, and whose hearts find satisfaction in the remembrance of God. For without doubt in the remembrance of God do hearts find satisfaction. (13:28)

Remember! Moses said to his people: "Call to mind the favor of God to you when He delivered you from the people of Pharaoh: they set you hard tasks and punishments, slaughtered your sons, and let your womenfolk live: therein was a tremendous trial from your Lord." (14:6)

Without adding, "So please God." and call thy Lord to mind when thou forgets, and say, "I hope that my Lord will guide me ever closer (even) than this to the right road." (18:24)

And keep thy soul content with those who call on their Lord morning and evening, seeking His Face; and let not thine eyes pass beyond them, seeking the pomp and glitter of this Life; nor obey any whose heart We have permitted to neglect the remembrance of Us, one who follows his own desires, whose case has gone beyond all bounds. (18:28)

(Unbelievers) whose eyes had been under a veil from remembrance of Me, and who had been unable even to hear. (18:101)

(This is) a mention of the Mercy of thy Lord to His servant Zakariya. (19:2)

Verily, I am God. There is no god but I: So serve thou Me (only), and establish regular prayer for celebrating My praise. (20:14)

Go, thou and thy brother, with My Signs, and slacken not, either of you, in keeping Me in remembrance. (20:42)

Say: "Who can keep you safe by night and by day from (the Wrath of) (God) Most Gracious?" Yet they turn away from the mention of their Lord. (21:42)

But you treated them with ridicule, so much so that (ridicule of) them made you forget My Message while you were laughing at them! (23:110)

(Lit is such a Light) in houses, which God hath permitted to be raised to honor; for the celebration, in them, of His name: In them is He glorified in the mornings and in the evenings, (again and again). (24:36)

Men whom neither merchandise nor any sale divert from the Remembrance of God and constancy in prayer and paying the poor-rate; they fear the day the hearts and eyes will be transformed (in a world wholly new), fear is for the Day when hearts and eyes will be transformed (in a world wholly new). (24:37)

Except those who believe, work righteousness, engage much in the remembrance of God, and defend themselves only after they are unjustly attacked. And soon will the unjust assailants know what vicissitudes their affairs will take! (26:227)

Recite what is sent of the Book by inspiration to thee, and establish regular Prayer: for Prayer restrains from shameful and unjust deeds; and remembrance of God is the greatest (thing in life) without doubt. And God knows the (deeds) that you do. (29:45)

O you who believe! Remember the Grace of God, (bestowed) on you, when there came down on you hosts (to overwhelm you): But We sent against them a hurricane and forces that you saw not: but God sees (clearly) all that you do. (33:9)

You have indeed in the Messenger of God a beautiful pattern (of conduct) for any one whose hope is in God and the Final Day, and who engages much in the Praise of God. (33:21)

And recite what is rehearsed to you in your homes, of the Signs of God and His Wisdom: for God understands the finest mysteries and is well acquainted (with them). (33:34)

For Muslim men and women,- for believing men and women, for devout men and women, for true men and women, for men and women who are patient and constant, for men and women who humble themselves, for men and women who give in charity, for men and women who fast (and deny themselves), for men and women who guard their chastity, and for men and women who engage much in God's praise,- for them has God prepared forgiveness and great reward. (33:35)

O you who believe! Celebrate the praises of God, and do this often. (33:41)

O men! Call to mind the grace of God unto you! is there a creator, other than God, to give you sustenance from heaven or earth? There is no god but He: how then are you deluded away from the Truth? (35:3)

Saad: By the Qur'an, Full of Admonition: (This is the Truth). (38:1)

Is one whose heart God has opened to Islam, so that he has received Enlightenment from God, (no better than one hard-hearted)? Woe to those whose hearts are hardened against celebrating the praises of God. They are manifestly wandering (in error)! (39:22)

God has revealed (from time to time) the most beautiful Message in the form of a Book, consistent with itself, (yet) repeating (its teaching in various aspects): the skins of those who fear their Lord tremble thereat; then their skins and their hearts do soften to the celebration of God's praises. Such is the guidance of God. He guides therewith whom He pleases, but such as God leaves to stray, can have none to guide. (39:23)

Those who reject the Message when it comes to them (are not hidden from Us). And indeed it is a Book of exalted power. (41:41)

In order that you may sit firm and square on their backs, and when so seated, you may celebrate the (kind) favor of your Lord, and say, "Glory to Him Who has subjected these to our (use), for we could never have accomplished this (by ourselves)." (43:13)

If anyone withdraws himself from remembrance of (God) Most Gracious, We appoint for him an evil one, to be an intimate companion to him. (43:36)

Therefore shun those who turn away from Our Message and desire nothing but the life of this world. (53:29)

And We have indeed made the Qur'an easy to understand and remember: then is there any that will receive admonition? (54:17)

But We have indeed made the Qur'an easy to understand and remember: then is there any that will receive admonition? (54:22)

And We have indeed made the Qur'an easy to understand and remember: then is there any that will receive admonition? (54:32)

And We have indeed made the Qur'an easy to understand and remember: then is there any that will receive admonition? (54:40)

And (oft) in the past, have We destroyed gangs like unto you: then is there any that will receive admonition? (54:51)

Has not the Time arrived for the Believers that their hearts in all humility should engage in the remembrance of God and of the Truth which has been revealed (to them), and that they should not become like those to whom was given Revelation aforetime, but long ages passed over them and their hearts grew hard? For many among them are rebellious transgressors. (57:16)

The Evil One has got the better of them: so he has made them lose the remembrance of God. They are the Party of the Evil One. Truly, it is the Party of the Evil One that will perish! (58:19)

O you who believe! When the call is proclaimed to prayer on Friday (the Day of Assembly), hasten earnestly to the Remembrance of God, and leave off business (and traffic): That is best for you if you but knew! (62:9)

And when the prayer is finished, then may you disperse through the land, and seek of the Bounty of God. and celebrate the Praises of God often (and without stint): that you may prosper. (62:10)

O you who believe! Let not your riches or your children divert you from the remembrance of God. If any act thus, the loss is their own. (63:9)

That We might try them by that (means). But if any turns away from the remembrance of his Lord, He will cause him to undergo a severe Penalty. (72:17)

But keep in remembrance the name of thy Lord and devote thyself to Him whole-heartedly. (73:8)

Verily this is an admonition; therefore, whoso will, let him take a (straight) path to his Lord! (73:19)

And celebrate the name or thy Lord morning and evening. (76:25)

Sources:

Mir Ahmed Ali, S. V. *The Holy Qur'an*. Elmhurst, NY: Tahrike Tarsile Qur'an Inc., 1995.

Yusuf Ali, Abdullah. *The Holy Qur'an: Text, Translation and Commentary*. Washington, DC: Islamic Center, 1978.

Appendix C

Dhikr of the Ninety-Nine Beautiful Names of God

1. The Beneficent	35. The Appreciative	69. The Able
2. The Merciful	36. The Most High	70. The Powerful
3. The Sovereign	37. The Most Great	71. The Expediter
4. The Holy	38. The Preserver	72. The Delayer
5. The Source of Peace	39. The Maintainer	73. The First
6. The Trusted	40. The Reckoner	74. The Last
7. The Protector	41. The Sublime One	75. The Manifest
8. The Mighty	42. The Generous One	76. The Hidden
9. The Compeller	43. The Watchful	77. The Governor
10. The Majestic	44. The Responsive	78. The Most Exalted
11. The Creator	45. The All-Embracing	79. The Source of All Goodness
12. The Evolver	46. The Wise	80. The Acceptor of Repentance
13. The Fashioner	47. The Loving	81. The Avenger
14. The Forgiver	48. The Glorious One	82. The Pardoner
15. The Subduer	49. The Resurrector	83. The Compassionate

16. The Bestower	50. The Witness	84. The Eternal Owner of Sovereignty
17. The Provider	51. The Truth	85. The Lord of Glory and Bounty
18. The Opener	52. The Trustee	86. The Equitable
19. The All-Knowing	53. The Most Strong	87. The Gatherer
20. The Constrictor	54. The Firm One	88. The Self-Sufficient
21. The Expander	55. The Guardian	89. The Enricher
22. The Abaser	56. The Praiseworthy	90. The Preventer
23. The Exalter	57. The Counter	91. The Distresser
24. The Honorer	58. The Originator	92. The Propitious
25. The Dishonorer	59. The Restorer	93. The Light
26. The All-Hearing	60. The Giver of Life	94. The Guide
27. The All-Seeing	61. The Bringer of Death	95. The Incomparable
28. The Judge	62. The Living	96. The Everlasting
29. The Just	63. The Self-Subsisting	97. The Supreme Inheritor
30. The Kind	64. The Finder	98. The Guide to the Right Path
31. The Aware	65. The Noble	99. The Patient
32. The Forebearing One	66. The Unique	
33. The Great One	67. The One	
34. The All-Forgiving	68. The Eternal	

Source: Qur'an

Appendix D

Selected Sayings of Dhikr (Remembrance)

La ilahah illallah (There is no God but God)—renewal of faith.

Allahu Akbar (God is the greatest).

Assalaamu alaikum (Peace be upon you)—by way of greetings.

Wa alaykumus salaam (Peace be upon you)—in reply to greetings.

Assalaamu alaikum Warahmatullahi Wabarakatuh (Peace and mercy and blessings of God be upon you).

Bismillah (In the name of God)—before making a beginning.

Bismilllahi Al-Rahmani Al-Rahim (In the name of God, the Beneficent, the Merciful).

JazakAllahu khair (May God reward you for the good)—expression of thanks.

BarakAllahu feekum (May God bless you)—when responding to someone's thanks.

Fi aman Allah (In the protection of God)—by way of saying good-bye.

Fi sabil Allah (For the sake of God)—when giving to charity.

Hadha min fadl rabbi (This is by the grace of my Lord).

Subhanallah (Glory be to God)—for praising something.

Insha Allah (If God wishes/God willing)—for expressing a desire to do something or for something to happen.

Astaghfir Allah (I seek forgiveness from God)—repenting for sins before God.

Al-Hamdu lillahi rabbil 'alamin (Praise be to God, the Lord of the worlds).

Maa shaa Allah (As God has willed)—for expressing appreciation for something good.

Al-Hamdulillah (All praise is for God)—for showing gratitude to God after success or even after completing anything.

A'udhu billah (I seek refuge in God).

Ya Allah (Oh God)—when in pain or distress, calling upon God and no one else.

Subhan Allah (Glory be to God)—when dismayed or shocked by something or glorifying God when seeing His creations.

Alaihi salaam (Peace be upon him)—whenever saying the name of a prophet.

RadiaAllahu anhu/anha (May God be pleased with him or her).

Rahimullah (May God have mercy on him or her).

Inna lillahi wa inna ilaihi raji'un (To God we belong, and to Him is our return)—an expression of sympathy of the news of a loss or someone's death.

La hawla wa la quwata illa Billah (There is no might or power except with God).

Subhan Allahi wa bi Hamdihi (Glory be to God, and praise Him).

Subhan Allahi 'l-adheem wa bi Hamdihi (Glory be to God, the Supreme, and praise Him).

Yur-hamok-Allah (May God have mercy on you)—when someone else sneezes.

Ohebok-fi-Allah (I love you for the sake of God)—when having love for someone.

Ummun-to-Billah (May God bless you with goodness)—when getting married (and other happy occasions).

Fi-umman-Allah (May God protect you)—when parting from someone.

Tawak-kalto-ul-Allah (I put my trust in God)—when a problem appears.

Na-uzo-Billah (God protect us)—when unpleasantness occurs.

Ta-barruk-Allah (May God bless you)—when pleasantness occurs.

La ilahah illa Huwa (None has the right to be worshipped but He).

Source: Qur'an and Hadiths

Appendix E

Selected Shi'a Hadiths on Dhikr

Kitab al-Kafi

Al-Husayn ibn Muhammad from Mu'alla ibn Muhammad from al-Washsha' from 'Abdallah ibn 'Ajlan from abu Ja'far (a.s.) who has said the following about the words of Allah, the Most Holy, the Most High. "Ask the people of Dhikr if you do not know." (16:43, 21:7 Holy Quran). The Holy Prophet (s.a.) has said, "I am the Dhikr and the Imams are the people of Dhikr." About the words of Allah, the Most Holy, the Most High that says, "It is a Dhikr for you and for your people and you all will be asked questions." (43:44) The Imams (a.s.) said, "We are his people and we will be questioned." (It seems that both the Holy Prophet (s.a.) is called Dhikr and the Holy Quran is also called Dhikr). (H 543, Ch. 20, h 1)

Al-Husayn ibn Muhammad has narrated from Mu'alla ibn Muhammad from Muhammad ibn 'Uwarma from Ali ibn Hassan from his uncle 'Abd al-Rahman ibn Kathir said that he asked Imam abu 'Abdallah (a.s.) about the meaning of the following words of Allah. "Ask the people of Dhikr if you do not know." (16:43, 21:7 Holy Quran) The Imams (a.s.) said, "Prophet Muhammad (s.a.) is Dhikr' and we are the people of Dhikr who will be asked." I also asked about, "It is a Dhikr for you and for your people and you all will be asked questions." (43:44) The Imams (a.s.) said, "It is a reference to us. We are the people of Dhikr and we will be asked questions." (H 544, Ch. 20, h 2)

Al-Husayn ibn Muhammad has narrated from Mu'alla ibn Muhammad from al-Washsha' who has said that said to Imam al-Rida (a.s.), "May Allah take my soul in service for your cause, what is the meaning of the words of Allah, 'ask the people of Dhikr if you do not know'"? (Qur'an 16:43; 21:7) The Imams (a.s.) said, "Dhikr' is Prophet Muhammad (s.a.) and we are his family (people) about whom questions will be asked." I further asked about, "Are you the ones to be questioned and we will be the ones to question?" The Imams (a.s.) said yes, that is true." I then asked, "Will it be right on us to ask you?" The Imams (a.s.) said, "Yes, it is so." I then asked, "Will it be a right on you to answer us?" The Imams (a.s.) said, "No, we will decide. We may or may not answer. Have you not heard the words of Allah, the Most Holy, the Most High that say, "This is a gift from us. You may (give to others and) oblige or keep without being held accountable." (38:39) (H 545, Ch. 20, h 3)

A number of our people have narrated from Ahmad ibn Muhammad from al-Husayn ibn Sa'id from al-Nadr ibn Suwayd from 'Asim ibn Hamid from abu Basir from Imam abu 'Abdallah (a.s.) who has said the following about the words of Allah, the Most Holy, the Most High. "It is a Dhikr for you and for your people and you all will be asked questions." (43:44) The Messenger of Allah is the Dhikr (reminder of Allah) and members of his family (a.s.) are the ones who will be asked questions and they are the people of Dhikr." (H 546, Ch. 20, h 4)

Ahmad ibn Muhamad has narrated from al-Husayn ibn Sa'id from Hammad from Rib'iy from Fudayl from abu 'Abdallah (a.s.) who has said the following about the words of Allah, the Most Holy, the Most High. "It is a Dhikr for you and for your people and you all will be asked questions." (43:44) The Imams (a.s.) said, "The Holy Quran is the 'Dhikr' and we are the ones who will be asked questions." (H 547, Ch. 20, h 5)

Muhammad ibn Yahya has narrated from Muhammad ibn al-Husayn from Muhammad ibn 'Isma'il from Mansur ibn Yunus from abu Bakr al-Hadrami who has said the following. "I was in the presence of Imam (a.s.) abu Ja'far (a.s.) and al-Ward brother of al-Kumayt came to see him.

He to the Imams (a.s.) said, "May Allah take my soul in service for your cause, I have chosen seventy questions and I do not know the answer even for one of them." The Imams (a.s.) said, "Not even one answer, O Ward?" He then said, "Yes, I do know the answer for one of them." The Imams (a.s.) asked, "What is it then?" He replied, "It is the words of Allah that say, 'Ask the people of Dhikr if you do not know who are they.'" The Imams (a.s.) replied, "We are the people of Dhikr." I then said, "Must we then ask you?" The Imams (a.s.) said, "Yes, you must ask us for answers." I then asked, "Must you then give us answers?" The Imams (a.s.) said, "We may or may not answer." (H 548, Ch. 20, h 6)

Muhammad ibn Yahya from Muhammad ibn al-Husayn from Safwan ibn Yahya from al-'Ala' ibn Razin from Muhammad ibn Muslim who had said that the following was said to abu Ja'far (a.s.) "These are people who think that the words of Allah, the Most Holy, the Most High. 'Ask the people of Dhikr if you do not know,' refers to the Jews and the Christians." The Imams (a.s.) asked, "Do they call you to their religion?" He (Muhammad ibn Muslim) has said that the Imams (a.s.) said, with his hand (pointing) to his chest, "We are the People of Dhikr (reminders of Allah) and we are the ones who must be asked questions." (H 549, Ch. 20, h 7)

A number of our people has narrated from Ahmad ibn Muhammad from al-Washsha' who has said that he heard Imam al-Rida say the following. "Imam Ali ibn al-Husayn has said that there are certain obligations for the Imams that are not obligatory for their followers and certain obligations of our followers are not obligatory for us. Allah, the Most Holy, the Most High has commanded them to ask us their questions saying, 'Ask the people of Dhikr if you do not know.' Thus, Allah has commanded them to ask us their questions but it is not obligatory for us to answer them. We may answer them or may not answer them if we may so decide." (H 550, Ch. 20, h 8)

Ahmad ibn Muhammad has narrated from Ahmad ibn Muhammad ibn abu Nasr who has said that he wrote a letter to Imam al-Rida (a.s.).

Of the issues for which he requested explanation in the letter was one about the following words of Allah, Most Holy, the Most High. "Ask the people of Dhikr (people who remind of Allah) if you do not know." The other question was about the words of Allah, the Most Holy, the Most High, "Not all believers have to become specialists in religious learning. Why do not some people from each group of believers seek to become specialists in religious learning and, after completing their studies, guide their group so that they will have fear of God?" (9:122) "Thus, it is obligatory for them to ask but it is not obligatory for you to answer." The Imams (a.s.) has said the following for the answer. "If they would not do what you would ask them, know that they are only following their (evil) desires. Who strays more than one who follows his desires without guidance from God?" (28:50) (H 551, Ch. 20, h 9)

Source: al-Kulayni, Muhammad ibn Ya'qub. "The Book about People with Divine Authority." In *Kitab Al-Kafi*, translated by Muhammad Sarwar. New York: Islamic Seminary Inc., 1999.

Other Shi'a Hadith Sources

1. Narrated from Imam as-Sadiq (a.s.), Allah Almighty said, "O son of Adam, remember Me within yourself and I will remember you within Myself. O son of Adam, remember Me in secret and I will remember you when (you are) in secret. O son of Adam, remember Me when in an assembly and I will remember you in an assembly which is better than your assembly." (*Bihar al-Anwar*, Vol. 93, No. 31, p. 158)

2. Allah said to Prophet Musa (a.s.), "Under no circumstance (should you) abandon My remembrance." (*Bihar al-Anwar*, Vol. 13, p. 342)

3. Imam Ali (a.s.) has said, "Remembrance is a source of great pleasure for the lovers (of Allah)." (*Ghurar al-Hikam* [Exalted Aphorisms and Pearls of Speech], No. 670)

4. The Holy Prophet (s) has said, "I urge you to recite the Quran and remember Allah frequently, for verily it (will result in) a remembrance for you in the heavens and a light for you in the earth." (al-Khisal, No. 13, p. 525)

5. According to Imam Ali (a.s.), "The one who occupies himself with the remembrance of Allah, Allah beautifies his remembrance (among people)." (Ghurar al-Hikam, No. 5235)

6. Imam Ali (a.s.) has said, "One who remembers Allah extensively is safe from hypocrisy; Remembrance of Allah throws Satan away." (Ghurar al-Hikam)

7. Imam Zain ul-'Aabideen (a.s.) says in a supplication, "O God! So defeat his (satan) authority over us through Thy authority, such that Thou holdest him back from us through the frequency of our supplications to Thee and we leave his trickery and rise up among those preserved by Thee from sin!" (al-Sahifah al-Sajjadiyyah: Dua', No.25)

8. Imam as-Sadiq (a.s.) said, "Verily the one who remembers Allah will never be struck by lightning." (Amali al-Saduq, No. 3, p. 375)

9. Imam Reza (AS) said: The one for whom the day of Ashura is a day of tragedy, grief and weeping, Allah The Mighty, The Glorious, shall make the Day of Judgment, a day of joy and happiness for him. (Bihar al-Anwar, Vol. 44, p. 284)

10. The Holy Prophet (p.b.u.h) said: O Fatimah! Every eye shall be weeping on the Day of Judgment except the eye which has shed tears over the tragedy of Hussein (AS) for surely, that eye shall be laughing and shall be given the glad tidings of the bounties and comforts of Paradise. (Bihar al-Anwar, Vol. 44; p. 293)

11. Imam Reza (AS) said (to one of his companions): If you desire that for you be the reward equivalent to that of those martyred along with Hussein (AS), then whenever you remember him say: 'Oh! Would that I

had been with them! A great achievement would I have achieved. (*Wasail al-Shia'h*, Vol.14, p. 502)

12. Imam as-Sadiq (AS) said: There is none who recites poetry about Hussein (AS) and weeps and makes others weep by means of it, except that Allah makes Paradise incumbent upon him and forgives his sins. (*Rijal al-Shaikh al-Tusi*, p. 289)

13. Imam Ali Ibn al-Husain (AS) used to say: Every Mu'min, whose eyes shed tears upon the killing of Hussein Ibn Ali (AS) and his companions, such that the tears roll down his cheeks, Allah shall accommodate him in the elevated rooms of Paradise. (*Yannaabe' al-Mawaddah*, p. 429)

14. Imam Sajjad (AS) said: Surely, I have never brought to mind the martyrdom of the children of Fatimah (AS) except that I have been choked with tears due to it. (*Bihar al-Anwar*, Vol. 46, p. 109)

15. Imam Baqir (AS) said: Amirul Mu'mineen Ali (AS), along with two of his companions, happened to pass by Karbala and as he did so, tears filled his eyes. He said (to them), "This is the resting place of their animals; and this is where their luggage shall be laid down; and it is here that their blood shall be shed. Blessed are you O Earth, that the blood of the beloved shall be spilled upon you." (*Bihar al-Anwar*, Vol. 44, p. 258)

16. Imam Baqir (AS) said: He who remembers us, or in whose presence, we are remembered, and (as a result) tears flow from his eyes, even though they may be in the measure of a wing of a mosquito, Allah shall construct for him a house in Paradise and make the tears a barrier between him and the fire (of hell). (*Al-Ghadeer*, Vol. 2, p. 202)

17. Imam as-Sadiq (AS) said: As for Ali Ibn al-Husain (AS), he cried over Hussein (AS) for twenty years (after the tragedy of Karbala); never would any food be placed before him except that he would begin to weep. (*Bihar al-Anwar*, Vol. 46, p. 108)

18. Imam as-Sadiq (AS), while sitting on the prayer mat prayed for the mourners and those going for the ziarat of the Ahlul Bayt (AS) as follows: O Lord, have mercy upon those eyes, which have shed tears in compassion for us; and upon those hearts, which have been restless and blistered for us; and upon those wailings, which have been for us. (*Bihar al-Anwar*, Vol. 98, p. 8)

19. Imam as-Sadiq (AS) said: O Zurarah! The sky had cried for forty days over (the martyrdom of) Hussein (AS). (*Mustadrak al-Wasail*, Vol. 1, p. 391)

20. Imam as-Sadiq (AS) said: The breath of one who is aggrieved upon the injustice and oppression subjected to us, is tasbeeh (glorification of Allah), and his concealing our secrets is jihad in the path of Allah. The Imam (AS) them added: This tradition ought to be written in gold. (*Amali al-Shaikh al-Mufid*, p. 338)

21. Imam as-Sadiq (AS) said: Allah has appointed to the grave of Imam Hussein (AS) four thousand anguished and grief-stricken angels, who weep over him (and shall continue to do so) up to the Day of Judgment. (*Kamil al-Ziyaraat*, p. 119)

22. Imam Reza (AS) said: He who sits in a gathering in which our affairs (and our path and aims) are discussed and revived, his heart shall not die on the day (Day of Judgment) when hearts shall die (of fear). (*Bihar al-Anwar*, Vol. 44, p. 278)

23. Imam Reza (AS) said: One who refrains from seeking his (worldly) desires on the day of Ashura, Allah shall grant him his desires of this world and the hereafter. (*Wasail al-Shia'h*, Vol. 14, p. 504)

24. Imam as-Sadiq (AS) said: One who weeps for Imam Hussein (AS), surely, the Imam (AS) observes him and seeks forgiveness for him and requests his holy fathers to (also) seek forgiveness for him. (*Bihar al-Anwar*, Vol. 44, p. 281)

25. Imam Ali (AS) said to Ibn Abbas: Once when he happened to pass by Karbala, Isa Jesus (AS) sat down and began to weep. His disciples, who were observing him, followed suit and began weeping too, but not comprehending the reason for this behavior; they asked him: "O Spirit of God! What is it that makes you weep?" Isa Jesus (AS) said: "Do you know what land this is?" The disciples replied: "No." He then said: "This is the land on which the son of the Prophet Ahmad (p.b.u.h) shall be killed." (*Bihar al-Anwar*, Vol. 44, p. 252)

26. Abu Baseer narrates that Imam Baqir (AS) said: The humans, the jinn, the birds, and the wild beasts (all) mourned and wept over (the tragedy which befell) Hussein Ibn Ali (AS). (*Kaamil al-Ziyaraat*, p. 79)

27. Imam Ali (a.s.) has said: O God, I verily seek nearness to You through remembrance of You, and I seek Your intercession by Yourself, and, I ask You, through Your Munificence, to draw me nearer to Yourself, and to motivate me to be grateful to You, and to inspire me with Your remembrance. (*Nahjul Balagha*, Du'a Kumayl)

Appendix F

Selected Sunni Hadiths on Dhikr

1. 'Abdullah ibn Busr reported a man said, "Messenger of Allah, the laws of Islam are too much for me. Tell me something I can cling to." He said, "Your tongue should remain moist with the remembrance of Allah." (at-Tirmidhi)

2. Abu'd-Darda' reported that the Messenger of Allah said, "Shall I inform you of the best of your actions and the purest of your property and the highest of your degrees and what is better for you than spending gold and silver and better for you than encountering the enemy and striking their necks and their striking your necks?" They said, "Yes, indeed!" He said, "Remembrance of Allah Almighty." Muadh ibn Jabal said, "There is nothing which saves from the punishment of Allah more than remembrance of Allah." (Ahmad, Ibn Abi'd-Dunya, at-Tirmidhi and Ibn Majah)

3. Abu Musa reported that the Messenger of Allah said, "If one man has some dirhams in his possession which he divides and another remembers Allah, the one who remembers Allah is better." One variant has, "There is no sadaqa better than remembrance of Allah." (at-Tabarani)

4. Anas ibn Malik reported that the Messenger of Allah said, "When you come upon the meadows of the Garden, graze in them." He was asked, "What are the meadows of the Garden?" "Circles of dhikr," he replied. (at-Tirmidhi)

5. Rafi' ibn Khadij reported that when his Companions met with him, at the end of it when the Messenger of Allah wanted to get up, he said, "Glory be to You, O Allah, and by Your praise. I testify that there is no god but Allah. I ask forgiveness of You and repent to You. I have acted badly and have wronged myself, so forgive me. Only You forgive wrong actions." They said, "Messenger of Allah, are these words which you originated?" "Yes," he replied, "Jibra'il came to me and said, "O Muhammad, they are the expiations of the gathering." (an-Nasa'i)

6. Abdullah ibn Amr ibn al-As said that he said, "There are certain words which someone can say in a gathering devoted to good or a gathering of dhikr by which Allah will seal the gathering as the page is sealed with a seal. They are as follows: 'Glory be to You, O Allah, and with Your praise. There is no god but You. I ask You for forgiveness and turn to You.'" (Abu Dawud and Ibn Hibban)

7. Abu Hurayra said, "I asked, 'Messenger of Allah, who will be the person happiest with your intercession on the Day of Rising?' The Messenger of Allah replied, 'I think that none would ask about this before you since I know your eagerness for hadith [learning]. The person happiest with my intercession on the Day of Rising will be the one who says: "There is no god but Allah" sincerely from his heart.'" (al-Bukhari)

8. Jabir reported that the Prophet said, "The best dhikr is 'La ilaha illa'llah,' and the best supplication is 'al-hamdu lillah'." (an-Nasa'i and Ibn Majah)

9. He reported that the Messenger of Allah said, "Renew your faith." He was asked, "Messenger of Allah, how do we renew our faith?" He replied, "Say often: 'There is no god but Allah.'" (Ahmad and at-Tabarani)

10. Ya'qub ibn Asim reported that two of the Companions of the Prophet heard the Prophet say, "No one at all says "There is no god but Allah alone with no partner. The kingdom and praise belong to Him and He has power over everything" sincerely with his soul, affirming it with

his heart, articulating it with his tongue but that Allah splits open the heaven so that He can look at the one on the earth who says it, and it is a right of the slave at whom Allah looks that He grant him his request." (an-Nasa'i)

11. Abu Hurayra reported that the Messenger of Allah said, "Anyone who says, 'Glory be to Allah and with His praise' a hundred times a day will have his sins fall away, even if they are like the froth of the sea." (Muslim and at-Tirmidhi)

12. Mus'ab ibn Sad (ibn Abi Waqqas) said that his father said, "We were with the Messenger of Allah when he asked, 'Are any of you able to earn a thousand good deeds every day?' One of those who was sitting there asked him, 'How can someone earn a thousand good deeds?' He said, 'Glorifying a hundred times is written as a thousand good deeds or a thousand errors fall away from him.'" (Muslim and an-Nasa'i)

13. Abu Hurayra reported that the Prophet passed by him when he was planting a seedling and he asked, "Abu Hurayra, what is that which you are planting?" He said, "Seedlings." He said, "Shall I not direct you to a seedling better than this? 'Glory be to Allah. Praise be to Allah. Allah is greater, and there is no god but Allah.' Each word of them will plant a tree for you in the Garden." (Ibn Majah)

14. Abdullah ibn Masud said, "Anyone who is tight-fisted about giving money, fears the struggle against the enemy and is wearied by the night should often say, "There is no god but Allah. Allah is greater. Praise be to Allah and glory be to Allah.'" (At-Tabarani)

15. 'A'isha bint Sad ibn Abi Waqqas related from her father that, together with the Messenger of Allah, he visited a woman and in front of her were some date-stones - or pebbles - which she was using to glorify Allah. He said, 'Shall I inform you what is easier for you than this - or better?' He said, 'Glory be to Allah by the number of things He has created in the heaven and glory be to Allah by the number of things He has created in

the earth and glory be to Allah by the number of things in between them and glory be to Allah by the number of things He has created. Then say, "Allah is greater" in the same way and "Praise be to Allah" in the same way, and "There is no god but Allah" in the same way and "There is no power nor strength except by Allah" in the same way.'" (Abu Dawud and at-Tirmidhi)

16. Mu'adh ibn Abdullah ibn Khubayb reported that his father said, "We went out on a very dark and rainy night looking for the Messenger of Allah to lead us in the prayer. We found him and he said, 'Speak.' I did not say anything. Then he said, 'Say,' and I did not say anything. Then he said, 'Say,' and I said, 'Messenger of Allah, what shall I say?' He said, 'Recite, "Say: He is God, One," and the suras of seeking refuge in the evening and the morning three times, it will be enough to protect you in respect of everything.'" (Abu Dawud, at-Tirmidhi, and an-Nasa'i)

17. Abu Hurayra said, "A man came to the Prophet and said, 'Messenger of Allah, what agony I suffered last night from a scorpion which stung me yesterday!' He said, 'If you had said in the evening, "I seek refuge with the perfect words of Allah from the evil of what He has created," it would not have harmed you." (Muslim)

18. 'Abdullah ibn Ghannam al-Bayadi reported that the Messenger of Allah said, "If anyone says in the morning, 'O Allah, whatever blessing comes to me or any of Your creation in the morning is from You alone with no partner; praise is Yours and thanks is to You' has fulfilled the thankfulness due for the day. If he says the like of that in the evening, he has fulfilled the thankfulness due for the night." (Abu Dawud and an-Nasa'i)

19. Ibn 'Umar said, "The Messenger of Allah did not omit these words in the evening and morning: 'O Allah, I ask You for pardon and wellbeing in this world and the Next. O Allah, I ask You for pardon and wellbeing in my deen and this world, my family and my property. O Allah, veil my defects and protect me from what I fear. O Allah, preserve me in front

of me and behind me, to my right and to my left, and above me. I seek refuge with Your might from unexpected harm from under me." (Abu Dawud, an-Nasa'i and Ibn Majah)

20. Abdullah ibn Amr ibn al-'As reported that the Prophet said, "There are two qualities in which a Muslim does not persevere in but that he will enter the Garden. They are easy but those who do them are few: After every prayer, he should glorify Allah ten times, praise Him ten times, and say the takbir ten times. That is 150 on the tongue and 150,000 in the balance. When he goes to bed, he should say the takbir 34 times, praise Allah 33 times and glorify Him 33 times. That is 100 on the tongue and a thousand in the balance.' I saw the Messenger of Allah count them. They asked, 'Messenger of Allah, how is it that they are easy and those who do them few?' He said, 'Shaytan comes to one of you when he goes to sleep and makes him fall asleep before he says them, and he comes when he is praying and reminds him of a need before he says them." (Abu Dawud, and at-Tirmidhi)

21. Abu Hurayra reported that the Messenger of Allah said, "If, when someone retires to his bed and says. 'There is no god but Allah alone with no partner. His is the Kingdom and praise is His. He has power over everything and there is no power or strength except by Allah. Glory be to Allah and praise be to Allah. There is no god but Allah, and Allah is greater,' he will be forgiven his sins or errors, even if they are like the froth of the sea." (an-Nasa'i)

22. 'Ubada ibn as-Samit reported that the Prophet said, "If someone wakes up at night and says, 'There is no god but Allah alone with no partner. The kingdom is His and His is the praise. He has power over everything. Praise belongs to Allah. Glory be to Allah. There is no god but Allah. Allah is greater. There is no strength or power except by Allah,' and then says, 'O Allah, forgive me' or makes supplication to Allah,' it will be answered. If he does wudu', then his prayer will be accepted." (al-Bukhari)

23. Abu Dharr reported that the Messenger of Allah said, "If, after the Fajr prayer, anyone says while his feet are still folded before speaking, 'There is no god but Allah alone with no partner. His is the kingdom and praise is His. He gives life and makes die, and He has power over everything' ten times, Allah will write for him ten good deeds, efface ten evil deeds from him, and raise him ten degrees, and that day he is protected from every very disliked thing, guarded against shaytan, and no sin will overtake him in that day unless it is associating with Allah." (At-Tirmidhi)

24. Al-Harith ibn Muslim at-Tamimi said, "The Prophet said to me, 'When you pray Subh, say seven times before speaking, 'O Allah, protect me from the Fire.' If you die on that day, Allah will write for you protection from the Fire. When you pray Maghrib, say seven times before speaking, 'O Allah, protect me from the Fire.' If you die that night, Allah will write for you protection from the Fire." (an-Nasa'i, and Abu Dawud)

25. Anas ibn Malik reported that the Messenger of Allah said, "If, when a man leaves his house, he says, 'In the name of Allah. I have relied on Allah and there is no power or strength except by Allah,' he will he told, 'It is enough for you. You have been guided, spared and protected,' and Shaytan will be kept far from him." (At-Tirmidhi, an-Nasa'i; and Ibn Hibban)

Source: Ibn Muhammd, al-Haafidh Shihabuddin Abu'l-Fadl Ahmad ibn Ali (known as Ibn Hajar al-'Asqalani, born AD 1372, died AD 1449). *Mukhtasar at-Targhib wa at-Tarhib*. Leicestershire: UK Islamic Academy, 2009.

Appendix G

Selected Examples of Recommended Supplications (Sunni and Shi'a Hadiths)

Supplication (Dhikr)	Arabic Transliteration	English Translation	Source
Before eating	Allahumma baa rik lanaa feemaa razaqtanaa wa qinaa azaaba al-naar	O God! Bless us on everything You give us, and avoid us from hellfire. And with the name of God.	Abu Bakr Ahmed ibn Muhammed (Ibn Sunni)
	Bismillah	In the name of God.	Imam Ali ibn Abi Talib
After eating	Alhamdulillah il-lathi at'amana wasaqana waja'alana Muslimeen	All praise belongs to God, Who fed us and quenched our thirst and made us Muslims.	Abu Bakr Ahmed ibn Muhammed (Ibn Sunni)
	Alhamdulillah	Praise be to God.	Imam Ali ibn Abi Talib

Before sleeping	Allahumma bismika ahyaa wa bismika amuutu	O God! In Your name I live, and in Your name I die.	*Sahih Muslim*, Hadith 6887
	Bismillahi amuutu wa ahyaa wa ila Allahi almaseeru. Allahumma! Amin ruaatee wa astur awratee wa 'addaannee 'amanatee	In the name of God do I die and live, and to God is the return. O God! Dispel my fears and hide my faults and (help me to) return what has been entrusted to me.	*Makarim al-Akhlaq*, 38
After waking up	Alhamdu lillahi llahi ahyana ba'da ma amatana wa ilaihin nushur	Praise to God, Who has given us life after He caused us to die, and to Him is the resurrection.	*Sahih Muslim*, Hadith 6887
	Sub'hanallahi Rabbin-Nabiyyeen, wa Ilahil Mursaleen, wa Rabbil Mustadh'afeen, wal Hamdu Lillahilladhee Yuhyil Mawta wa Huwa Alaa Kulli Shay'in Qadeer.	All glory be to God the Lord of the prophets, the God of the messengers, and the Lord of the enfeebled ones. All praise be to God Who gives life to the dead, and He has power over all things.	Imam Ja'far as-Sadiq

Before entering restroom	Bismillahi Allahumma inni a'udhu bika minal khubuthi wal khaba'ith	O God! I seek refuge with You from all offensive and wicked things (evil deeds and evil spirits).	*Sahih Bukhari*, Hadith 142
	Bismillahi wa billahi a'dhu billahi min alrrijsi alnnajisi alkhabethi almukhubuthi alshshaytani alrrajeemi	O God! I seek refuge with you from the filth of the impurity of the evil of the reviled Shaitan. O God! Pull away from me all uncleanliness and protect me from the accursed Shaitan.	Al-Faqih 1:23/25
After leaving restroom	Ghufranaka al-hamdu lillahil ladhi adh-haba annil adhaa wa aafani	I seek Your forgiveness. All praises are due to God Who has taken away from me the discomfort and granted me comfort.	*Ibn Majah*, Hadith 300
	Alhamdu lillahi allethee akhraja anni 'adahu wa abkee fi quwwathu fayalaha min ni'matin la yukaddaru alkadeeruna kadraha	Praise be to God, the One who removed from me its filth and left me its strength. What a (great) blessing it is—the real value of which cannot be fully appreciated by anyone.	Al-Faqih 1:23/25
Beginning of wudu (ablution)	Bismillah	In the name of God.	*Ibn Majah*, Hadith 1062
	Bismillahi wa billahi wal hamdu lil lahil lazi ja'alal ma'a tahura wa lam yaj alhu najisa	I begin my ablution in the name of God. All praise is due to God, Who made water purifying, and not najis (impure).	Ayatullah al Uzma Sayyid Ali al-Husaini Sistani, Duas.org

Ending of wudu (ablution)	Ashadu an-La ilaha illallahu wahdahu la sharika lahu wa ashhadu anna Muhammadan 'abduhu wa rasoolu	I testify that there is no God besides God; He is alone; He has no partner; and I testify that Muhammad is indeed His bondsman and apostle.	*Sahih Muslim*, Hadith 554
	Ashhadu an la ilaha illal-lahu wahdahu la shareeka lah, wa-ashhadu anna Muhammadan aabduhu warasooluh	I bear witness that none has the right to be worshipped except God, alone without partner, and I bear witness that Muhammad is His slave and messenger.	Declaration of Faith
Entering house	Bismillahi walajna, wa bismillahi kharajna, wa alallahi rabbina tawakkalna	In the name of God we enter, and in the name of God we exit, and upon God our Lord we rely.	*Abu Dawud*, Hadith 5096
	Assalamu alayna min Rabbina	Peace be on us from our Lord.	Imam Ali ibn Abi Talib
Leaving house	Bismillahi, tawakkaltu ala llahi, la hawla wa la quwwata illa billah	In the name of God, I rely upon God; there is no power and no strength except with God.	*Abu Dawud*, Hadith 5095
	Bismillahi, amanta billahi, wa tawakkaltu ala llahi, ma sha'allah la hawla wa la quwwata illa billah	In the name of God, I rely upon God and trust in God and that there is no power or strength except with God.	Imam Musa al-Kazim, *Kitab Al-Kafi*

Entering mosque	Allahummaftah li abwaba rahmatika	O God! Open to me the gates of Your mercy.	*Ibn Majah*, Hadith 772
	Allahumma, ghfirli bima azhnabtu wa aftah li abwaba rahmatika	O God, forgive me my sins and open to me the doors of Your mercy.	Amali al-Tusi, 2:209 (*Bihar al-Anwar*, Vol. 81, p. 22)
Leaving mosque	Allahumma inni as'aluka min fadlika	O God! I ask of You from Your bounty.	*Ibn Majah*, Hadith 772
	Allahumma, ghfirli bima azhnabtu wa iftah li abwaba rezkika	O God, forgive me my sins and open to me the doors of Your favor.	Amali al-Tusi, 2:209 (*Bihar al-Anwar*, Vol. 81, p. 22)

References

Abi Talib, Imam Ali ibn. *Nahjul Balagha*. Translated by Farouk Ebeid. Beirut, Lebanon: Dark Al-Kitab Al-Lubnani, 1989.

Administrator. *Fatima Al-Zahra (as), the Lady of Light*. The WorldForum for Proximity of Islamic Schools of Thought, May 2010.

Al-Ashqar, Umar S. *The World of the Jinn and Devils*. Riyadh, Saudi Arabia: International Islamic Publishing House (IIPF), 2005.

Al-Hakim, Ayatullah Sayyid Muhammad Baqir. *The Role of the Ahl Al-Bayt in Building the Virtuous Community Book Eight: The System of Devotional Acts of the Virtuous Community*. London: Ahlul Bayt World Assembly (ABWA) Publishers, 2011.

Al-Haythami, Ahmad ibn Hajar. *Al-Sawa'iq al-Muhriqah (Loud/Frightening Lightning)*. Maktabat al-Ma'arif, 1965.

Ali, Abdullah Yusuf. *The Holy Qur'an: Text, Translation, and Commentary*. Washington, DC: The Islamic Center, 1978.

Ali, S.V. Mir Ahmed. *The Holy Qur'an*. Elmhurst, New York: Tahrike Tarsile Qur'an Inc., 1995.

Al-Jawziyya, Imam Ibn Qayyim. *Merits of Remembrance of Allah*. Translated by Rafique Abdur Rehman. United Kingdom: Darul Ishaat, 2007.

Al-Khattab, Nasiruddin. *Musnad Imam Ahmad ibn Hanbal*. Vols. 1–3. Riyadh: Darussalam, 2012.

Al-Khazraji, Khalid; Muhammad Ghoneim, and M. S. M. Saifullah. *On the Nature of Hadith Collections of Imam al-Bukhari and Muslim*. Islamic Awareness, August 24, 2005.

Al-Kulayni, Muhammad ibn Ya'qub. "The Book about People with Divine Authority." In *Kitab Al-Kafi*. Translated by Muhammad Sarwar. New York: Islamic Seminary Inc., August 15, 1999.

Al-Mufid, Shaykh. *Kitab al-Irshad: The Book of Guidance into the Lives of the Twelve Imams*. 2nd ed. Translated by I. K. A. Howard, University of Edinburgh. Qum, Iran: Ansariyan Publications, 2004.

Al-Munajjid, Muhammad Salih. *Dealing with Worries and Stress*. Zad Group, January 26, 2015.

Al-Musawi, Hashim. *The Shia: Their Origins and Beliefs*. Translated by Dr. Hamid S. Atiyyah. Beirut: Al-Ghadeer Center for Islamic Studies, 1996.

Al-Qahtani, Sa'id bin Wahf. *Fortress of the Muslim: Invocations from the Qur'an and Sunnah*. 2nd ed. Riyadh: Darussalam, 2004.

Al-Qasim, Sheikh Abdul Muhsin Ibn Muhammad. *The Battle of Uhud: Victory—Not Defeat*. The Message of Islam. Accessed June 7, 2012 islamicstudies.islammessage.com.

Al-Qazwini, Imam Muhammad bin Yazeed ibn Majah. *Sunan Ibn Majah*. Translated by Nasriddin al-Khattab. Riyadh: Darussalam, 2007.

Al-Sadiq, Imam Ja'far. *The Lantern of the Path*. Rockport, MA: Element Books Ltd., November 1991.

Al-Sajjad, Imam Ali Ibnul-Husayn Zaynul-Aa'bideen. *Al-Sahifah Al-Sajjadiyyah Al-Kamilah (The Psalms of Islam)*.4th ed. Translated by William C. Chittick. Qum, Iran: Ansariyan Publications, 2006.

Alsamail, Ali. *Imam Al-Jawad (AS): The Manifestation of Magnanimity*. London: Ahlulbayt Islamic Mission, 2012.

Al-Suyuti, Imam Jalal Al-Din. *Tarikh al-Khulafa*. Beirut: Dar al-Kitab al-Arabi, 2002.

Al-Suyuti, Imam Jalal Al-Din. *The Remembrance of God: The Outcome of Contemplation over Loud Dhikr*. Translated by Sajeda Maryam Poswal. Bristol, England: Amal Press, 2008.

Al-Tabari, Abu Ja'far Muhammad ibn Jarir. *The History of al-Tabari; the Caliphate of Yazid. B. Mu'awiyah*. Vol. 19. Translated by I. K. A. Howard. Albany, NY: State University of New York Press, 1990.

Al-Taftazani, Allama Sa'd al-Din. *Sharh al-Aqa'id al-Nasfiyya*. Karachi: Maktaba Khair Kathir, n.d.

Al-Tirmidhi, Hafiz Abu Elsa. *Jami' al-Tirmidhi*. Vols. 1–6. Translated by Abu Khaliyl. Dar-us-Salam, 2007.

Altmann, E. M., and C. D. Schunn. "Decay versus Interference: A New Look at an Old Interaction." *Psychological Science*, 23, no. 11, (2012): 1435–1437.

Amini, Ayatullah Ibrahim. *Self Building: An Islamic Guide for Spiritual Migration towards God*. Translated by Sayyid Hussein Alamdar. Qum: Ansariyan Publications, 1997.

Ansariyan, Allama Hussein. *Ahl Al-Bayt: The Celestial Beings on the Earth*. Translated by Dr. Ali Akbar Aghili Ashtiani. Qum: Ansariyan Publications, 2007.

Ayati, Dr. Ibrahim. *A Probe into the History of Ashura*. Jamaica, New York: Imam Al Khoei Islamic Center, 1985.

Badaur, Dr. Abdelfattah Mohsen. *Peace Be Upon Islam*. Bloomington, Indiana: Trafford Publishers, 2011.

Bennison, Amira K. *The Great Caliphs: The Golden Age of the Abbasid Empire*. New Haven, CT: Yale University Press, 2009.

Bewley, Aisha. "Glossary of Islamic Terms." In *The Sunnah and the Science of Hadith*, Dr. Norlain bint Muhammad Dindang. Riyadh, Saudi Arabia, July 27, 2004.

Bilgrami, Sayed Tahir. *Essence of Life, A Translation of Ain al-Hayat by Allama Mohammad Baqir Majlisi*. Qum: Ansarian Publications, 2005.

Brown, Daniel W. *Rethinking Tradition in Modern Islamic Thought (Cambridge Middle East Studies)*. Cambridge University Press, 1999.

Bucaille, Maurice. *Mummies of the Pharaohs: Modern Medical Investigations*. New York: St. Martins Press, 1990.

Chang, Lulu. "Americans Spend an Alarming Amount of Time Checking Social Media on Their Phones." *Digital Trends* (June 13, 2015).

Chittick William C. *Ibn 'Arabi: Heir to the Prophets*. London: Oneworld Publishers, 2005.

Cognitive Psychology and Cognitive Neuroscience. Boulder, Colorado: University of Colorado, 2013.

Collection of Imam Shafi'i Poetry. Beirut: Dar al-Kitab al-Arabi, 1993.

Corbin, Henry. *History of Islamic Philosophy*. London: Kegan Paul International, 1993.

Cornell, Vincent J. *Voices of Islam: Voices of the Spirit.* Vol. 2. Westport, Connecticut: Prager Publishers, 2007.

Dodge, Christine Huda. *The Everything Understanding Islam Book.* 2nd ed. Avon, Massachusetts: Adams Media, 2009.

Donner, Fred. *Muhammad and the Believers: At the Origins of Islam.* Cambridge: The Belknap Press of Harvard University Press, 2010.

Elhadj, Elie. *The Islamic Shield: Arab Resistance to Democratic and Religious Reforms.* Brown Walker Press, 2007.

El-Naggar, Dr. Zaghloul. *The Human Heart in the Glorious Qur'an.* Committee on Scientific Notions in the Noble Qur'an, Supreme Council on Islamic Affairs. Cairo, Egypt. www.elnaggarzr.com.

Fitzpatrick, Coeli PhD, and Adam Hani Walker. *Muhammad in History, Thought, and Culture: An Encyclopedia of the Prophet of God.* Vols. 1–2. Santa Barbara, California: ABC-CLIO Publishers, 2014.

Ford, David R. *Jews, Christians, and Muslims Meet around Their Scriptures: An Interfaith Practice for the 21st Century.* Rome: Cambridge University Press, April 5, 2011.

Foucault, Michel. "What Is Enlightenment?" In *The Essential Foucault*, eds. Paul Rabinow and Nikolas Rose. New York: The New Press, 2003, p. 43–57.

Ghazzal, Zouhair. "The Ulama: Status and Fuction." In *A Companion to the History of the Middle East*, Youssef M. Choueiri. Wiley-Blackwell, 2005.

Hanne, Eric J. *Putting the Caliph in His Place: Power, Authority, and the Late Abbasid Caliphate.* Fairleigh Dickinson, 2007.

Hass-Cohen, Noah, and Joanna Clyde Findlay. *Art Therapy and the Neuroscience of Relationships, Creativity, and Resiliency: Skills and Practices*. W.W. Norton and Company, July 6, 2015.

Haykal, Muhammad Husayn. *The Life of Muhammad*. Translated by Isma'il Ragi Al-Faruqi. Oak Brook, Illinois: American Trust Publications, 2005.

Hebrew Praise and Worship Words. Just Worship. www.justworship.com.

Hilli, Jamal al-Din ibn Yusuf Allamah. *Certainty Uncovered (Kashf al-Yaqin*

Virtues of Imam Ali). Translated by Dr. Ali Akbar Aghili Ashtiani. Qum: Ansariyan Publications, 2007.

Horney, Karen. *Neurosis and Human Growth: The Struggle toward Self-Realization*. New York: W. W. Norton and Company, 1991.

Hussain, Irshad. "Shaykh Muhammad Jawad Mughniyyah: A Jurisprudent." *Al Taqrib: A Journal of Islamic Unity*, no. 4 (Winter 2009).

Ibn Abi Talib, Imam Ali. *Nahjul Balagha (Peak of Eloquence): Sermons and Letters of Imam Ali Ibn Abi Talib*. 12th ed. Islamic Seminary Publications, 1999.

Ibn 'Arabi, Muhyiddin. *Book of the Quintessence Concerning What Is Indispensable for the Spiritual Seeker*. Cairo: Muhammad 'Ali Sabih and Sons, 1967.

Ibn Kathir. Hafiz. *Al-Bidaya wa al-Nihaya*. Vol. 8. Beirut: Maktaba al-Ma'arif, 1999.

Ibn Muhammd, al-Haafidh Shihabuddin Abu'l-Fadl Ahmad ibn Ali (known as Ibn Hajar al-'Asqalani, born AD 1372, died AD 1449).

Mukhtasar at-Targhib wa at-Tarhib. Leicestershire: UK Islamic Academy, 2009.

Ibn Shahrashub, Muhammad ibn Ali. *Manaqib Ali Abi Talib.* Qum: Allamah Publications, 1959.

Ja'fari, Sayyid Husayn Muhammad. *The Origins and Early Development of Shia Islam.* CreateSpace, October 12, 2014.

Jaffer, Mohammed Yusuf. *Thaqalain—Part 9.* Quran and Hadith Regarding Ahlel Bait. Accessed April 17, 1998 www.najah.info.

Jaffery, Sarah. *United Nations on Imam Ali ibn Abi Talib.* Ahlul-Bayt Student Association, November 16, 2012.

Kasmai-Nazeran, Sayedeh. "Reaching Perfection: An Islamic Perspective." *Islamic Insights* (June 9, 2008).

Kermalli, Jameel. *Islam the Absolute Truth: A Comprehensive Approach to Understanding Islam's Beliefs and Practices.* Sanford, Florida: Zahra Foundation, 2008.

Keys to Powerful Living: Praise. The Christian Broadcasting Network. CBN.com.

Khan, Dr. Muhammad Muhsin. *Sahih Al-Bukhari.* Vols. 1–9. Al-Medina Al-Munauwara: Islamic University, 1994.

Kompridis, Nikolas. "So We Need Something Else for Reason to Mean." *International Journal of Philosophical Studies* 8, no. 3 (2000): 271–295.

Lalani, Arizna R. *Early Shi'i Thought: The Teachings of Imam Muhammad Al-Baqir.* London, 2000.

Lally, P., C. H. M. van Jaarsveld, H. W. W. Potts, and J. Wardle. "How Are Habits Formed: Modelling Habit Formation in the Real World." *European Journal of Social Psychology* 40, no. 6 (October 2010): 998–1009.

Lari, Sayyid Mujtaba Musavi. *Imamate and Leadership: Lessons on Islamic Doctrine (Book Four)*. Translated by Hamid Algar. Tehran: Foundation of Islamic Cultural Propagation in the World, 1996.

Lawson, Todd. *Gnostic Apocalypse and Islam*. London: Routledge, 2012.

MacDonald, Duncan B. *Development of Muslim Theology, Jurisprudence, and Constitutional Theory*. London: Routledge, 1903.

Machiavelli, Niccolo. *The Prince*. New York: Bantam, 1966.

Majlisi, Mohammad Baqir. *Bihar al-Anwar (Ocean of Lights)*. Beirut: Dar Ihya al-Turath al Arabi Publications, 1983.

Majlisi, Mohammad Baqir. *Hayat Al Qulub*. Vols. 2–3. Qum: Ansariyan Publications, 2003.

Mander, Jason. *Daily Time Spent on Social Networks Rises to 1.72 Hours*. www.globalwebindex.net/blog/daily-time-spent-on-social-networks-rises-to-1-72-hours. January 26, 2015.

Mavani, Hamid. *Religious Authority and Political Thought in Twelver Shi'ism: From Ali to Post-Khomeini*. London: Routledge, 2013.

McCraty, Rollin, Raymond Trevor Bradley, and Dana Tomasino. "The Heart Has Its Own 'Brain' and Consciousness." In5d Esoteric Metaphysical Spiritual Database. in5d.com. January 10, 2015.

Meier, Beat, Sibylle Matter, Brigitta Baumann, Stefan Walter, and Thomas Koenig. "From Episodic to Habitual Prospective Memory: ERP-Evidence for a Linear Transition." *Frontiers in Human Neuroscience*. Vol. 8, Article 489 (July 2, 2014): 1-13.

Mercado, Leonardo N. "The Return of Imam Mahdi and Jesus Christ: A Comparative Eschatology." In *The Bright Future*, Dr. S. Razi Moosavi Gilani. Bright Future Publication, October 7, 2014.

Mirza, Kaukab Ali. *The Great Muslim Scientist and Philosopher Imam Jafar ibn Mohammed As-Sadiq*. 2nd ed. Translated by Kaukab Ali Mirza. Ontario: Willowdale Publishers, 1997.

Mufti, Imam Kamil. *Keeping God in the Heart*. IslamReligion.com. May 7, 2012.

Mugniyyah, Shaykh Muhammad Jawad. *Ahl al-Bayt (Shi'a 12 Imams) and Infallibility*. Accessed March 15, 2010 www.Free-Minds.org.

Muhaiyaddeen, M.R. Bawa. *Dhikr: The Remembrance of God*. Philadelphia, Pennsylvania: The Fellowship Press, 1999.

Muir, Sir William. *The Life of Mohammad from Original Sources*. Edinburgh: Adamant Media Corporation, 1912.

Muslim, Imam Abul-Husain. *Sahih Muslim*. Vols. 1–7. Translated by Nasiruddin al-Khattab. Dar-us-Salam Publications Inc., 2007.

Mutahhari, Ayatollah Murtaza. *Wilayat the Station of the Master*. Tehran: World Organization for Islamic Services, 1982.

Mutahhari, Ayatollah Murtada. *Man and Universe*. Pakistan: Islamic Seminary Publications, 1990.

Mutahhari, Ayatullah Murtada. *Understanding the Uniqueness of the Qur'an*. Creatspace, September 9, 2014.

Mutahhari, Murtada. *Polarization around the Character of 'Ali Ibn Abi Talib*. Tehran: World Organization for Islamic Services, 1981.

Nasr, Vali. *The Shia Revival: How Conflicts within Islam Will Shape the Future*. W.W. Norton and Company Inc., 2006.

Nomani, Allama Shibli. *Sirat-un-Nabi: The Life of the Prophet*. Vols. 1–7. Translated by Syed Suleiman Nadwi. New Delhi: Kitab-Bhavan Publishers, 2000.

Olowu, Morufudeen O. *Dhikr (Remembrance): The Sufis Perspective*. Bloomington, Indiana: Xlibris, 2009.

Petronzio, Matt. *US Adults Spend 11 Hours per Day with Digital Media*. Statista: The Statistics Portal. March 5, 2014.

Praising God. All About God Ministries Inc. Peyton, Colorado. www.allaboutgod.com.

Qummi, Shaykh Abbas. *Mafatih Al-Jinan 1–2 (Keys to the Garden of Paradise)*. Qum: Ansariyan Publications, 2010.

Qara'ati, Muhsin. *A Commentary on Prayer*. 2nd ed. Translated by Mansoor L. Limba. Tehran: Ahlul Bayt Word Assembly, 2014.

Razwy, Sayed Ali Asgher. *A Restatement of the History of Islam and Muslims*. 2nd ed. The World Federation of Khoja Shia Ithna-Asheri Muslim, 2001.

Reis, Dr. David. *Shi'ite Identity Formation: Martyrdom through Collective Memory*. University of Oregon, 2013.

Renard, John. *Seven Doors to Islam: Spirituality and the Religious Life of Muslims*. Berkeley and Los Angeles: University of California Press, 1996.

Rich, Tracey R. *Prayers and Blessings*. Judaism 101. www.jewfaq.org/prayer.htm.

Richter, Felix. *Americans Use Electronic Media 11+ Hours a Day.* Statista: The Statistics Portal. March 13, 2015.

Rizvi, Hujjatul Islam Wal Muslimeen al-Haj Sayyid Muhammad Rizvi. *Islamic Correspondence Course: Advanced Book Two.* Dar Es Salaam, Tanzania: Bilal Muslim Mission of Tanzania, 2008.

Rizvi, Sayyid Sa'eed Akhtar. *Imamate: Vicegerency of the Prophet.* CreateSpace, 2014.

Rodinson, Maxime. *Muhammad: Prophet of Islam.* London: Tauris Parke Paperbacks, 2002.

Rodriguez, Angel Manuel. *Posture during Prayer.* Biblical Research Institute, General Conference of Seventh-Day Adventists. April 2004. webcache.googleusercontent.com.

Rosenbloom, Lila. *Jewish Remembrance: Yom Hashoah, the Zionists, and the Shofar.* College Park: University of Maryland, 2009.

Sarwar, Muhammad. *Kitab Al-Kafi.* Compiled by Thiqatu al-Islam, Abu Ja'far Muhammad ibn Ya'qub al-Kulayni. Islamic Seminary Inc., 2013.

Scott, Martin, and Stephen Sale. "Consumers Use Smartphones for 195 Minutes per Day, But Spend Only 25% of That Time on Communications." *Knowledge Centre* (May 2, 2014).

Shahin, Badr. *Lady Zaynab (Peace Be upon Her).* Qum: Ansaryian Publications, 2002.

Shakir, Ahmad, and Hamza Ahmad al-Zayn. *Al-Musnad Ahmad bin Hanbal.* Cairo: Dar-al-Hadith, 1995.

Shaltoot, Mahmood. *Verdict by His Excellency Shaikh al-Akbar Mahmood Shaltoot, Head of the al-Azhar University, on Permissibility of Following* 'al-Shia al-Imamiyyah' School of Thought. Accessed July 6, 1959 www.al-Islam.org.

Sharaf al-Din. Abd al-Husayn. *Al-Fusul al-Muhimmah fi Talif al-Ummah*. Rabitat al-Thaqafah wa-al-Alaqat al-Islamiyah, Idarat al-Tarjamah wa-al-Nashr, 1996.

Shaykh al-Saduq (Ibn Babawayh al-Qummi). *Kitab al-Tawhid: The Book of Divine Unity*. Translated by Ali Adam. Birmingham, United Kingdom: AMI Press, Al-Mahdi Institute, 2013.

Shirazi, Abd al-Karim Bi-Azar. "Imam Ali and the Caliphs: Their Relationship and Interaction." Translated by D. D. Sodagar. *Al-Taqrib: A Quarterly Journal of Islamic Unity* 2, no. 3. (Winter 2008).

Shulman, David, and Guy G. Stroumsa. *Self and Self-Transformation in the History of Religions*. Oxford University Press, 2002.

Siddiqui, Abdul Hamid. *Sahih Muslim: English Translation*. Vols. 1–4. Lahore: Sh. Muhammad Ashraf, 1973–1975.

Siddiqui, Muhammed Zubayr. *Hadith Literatures: Its Origin, Development, and Special Features*. Islamic Book Trust, 2006.

Tabari, Ahmad ibn 'Abd Allah. *Dhakha'ir al-'Uqba*. Qum: Maktabat al-Amin, 2001.

Tabarsi, Shaykh Abu Ali al-Fadl. *Tafsir Majma' al-Bayan*. Vol. 27. Tehran: Intesharat-e-Farahani, 1981.

Tahmasebi, Muhammad Husayn. *Imam Ali: Sunshine of Civilized Islam*. CreateSpace, 2013.

Tenik, Ali, Dr. Harran U. Ilahiyat Fakultesi, Vahit Goktas, and Dr. Ankara U. Ilahiyat Fakultesi. "Importance and Effects of Remembrance (Dhikr) in Socio-Psychological Terms." *AUIFD* 49 (2008): 217–236.

The Encyclopedia of Islam. Vol. 7. Leiden: E. J. Brill, 1965–1986.

The Holy Bible: New International Version. London: Hodder and Stoughton, 2011.

The Prophet's Biography. Department of Islamic Resources. 2006. www.islamhouse.com.

Tulving, E. "How Many Memory Systems Are There?" *American Psychologist* 40, no. 4 (1985): 385–398.

Tulving, Endel. "Episodic and Semantic Memory." In *Organization of Memory*, 381–402. New York: Academic Press, 1972.

Turfe, Tallal Alie. *Children of Abraham: United We Prevail, Divided We Fail.* Bloomington, Indiana: iUniverse, 2013.

Turfe, Tallal Alie. *Energy in Islam: A Scientific Approach to Preserving Our Health and the Environment.* Elmhurst, New York: Tahrike Tarsile Qur'an Inc., 2010.

Turfe, Tallal Alie. *Know and Follow the Straight Path: Finding Common Ground between Sunnis and Shi'as.* Bloomington, Indiana: iUniverse, 2015.

Turfe, Tallal Alie. *Patience in Islam: Sabr.* Elmhurst, New York: Tahrike Tarsile Qur'an Inc., 1996.

Turfe, Tallal Alie. *Unity in Islam: Reflections and Insights.* Elmhurst, New York: Tahrike Tarsile Qur'an Inc., 2004.

Vaughan-Lee, Llewellyn. "The Dhikr as an Archetype of Transformation." *Sound Journal* (October 2012).

Vogel, Edward K., and Trafton Drew. "Why Do We Forget Things?" *Scientific American* (November 4, 2008).

Wallace, Kelly. *Teens Spend a "Mind-Boggling" 9 Hours a Day Using Media.* November 3, 2015. www.cnn.com/2015/11/03/health/teens-tweens-media-screen-use-report.

Watt, William Montgomery. *Islamic Political Thought: The Basic Concepts.* Edinburgh: University Press, 1968.

Wesson, Kenneth. "Learning and Memory: How Do We Remember and Why Do We Often Forget?" March 2, 2012. Brainworldmagazine.com.

Za'l, Hafiz Abu Tahir Zubair 'Ali. *Sunan Abu Dawud.* Vols. 1–5. Riyadh: Darussalam, 2008.

Za'l, Hafiz Abu Tahir Zubair 'Ali. *Sunan An-Nasa'i.* Vols. 1–6. Riyadh: Darussalam, 2007.

Zaynali, Gulam Husayn. *The Twelve Imams in the Sunni Sources: Fiqh ul-Hadith.* Translated by Ahmad Rezwani. Edited by Mahdi Baqi. Qum, Iran: Dar ul-Hadith Scientific Cultural Institute, 2010.

Index of Subjects and Names

A

Abdullah bin Rawahah ibn Tha'labah, 141
Abdullah bin Ubay, 137
Abi Talib, Imam Ali ibn, 13, 17, 27, 33, 35, 56, 87–88, 135, 136, 137, 139, 141, 142, 143
Abraham (prophet), 20, 21, 29, 30, 36, 83–84, 175
Abu Talib, 92, 174
action, as phase of psychology of dhikr, 112, 113, 115–116
adhan (first call to prayer), 57
admonition (*maw'idhah*), 173
afternoon prayer (*al'-asr*), 43
Ahl al-Bayt (Household of Prophet Muhammad), xxv, 12, 13, 15, 20, 21, 22, 23, 25, 26, 49–50, 89–90, 97, 102, 104
Ahl al-Dhikr, 22–23
Ahl Aql (People of Intellect), 23
Ahl Ilm (People of Knowledge), 23
al'-asr (afternoon prayer), 43
Al-Baqir, Imam Muhammad, 179
Al-Baqir, Mohammad, 109–110
al-fajr (dawn prayer), 43
al-Fatiha, 15–16, 17
Al-Ghaffar (the All-Forgiving), 42
Ali al-Asghar, 97
Al-Kulayni, Muhammad ibn Ya'qub, 49–50

al-maghrib (evening prayer), 43
Al-Mahdi, Imam Muhammad, 172, 174, 175, 176, 177, 179
alms, 31, 34–35
al-sadr (chest), 163
Al-Sahifah Al-Sajjadiyyah Al-Kamilah (*The Psalms of Islam*) (Imam Ali Ibnul-Husayn Zaynul-Aa'bideen), 33
Al-Sajjad, Imam Ali Ibnul-Husayn Zaynul-Aa'bideen, 33
Al-Shafi'i (imam), 13
al-thaqalayn (two weighty things), 21, 25, 26
Altmann, E. M., xxiv
Amru ibn Abd Wid, 140, 141
Angel Gabriel, 92
angels, as Article of Faith, 29, 110
Antichrist, 174
Articles of Faith (*Usul al-Din*), 26, 27, 28–31
Ashura, xxv, 97, 101
As-Sadiq, Imam Ja'far, 24, 33, 106, 120, 185
Awaited One, *dhikr* (remembrance) of in Abrahamic faiths, 175–176
awareness, 78
Ayat al-Kursi, 41
'ayn (perception), 71, 76–78, 117
ayn al-yaqin (perception of certainty), 117, 118

B

Badr, Battle of, 134–136
battles, Islamic, 134–144
bayan (explanation), 173
Beautiful Names of God, xxv, 42, 128, 130, 132, 202–203
to become nearer to God (*kurbatan illalah*), 53
belief in God, as Article of Faith, 29
Beliefnet.com survey, 166
believer (*mu'min*), 159
benefits, of dhikr, 51, 59–60
blessed (*berakhah* in Hebrew), 168
blessing (*ni'mah*)
    importance of counting, 2
    straight path as, 16
    upon Ahl-al-Bayt, 13–14
body, as door of dhikr, 61, 62
books of God, as Article of Faith, 28, 29, 79–81
brain, 65–66
Branches of Faith (*Furu' al-Din*), 26, 27, 28
brotherhood, 54, 103, 145, 149, 150, 152, 158, 159
Bucaille, Maurice, 103

C

call for prayer (*adhan*), 57
certainty (dhikr of *al-yaqin*), as stage of psychology of dhikr, 116, 117
certainty (*yaqin* or *al-yaqin*), 111, 116, 117–120
certainty of truth (*haq al-yaqin*), 162
chapter (*sura*), 15
charitable deeds, 36
chest (*al-sadr*), 163
Christianity, 165, 166, 170–171, 174, 175
Christians, 23, 165–166, 168, 170, 171, 175
circumambulation prayer (*towwaf*), 32

cloak (*kisa*), 97
cognition (*ma'rifah*), 70, 71
Common Sense Media, xix
community (Ummah), 26, 104, 158
complacency, 9
compulsory prayers (*wajib*), 32, 33
confession of faith (*tahlil*), as effect of dhikr, 55, 56–57, 122
consciousness, 71, 72
consciousness of God (*taqwah*), 52–53
constancy, as phase of psychology of dhikr, 112, 113, 116
contemplation (*fikr*), 71, 74–76
contentment (*qana'a*), 29, 52
Cowen and Company survey, xix
creatures, 105–111

D

daily prayer (*salat wajib*), 15, 32, 41, 43, 56, 115
Daniel, 168
David (prophet), 80, 85, 107
dawn prayer (*al-fajr*), 43
Day of Judgment (*Yawm al-Qiyamah*), 4, 30, 172
death, 30–31, 117–118
death prayer (*mayyit*), 32
declaration of faith that declares belief in the oneness of God and the acceptance of Muhammad as God's Prophet (*shahada*), 56
Deuteronomy, 167, 169
devil (*Shaytan*), 108
devotion (*ikhlas*), 29
dhikr (remembrance)
    additional words for, 1, 166
    advantages of reciting, 60
    of Ahl al-Bayt, 49–50
    of Beautiful Names of God, 42
    benefits of, 59–60
    blessings of, 1–4

disadvantages of not reciting, 60–61
doors of, 61
easy steps to, 40–42
effects of, 55–59
as emanating from at least three levels, 121–122
energy of, 5–11
eschatology of, 172–179
meanings of, xxiii, 1, 45, 52
monotheistic aspects of, 165–171
need of wake-up call for, xxii
philosophy of, 70–78
power of, 126–133
practice of, 40
praises for, 41, 56
psychology of, 112–125
purpose of, 78
as remedy for selected character disorders, 2
as remembering others, 180–186
selected occurrences of in Qur'an, 191–192
selected Qur'anic verses on, 193–201
selected sayings of, 204–206
straight path of, 12–26
theology of, 27–37
transformation of, 160–164
types of, 39
virtues of, 51–55
dhikr (reminder), Qur'an as, 126–127
dhikr al-lisan (tongue), as stage of psychology of dhikr, 116, 117, 120, 121
dhikr al-qalb (heart), as stage of psychology of dhikr, 116, 117, 120, 121
dhikr of al-yaqin (certainty), as stage of psychology of dhikr, 116, 117
dialogue
importance of, 150, 151, 152, 155, 157
with non-Muslims, 145, 148

Dickens, Charles, 104
direct remembrance, 6
diversity, as hallmark of dhikr, 145, 146, 155–159
du'as (supplications), 19, 31, 32–33, 39, 40, 44–45, 123, 221–225

E

ears, as door of dhikr, 61, 62
ease, as hallmark of dhikr, 145, 146, 150–155
effects, of dhikr, 51, 55–59
Eid prayers, 7
electronic media, use of, xx–xxi
Ello, xix, xx
empathy, 181–183
encoding, as stage of human memory process, 63, 64
endurance (sabr), 52, 53
episodic memory, 121, 122, 123, 124
eschatology, of dhikr, 172–179
evening prayer (al-maghrib), 43
exalting (takbir), as effect of dhikr, 55, 56, 57
Exodus, 168-169
explanation (bayan), 173
eyes, as door of dhikr, 61, 62

F

Facebook, xvii, xix, xx
faith (iman), 11, 111
false messiahs, 174, 175
fasting (sawm), 31, 34, 74
Fatima, 13, 41
fikr (contemplation), 71, 74–76
first call to prayer (adhan), 57
flexibility, as hallmark of dhikr, 145, 146, 149–150
follower (Shi'a), 21
forgetfulness (nisyan), 18, 121, 130

forgiveness (*istighfar*), as effect of dhikr, 55, 56, 59
forgiveness (*istighfar*), as virtue of dhikr, 52
Friday Prayer, 43
fu'aad (inner heart), 163
Furu' al-Din (Branches of Faith), 26, 27, 28

G

Gandhi, Mahatma, 104
generosity (*infaq*), 29
gentleness (*hilm*), 97
Ghadir Khumm, 83, 94
Gibbon, Edward, 104
gift (*hadiyya*), 16
Global WebIndex, xix
glorification/glorifying (*tasbih*), 55, 56, 58, 105, 106, 122
God
    belief in, as Article of Faith, 29
    belief in unity of, 29
    fear of, 68
    glorification of (*tasbih*), 105
    justice of, 29
    mutual relationship between God and mankind, 38
    oneness of (*tawhid*), 102
    remembrance of, as type of dhikr, 39
God wills (*mash'iah*), 131
God's protection (*isti'adhah*), 59
Gospel (*injil*), 79, 80, 81
gratitude (*shukr*), 29, 52, 53, 54–55, 161
guidance (*hidaya*), 16, 17, 18
guide us (*ihdina*), 16

H

habitual memory, 121, 122, 124–125
hadiths (traditions)
    Shi'a hadith that confirms that al-thaqalayn refers to the Qur'an and Ahl al-Bayt, 24–25
    Shi'a hadiths collected/recorded by Muhammad ibn Y'qub al-Kulayni, 49–50
    Shi'a hadiths on dhikr, 46–48, 207–214
    Shi'a hadiths that confirm that Ahl al-Bayt is that of Prophet Muhammad and his progeny, 25
    Shi'a hadiths that recollect tragedy of Karbala, 100–101
    Shi'a hadiths that record dhikr of blessings upon Ahl-al-Bayt, 15
    Sunni hadiths confirming blessing and peace that corresponds with Prophet's declaration, 13
    Sunni hadiths on dhikr, 215–220
    Sunni hadiths that confirm that Ahl al-Bayt is that of Prophet Muhammad and his progeny, 25
    Sunni hadiths that confirm that al-thaqalayn refers to Qur'an and Ahl al-Bayt, 21
    Sunni hadiths that embrace memory of Imam Hassan and Imam Hussein, 99–100
    as type of dhikr, 39
hadiyya (gift), 16
Hajj (pilgrimage), 7, 31, 32, 36, 44
hands, as door of dhikr, 61
haq (truth), 117
haq al-yaqin (certainty of truth), 162
haq al-yaqin (truth of certainty), 117
Hassan, Imam, 13
hawqala (might and power), as effect of dhikr, 55, 56, 58–59
heart

attributes of, 68
as door of dhikr, 61, 62, 66–67
purification of, 69
qalb, 163
role of, 110
rust of, 109
heart (*dhikr al-qalb*), as stage of psychology of dhikr, 116, 117, 120, 121
Hebrew praises, 168–169
hereafter, xxiii, xxvi, 28, 29, 30, 33, 71, 118, 120, 133, 177, 185
hidaya (guidance), 16, 17, 18
hilm (gentleness), 97
Holocaust, 169
Household of Prophet Muhammad (Ahl al-Bayt), xxv, 12, 13, 15, 20, 21, 22, 23, 25, 26, 49–50, 89–90, 97, 102, 104
Hugo, Victor, 104
Hunayn, Battle of, 134, 142–144
Hussein, Imam Ali ibn, 89

I

ibadat (worship), 76, 163
Ibn Abbas, 143
Ibn al-Jawzi, Abu'l-Faraj, 108
IDC survey, xxi
idraq an-nafs (self-realization), 21, 120, 178, 188
ihdina (guide us), 16
ihsan (perfection), 78, 163–164, 188
ijtihad (reasoning), 73–74, 149
ikhlas (devotion), 29
ilm (knowledge), 71, 72–73, 117, 145, 146
'ilm al-yaqin (knowledge of certainty), 117
Imam Hussein ibn Ali/Imam Hussein, xxv, 13, 88–89, 96–104, 132, 174
Imamat, as Article of Faith, 29
imams, supplications (*du'as*) of, 87–88
iman (faith), 11, 111
iman (inner faith), 163

impure self (*nafs al-ammarah*), 72
inanimate objects, 105, 107
indirect remembrance, 7
Infallible Imams, 17, 21, 23, 26, 109, 171
infaq (generosity), 29
Informate Mobile Intelligence survey, xvii
Injil, 22, 23
injil (Gospel), 79, 80, 81
inner faith (*iman*), 163
inner heart (*fu'aad*), 163
insensitivity, 9
intention (*niyyah*), 5–6, 114
interreligious understanding, 171
iqama (second call to prayer), 57
Isaac, 83–84
Ishmael, 83–84
Islam
    belief in the end of the world, 174
    defined, 27–28
    unity in, 145–159
Islamic battles, 134–144
Islamic personality, 19, 111, 112, 113, 116, 176, 177, 178, 179, 183, 187–188
isti'adhah (God's protection), 59
istighfar (forgiveness), as effect of dhikr, 55, 56, 59
istighfar (forgiveness), as virtue of dhikr, 52
istirja' (return), 133

J

Jacob (prophet), 174
Jesus (prophet), 21, 30, 80, 87, 99, 172, 174, 175, 176
Jews, 23, 142, 165–166, 168, 169, 171, 175
jihad (struggle), 31, 37
Job (prophet), 74–75
Jonah (Yunus) (prophet), 85–86

Joseph (prophet), 91–95, 174
Judaism, 165, 166, 169, 175
justice, as virtue of dhikr, 52, 54

K

Karbala, tragedy at, xxv, 96–104
Khadijah, 92, 174
khalifa (representative), 102
Khandaq, Battle of, 134
Khaybar, Battle of, 134, 139–141, 142
Khomeini, Grand Ayatollah, 155
khums principle of alms, 35
kisa (cloak), 97
Kitab Al-Kafi (Muhammad ibn Ya'qub al-Kulayni), 49–50, 207–209
knowledge (*ilm*), 71, 72–73, 117, 145, 146
knowledge of certainty (*'ilm al-yaqin*), 117
kurbatan illalah (to become nearer to God), 53
Kursi (Throne or Seat), 42

L

law (*shari'a*), 149
lawh al-mahfuz (preserved tablet), 81
laziness, 9
lethargy, 9
light (*nur*), 16
lisan (tongue), 163
loud utterance, 6, 7
Loving, as one of God's beautiful names, 132
Luke, 167

M

ma'ad (resurrection), 30
major jihad, 37
Major Prophets, 30
makeup prayer (*qadha*), 32
mandatory prayers (*wajib*), 32, 33
Mandela, Nelson, 104
ma'rifah (cognition), 70, 71

mash'iah (God wills), 131
Mason and Nielson survey, xviii
maw'idhah (admonition), 173
mayyit (death prayer), 32
meditation, 78
memory, xxv, 63–64. *See also* episodic memory; habitual memory; semantic memory
mercy (*rahmah*), 111, 145, 146, 148–149
mercy, as virtue of dhikr, 52, 54
Messiah, 171, 175
Messiah (*Moshiach* or Anointed One), 175
messiahs, false messiahs, 174, 175
miftah al-falah (success), 52, 74
miftah al-faraj (relief), 52, 74
might and power (*hawqala*), as effect of dhikr, 55, 56, 58–59
minor jihad, 37
miracles, 82
misbaha (prayer beads), 1
monotheistic aspects, of *dhikr* (remembrance), 165–171
Muhammad (prophet). *See* Prophet Muhammad
mu'min (believer), 159
mustaqim (straight), 17
Mutahhari, Ayatullah Murtada, 107

N

nafs al-ammarah (impure self), 72
nafs al-mutma'inna (serene self), 162
nafs al-mutma'innah (pure self), 72
nafs al-mutma'innah (tranquil self), 119
nawafil (recommended prayers), 32
nawafil (supererogatory prayers), 32
nazr (prayer that becomes mandatory upon one's taking an oath or making a solemn promise to God), 32
negative energy, 6, 8–11

Nehemiah, 167
Nielsen Company survey, xx, xxi
night prayer (*al-'isha*), 43
ni'mah (blessing)
    importance of counting, 2
    straight path as, 16
    upon Ahl-al-Bayt, 13–14
Ninety-Nine Beautiful Names of God, xxv, 42, 128, 130, 132, 202–203
nisyan (forgetfulness), 18, 121, 130
niyyah (intention), 5–6, 114
noon prayer (*al-zuhr*), 43
nur (light), 16

O

objects, 105, 107
obligatory charitable payment (*zakat* and *khums*), 35
oneness of God (*tawhid*), 39, 102

P

parts (*rakats* or *rik'ats*), 15, 43
Passover, 169
patience (*sabr*), 11, 19, 29, 37, 43–44, 52–53, 74, 119, 124, 179
perception ('*ayn*), 71, 76–78, 117
perception of certainty (*ayn al-yaqin*), 117, 118
perfection (*ihsan*), 78, 163–164, 188
piety (*taqwah*), 29, 34
pilgrimage (Hajj), 7, 31, 32, 36, 44
pluralism, 156–157
positive energy, 6–8, 10
praising (*tahmid*)
    as effect of dhikr, 55, 56, 57–58, 122
    as part of unified perception, 78
prayer beads (*misbaha*), 1
prayer(s) (*salat*)
    afternoon prayer (*al-'asr*), 43
    as Branch of Faith, 31
    call for prayer (*adhan*), 57
    circumambulation prayer (*towwaf*), 32
    classifications of, 32
    common ground and common principle among Christians, Jews, and Muslims in, 165–166
    as compulsory in Islam, 31, 33
    compulsory prayers (*wajib*), 32, 33
    daily prayers, 15, 32, 41, 43, 56, 114
    dawn prayer (*al-fajr*), 43
    death prayer (*mayyit*), 32
    Eid prayers, 7
    evening prayer (*al-maghrib*), 43
    as form of *dhikr*, xxiv
    Friday Prayer, 43
    importance of group prayer, 7
    makeup prayer (*qadha*), 32
    mandatory prayers (*wajib*), 32, 33
    night prayer (*al-'isha*), 43
    noon prayer (*al-zuhr*), 43
    prayer that becomes mandatory upon one's taking an oath or making a solemn promise to God (*nazr*), 32
    prescribed prayers, 43–44
    reasons cited for not praying, xvii–xix
    recommended prayers (*nawafil*), 32
    second call to prayer (*iqama*), 57
    sign prayer (*salat ayat*), 32
    supererogatory prayers (*nawafil*), 32
preparation, as phase of psychology of dhikr, 112, 113, 114–115
preremembrance, as phase of psychology of dhikr, 112, 113
preserved tablet (*lawh al-mahfuz*), 81
Prophet Abraham, 20, 21, 29, 30, 36, 83–84, 175
Prophet David, 80, 85, 107
Prophet Jacob, 174

Prophet Jesus, 21, 30, 80, 87, 99, 172, 174, 175, 176
Prophet Job, 74–75
Prophet Jonah (Yunus), 85–86
Prophet Joseph, 91–95, 174
Prophet Moses, 21, 30, 80, 84–85, 101, 102
Prophet Muhammad
    blessings as given to, 12–13, 15
    dhikr as taught by, 41
    farewell sermon of, 83, 94–95
    as final prophet, 122
    as a follower (Shi'a), 21
    as inspired by story of Joseph, 91–95
    knowledge as important to, 73
    miracles of, 82, 107
    mission of mercy of, 148
    as one of five Major Prophets, 30
    as purified by God, 14
    Qur'an as revealed to, 22, 80, 81, 127, 173, 174
    as receiving guidance (*hidaya*) from God, 17
    as underscoring importance of group prayer, 7
Prophet Noah, 20, 21, 30
Prophet Zachariah, 86
prophets. *See also specific prophets*
    belief in, as Article of Faith, 29
    number of, 30
    role of, 30, 38, 81–87, 83
Psalms (*zabur*), 79, 80, 81, 85, 168-170
pure heart (*qalbun saleem*), 162
pure self (*nafs al-mutma'innah*), 72
purification, 78

Q

qadha (makeup prayer), 32
qalb (heart), 163
qalbun saleem (pure heart), 162
qana'a (contentment), 29, 52

Qur'an
    aim of, 127
    as from God and about God, 126
    as one of four books of God, 79, 80, 81
    as revealed to Prophet Muhammad, 22, 80, 81, 127, 173, 174
    role of, 129
    scientific wonders mentioned in, 81
    selected occurrences of dhikr in, 191–192
    selected verses on dhikr in, 193–201
    theme of, 127
    praises of dhikr, 45

R

rahmah (mercy), 111, 145, 146, 148–149
rahmatun-lelalamin (mercy for the universe), 15
Rajab, 34
rakats (units or parts), 15, 33, 54
Ramadan, 34, 44, 74, 74–75
Ramses II, 103
reasoning (*ijtihad*), 71, 73–74, 149
recitation
    importance of, xxii
    as part of unified perception, 78
    as type of dhikr, 39
recommended prayers (*nawafil*), 32
reinforcement, as stage of human memory process, 63, 64
reliance (*tawakkul*), 29, 133
relief (*miftah al-faraj*), 52, 74
remember (*zakar* in Hebrew), 166
"Remember: A Poem" (Turfe), xiii
remembering, forgetting as counterpart to, xxiv
remembrance
    as integral part of worship, xxv
    as phase of psychology of dhikr, 112, 113–114

remembrance (*dhikr*). *See* dhikr (remembrance)
reminder (*dhikr*), Qur'an as, 126–127
reminder (*tadhkeer*), 173
representative (*khalifa*), 102
resurrection (*ma'ad*), 30
retrieval, as stage of human memory process, 63, 64
return (*istirja'*), 133
Revelation, 170
rik'ats (parts), 15, 43
Rosh Hashanah, 169
ruh (soul), 66

S

Sabbath, 169
sabr (endurance), 52, 53
sabr (patience), 11, 19, 29, 37, 43–44, 52–53, 74, 119, 124, 179
Sacred Mosque (Ka'bah), 36
sacrifice, 181, 183–184
sadaqah (voluntary charity), 36
Sahih Bukhari, 23–24
Sahih Muslim, 25
Sa'id ibn Al-'As ibn Sa'id, 135
salat (prayer(s)). *See* prayer(s) (*salat*)
salat ayat (sign prayer), 32
salat wajib (daily prayer), 15, 32, 41, 43, 56, 115
Samuel (2), 167
sawm (fasting), 31, 34, 74
Schunn, C. D., xxiv
scientific wonders, 81
second call to prayer (*iqama*), 57
self-actualization, 19, 53, 66
self-awareness, 52, 66
self-centeredness, 9, 178
self-confidence, 52
self-criticism, 178, 179
self-forgiveness, 178
self-fulfillment, 177
self-realization (*idraq an-nafs*), 21, 120, 178, 188
self-refinement (*tazkiya*), 29
self-respect, 52, 103, 178
self-sacrifice, 36, 37, 178
semantic memory, 121, 122, 123, 124
serene self (*nafs al-mutma'inna*), 162
Sermon on the Night of Ashura at Karbala (Imam Hussein), 88–89
Sha'ban, 34
shahada (declaration of faith that declares belief in the oneness of God and the acceptance of Muhammad as God's Prophet), 56
shari'a (law), 149
Shaytan (devil), 108
Shi'a
adherence of to principle of khums and zakat, 35
belief in occultation of, 174
examples of prophets who were, 20–21
expansion of shahada for, 56
as followers of Prophet Noah, 20
hadith that confirms that al-thaqalayn refers to the Qur'an and Ahl al-Bayt, 24–25
hadiths collected/recorded by Muhammad ibn Ya'qub al-Kulayni, 49–50
hadiths on dhikr, 46–48, 207–214
hadiths that confirm that Ahl al-Bayt is that of Prophet Muhammad and his progeny, 25
hadiths that recollect tragedy of Karbala, 100–101
hadiths that record dhikr of blessings upon Ahl-al-Bayt, 15
versus Sunni, 152, 155

Shi'a (follower), 21
shukr (gratitude), 29, 52, 53, 54–55, 161
shukr (thankful), 163
sight, 76, 77
sign prayer (*salat ayat*), 32
silent utterance, 6, 7
sirat al mustaqim (straight path), 16, 18, 19–20, 21, 25, 82, 89, 163, 176
smartphones, use of, xvii, xviii, xxi–xxii, xxv, 114
smell, 76, 77
social media, xvii, xix, xxv
soul (*ruh*), 66
sound, 76, 77
spirit, as door of dhikr, 61, 62
storage, as stage of human memory process, 63, 64
straight (*mustaqim*), 17
straight path (*sirat al mustaqim*), 16, 18, 19–20, 21, 25, 82, 89, 163, 176
struggle (*jihad*), 31, 37
success (*miftah al-falah*), 52, 74
successor (*wasi*), 17
Sunni
    hadiths confirming blessing and peace that corresponds with Prophet's declaration, 13
    hadiths on dhikr, 215–220
    hadiths that confirm that Ahl al-Bayt is that of Prophet Muhammad and his progeny, 25
    hadiths that confirm that al-thaqalayn refers to Qur'an and Ahl al-Bayt, 21
    hadiths that embrace memory of Imam Hassan and Imam Hussein, 99–100
    versus Shi'a, 152, 155
    verses of on dhikr, 48–49
supererogatory prayers (*nawafil*), 32
supplications (*du'as*), 19, 31, 32–33, 39, 40, 44–45, 123, 221–225
sura (chapter), 15

T

tadhkeer (reminder), 173
tahlil (confession of faith), as effect of dhikr, 55, 56–57, 122
tahmid (praising)
    as effect of dhikr, 55, 56, 57–58, 122
    as part of unified perception, 78
takbir (exalting), as effect of dhikr, 55, 56, 57
taqwah (consciousness of God), 52–53
taqwah (piety), 29, 34
tasbih (glorification/glorifying), 55, 56, 58, 105, 106, 122
Tasbih Fatima, 41, 58
taste, 76, 77
tawakkul (reliance), 29, 133
tawhid (oneness of God), 39, 102
tazkiya (self-refinement), 29
thankful (*shukr*), 163
thikr, as another word for dhikr, 1
thought processes, 65
time management, xxii
tolerance, as hallmark of dhikr, 145, 146, 148
tongue (*dhikr al-lisan*), as stage of psychology of dhikr, 116, 117, 120, 121
tongue (*lisan*), 163
tongue, as door of dhikr, 61, 62
Torah, 22, 23, 79, 80, 81
touch, 76, 77
towwaf (circumambulation prayer), 32
tranquil self (*nafs al-mutma'innah*), 119
truth (*haq*), 117
truth of certainty (*haq al-yaqin*), 117
Twitter, xvii, xix
two weighty things (*al-thaqalayn*), 21, 25, 26

U

Ubaid Allah ibn Ziyad, 98
Uhud, Battle of, 134, 136–139
Umar ibn Sa'ad, 98
Umm al-Kitab (Mother of the Book), 127
Ummah (community), 26, 104, 158
units (*rakats*), 33
unity, in Islam, 145–159
Usul al-Din (Articles of Faith), 26, 27, 28–31

V

virtues, of dhikr, 51–55
Vogel, Edward K., xxiv
voluntary charity (*sadaqah*), 36

W

wajib (compulsory/mandatory prayers), 32, 33
Walid ibn 'Utbah, 135
wasi (successor), 17
wisdom, as hallmark of dhikr, 145, 146–147
Wise Reminder, 147
worship (*ibadat*), 76, 163

Y

Yahya (John), 86
yaqin or *al-yaqin* (certainty), 111, 116, 117–120
Yawm al-Qiyamah (Day of Judgment), 4, 30, 172
Yazid, 96, 98, 99, 102, 103, 104

Z

zabur (Psalms), 79, 80, 81, 85
zakat principle of alms, 35
zekr, as another word for dhikr, 1
zikr, as another word for dhikr, 166

TRUE DIRECTIONS

An affiliate of Tarcher Perigee

OUR MISSION

Tarcher Perigee's mission has always been to publish books that contain great ideas. Why? Because:

GREAT LIVES BEGIN WITH GREAT IDEAS

At Tarcher Perigee, we recognize that many talented authors, speakers, educators, and thought-leaders share this mission and deserve to be published – many more than Tarcher Perigee can reasonably publish ourselves. True Directions is ideal for authors and books that increase awareness, raise consciousness, and inspire others to live their ideals and passions.

Like Tarcher Perigee, True Directions books are designed to do three things: inspire, inform, and motivate.

Thus, True Directions is an ideal way for these important voices to bring their messages of hope, healing, and help to the world.

Every book published by True Directions– whether it is non-fiction, memoir, novel, poetry or children's book – continues Tarcher Perigee's mission to publish works that bring positive change in the world. We invite you to join our mission.

For more information, see the True Directions website:

www.iUniverse.com/TrueDirections/SignUp

Be a part of Tarcher Perigee's community to bring positive change in this world! See exclusive author videos, discover new and exciting books, learn about upcoming events, connect with author blogs and websites, and more! www.tarcherbooks.com